MULTICULTURAL |

JAMES A. BANKS, *Series Editor*

Reclaiming the Multicultural Roots of U.S. Curriculum:
Communities of Color and Official Knowledge
in Education
WAYNE AU, ANTHONY L. BROWN, AND DOLORES CALDERÓN

Human Rights and Schooling: An Ethical Framework for
Teaching for Social Justice
AUDREY OSLER

We Can't Teach What We Don't Know:
White Teachers, Multiracial Schools, Third Edition
GARY R. HOWARD

Teaching and Learning on the Verge:
Democratic Education in Action
SHANTI ELLIOTT

Engaging the "Race Question":
Accountability and Equity in U.S. Higher Education
ALICIA C. DOWD AND ESTELA MARA BENSIMON

Diversity and Education: A Critical Multicultural Approach
MICHAEL VAVRUS

First Freire: Early Writings in Social Justice Education
CARLOS ALBERTO TORRES

Mathematics for Equity:
A Framework for Successful Practice
NA'ILAH SUAD NASIR, CARLOS CABANA, BARBARA SHREVE,
ESTELLE WOODBURY, AND NICOLE LOUIE, EDS.

Race, Empire, and English Language Teaching:
Creating Responsible and Ethical Anti-Racist Practice
SUHANTHIE MOTHA

Black Male(d): Peril and Promise in the Education of
African American Males
TYRONE C. HOWARD

LGBTQ Youth and Education: Policies and Practices
CRIS MAYO

Race Frameworks:
A Multidimensional Theory of Racism and Education
ZEUS LEONARDO

Reaching and Teaching Students in Poverty:
Strategies for Erasing the Opportunity Gap
PAUL C. GORSKI

Class Rules:
Exposing Inequality in American High Schools
PETER W. COOKSON JR.

Teachers Without Borders? The Hidden Consequences of
International Teachers in U.S. Schools
ALYSSA HADLEY DUNN

Streetsmart Schoolsmart:
Urban Poverty and the Education of Adolescent Boys
GILBERTO Q. CONCHAS AND JAMES DIEGO VIGIL

Americans by Heart: Undocumented Latino Students and
the Promise of Higher Education
WILLIAM PÉREZ

Is Everyone Really Equal? An Introduction to Key
Concepts in Social Justice Education
ÖZLEM SENSOY AND ROBIN DIANGELO

Achieving Equity for Latino Students: Expanding the
Pathway to Higher Education Through Public Policy
FRANCES CONTRERAS

Literacy Achievement and Diversity:
Keys to Success for Students, Teachers, and Schools
KATHRYN H. AU

Understanding English Language Variation
in U.S. Schools
ANNE H. CHARITY HUDLEY AND CHRISTINE MALLINSON

Latino Children Learning English: Steps in the Journey
GUADALUPE VALDÉS, SARAH CAPITELLI, AND LAURA ALVAREZ

Asians in the Ivory Tower: Dilemmas of Racial Inequality
in American Higher Education
ROBERT T. TERANISHI

Our Worlds in Our Words: Exploring Race, Class, Gender,
and Sexual Orientation in Multicultural Classrooms
MARY DILG

Culturally Responsive Teaching:
Theory, Research, and Practice, Second Edition
GENEVA GAY

Why Race and Culture Matter in Schools:
Closing the Achievement Gap in America's Classrooms
TYRONE C. HOWARD

Diversity and Equity in Science Education:
Research, Policy, and Practice
OKHEE LEE AND CORY A. BUXTON

Forbidden Language:
English Learners and Restrictive Language Policies
PATRICIA GÁNDARA AND MEGAN HOPKINS, EDS.

The Light in Their Eyes:
Creating Multicultural Learning Communities,
10th Anniversary Edition
SONIA NIETO

(continued)

The Flat World and Education: How America's
Commitment to Equity Will Determine Our Future
LINDA DARLING-HAMMOND

Teaching What Really Happened:
How to Avoid the Tyranny of Textbooks and
Get Students Excited About Doing History
JAMES W. LOEWEN

Diversity and the New Teacher:
Learning from Experience in Urban Schools
CATHERINE CORNBLETH

Frogs into Princes: Writings on School Reform
LARRY CUBAN

Educating Citizens in a Multicultural Society,
Second Edition
JAMES A. BANKS

Culture, Literacy, and Learning:
Taking Bloom in the Midst of the Whirlwind
CAROL D. LEE

Facing Accountability in Education:
Democracy and Equity at Risk
CHRISTINE E. SLEETER, ED.

Talkin Black Talk:
Language, Education, and Social Change
H. SAMY ALIM AND JOHN BAUGH, EDS.

Improving Access to Mathematics:
Diversity and Equity in the Classroom
NA'ILAH SUAD NASIR AND PAUL COBB, EDS.

"To Remain an Indian": Lessons in Democracy from a
Century of Native American Education
K. TSIANINA LOMAWAIMA AND TERESA L. MCCARTY

Education Research in the Public Interest:
Social Justice, Action, and Policy
GLORIA LADSON-BILLINGS AND WILLIAM F. TATE, EDS.

Multicultural Strategies for Education and Social Change:
Carriers of the Torch in the United States and South
Africa
ARNETHA F. BALL

Un-Standardizing Curriculum: Multicultural Teaching in
the Standards-Based Classroom
CHRISTINE E. SLEETER

Beyond the Big House:
African American Educators on Teacher Education
GLORIA LADSON-BILLINGS

Teaching and Learning in Two Languages:
Bilingualism and Schooling in the United States
EUGENE E. GARCÍA

Improving Multicultural Education:
Lessons from the Intergroup Education Movement
CHERRY A. MCGEE BANKS

Education Programs for Improving Intergroup Relations:
Theory, Research, and Practice
WALTER G. STEPHAN AND W. PAUL VOGT, EDS.

Walking the Road:
Race, Diversity, and Social Justice in Teacher Education
MARILYN COCHRAN-SMITH

City Schools and the American Dream:
Reclaiming the Promise of Public Education
PEDRO A. NOGUERA

Thriving in the Multicultural Classroom:
Principles and Practices for Effective Teaching
MARY DILG

Educating Teachers for Diversity:
Seeing with a Cultural Eye
JACQUELINE JORDAN IRVINE

Teaching Democracy:
Unity and Diversity in Public Life
WALTER C. PARKER

The Making—and Remaking—
of a Multiculturalist
CARLOS E. CORTÉS

Transforming the Multicultural Education
of Teachers: Theory, Research, and Practice
MICHAEL VAVRUS

Learning to Teach for Social Justice
LINDA DARLING-HAMMOND, JENNIFER FRENCH, AND
SILVIA PALOMA GARCIA-LOPEZ, EDS.

Culture, Difference, and Power
CHRISTINE E. SLEETER

Learning and Not Learning English:
Latino Students in American Schools
GUADALUPE VALDÉS

The Children Are Watching:
How the Media Teach About Diversity
CARLOS E. CORTÉS

Multicultural Education, Transformative Knowledge,
and Action: Historical and Contemporary Perspectives
JAMES A. BANKS, ED.

RECLAIMING THE MULTICULTURAL ROOTS OF U.S. CURRICULUM

COMMUNITIES OF COLOR AND OFFICIAL KNOWLEDGE IN EDUCATION

WAYNE AU
ANTHONY L. BROWN
DOLORES CALDERÓN

AFTERWORD BY MICHAEL DUMAS

TEACHERS COLLEGE PRESS
TEACHERS COLLEGE | COLUMBIA UNIVERSITY
NEW YORK AND LONDON

Published by Teachers College Press, 1234 Amsterdam Avenue, New York, NY 10027

Copyright © 2016 by Teachers College, Columbia University

Cover design by adam b. bohannon. Photo by Aaron Escobar, Wikimedia Commons.

Library of Congress Cataloging-in-Publication Data

Names: Au, Wayne, 1972- author. | Brown, Anthony Lamar, author. | Aramoni Calderón, Dolores, author.
Title: Reclaiming the multicultural roots of U.S. curriculum : communities of color and official knowledge and education / Wayne Au, Anthony L. Brown, Dolores Calderón ; afterword by Michael Dumas.
Description: New York, NY : Teachers College Press, 2016. | Series: Multicultural education series | Includes bibliographical references and index.
Identifiers: LCCN 2016015808 (print) | LCCN 2016027372 (ebook) | ISBN 9780807756782 (pbk. : alk. paper) | ISBN 9780807756799 (hardcover : alk. paper) | ISBN 9780807773932 (ebook)
Subjects: LCSH: Education—Curricula—Social aspects—United States. | Curriculum change—United States. | Multicultural education—United States.
Classification: LCC LB1570 .A94 2016 (print) | LCC LB1570 (ebook) | DDC

ISBN 978-0-8077-5678-2 (paper)
ISBN 978-0-8077-5679-9 (hardcover)
ISBN 978-0-8077-7393-2 (ebook)

Printed on acid-free paper
Manufactured in the United States of America

23 22 21 20 19 18 17   8 7 6 5 4 3 2

Contents

Series Foreword   James A. Banks   ix

1. **The Peculiar Sensation of Curriculum History:**
   Challenging the Canon of Curriculum Studies   1

   Understanding the Context of Curricular Silence   3

   The Master Narrative at the Foundation of Curriculum Studies   4

   Digging in the Crates: A Guiding Metaphor to Critical
      Revisionist Curricular History   11

   Theoretical Lenses   13

   The Chapters   15

2. **Education for Colonization or Education for Self-Determination?**
   Early Struggles over Native American Curricular Sovereignty   18

   Indigenous Curriculum for All of Time   19

   The Advent of "Indian Education" Under the Federal Indian
      Policies of the United States   20

   Curricular Genocide and Curricular Self-Determination:
      The Challenges of Native Curricular Discourse   23

   Curricular Discourse During Colonial Times   25

   Curricular Self-Determination in the Context of Colonization   26

   Federal Off-Reservation Boarding Schools   29

   Curricular Genocide and the Assault on Indian Identity   31

   Rebelling Against Curricular Genocide   37

   Reappropriation, Survival, and National Resistance
      Through Schooling   38

   Indian Education and the Progressive Era of
      Curriculum Reform   40

   Conclusion   43

3. Cultural Maintenance or "Americanization"?
    Transnational Curriculum and the "Problem" of
    Chinese American and Japanese American Education
    in the Early 20th Century   46

    Asian America and the Focus of this Chapter   48

    Historical Context for Chinese and Japanese American
        Curricular Discourse   49

    Early Chinese American Transnational Curricular Discourse   51

    Early Japanese American Transnational Curricular Discourse   65

    Conclusion   77

4. Colonial Legacies: Shaping the Early Mexican American
    Discourse in Texas and New Mexico   80

    Mexican Americans and the Focus of This Chapter   83

    Colonial Origins of Mexican American Curricular Discourse   84

    The Context of New Mexico   85

    The Context of Texas   89

    Mexican American Racial Ambiguity and the Impact
        on Schooling   92

    From Colonization to Segregation in Schools:
        Two Sides of the Same Coin   96

    Eugenics, IQ Testing, and the Segregation of Mexicans
        and Mexican Americans   102

    Challenging and Resisting Segregated Schooling   103

    Early Life and Educational Trajectory of George I. Sánchez 104

    The Many Influences on the Work and Life of George I. Sánchez 106

    Conclusion   112

5. African American Curriculum History:
    A Revisionist Racial Project   114

    The Context of African American Curricular Revision   115

    The Nadir: Theology, Science, and Curriculum   116

    African American Image Making and the U.S. Curriculum   120

    Children's Literature and the Curriculum of Race Making   121

    Textbooks and Race Making   124

    Reconstructing the "Negro": A Revisionist Ontological Project 128

    Journal of Negro Education as Countercurricular Space   129

The Critical Appraisals of the *Journal of Negro Education*   129

Against Anti-Black Curriculum:
   Textbooks, Encyclopedias, and Children's Literature   140

Concluding Thoughts on African American Curricular History   144

6. Conclusion   **146**

Afterword: What We Must Know   Michael Dumas   151

Notes   **153**

References   **155**

Index   **169**

About the Authors   **180**

Series Foreword

This informative, timely, and engaging book describes the ways in which the perspectives, insights, and histories of communities of color have been marginalized and silenced in the foundations of curriculum studies discourse. The project of Au, Brown, and Calderón is to remedy the invisibility of marginalized groups of color in the curriculum studies discourse by chronicling their educational histories, struggles, and victories. Using case studies that focus on the history of the schooling experiences of Native Americans, Chinese Americans, Japanese Americans, Mexican Americans, and African Americans, the authors document the long and poignant journeys that these groups have pursued to attain cultural recognition, structural inclusion, and self-determination.

The illuminating educational histories of the five ethnic groups depicted in this book are linked by a number of overarching and compelling themes. They include the ways in which each group experienced powerful and destructive forces to assimilate into U. S. society and to develop strong national loyalties while being denied structural inclusion and full citizenship. These groups were also victimized by mainstream institutionalized knowledge that depicted them as intellectually inferior to Whites, by being forced to attend segregated and inferior schools, and by a school curriculum that reinforced the negative images of them that were constructed by mainstream scholars and textbook writers that were widespread within schools and the popular culture.

A cogent and significant theme that unifies the case studies in this book is the powerful ways in which each of the five groups resisted victimization and oppression and pursued self-determination, cultural maintenance, and agency. Chinese and Japanese American communities established schools that taught their languages and cultures. Scholars of color played major roles in contesting stereotypes and misconceptions about their groups by creating transformative and oppositional knowledge (Banks, 1993). They constructed counternarratives that contested mainstream narratives that were detrimental to students and communities of color. George I. Sánchez (Murillo, 1996) challenged the widely held belief that Hispanic students were intellectually inferior to Whites; he described how Hispanic students were victimized by tests that were not in their home language. Carter G. Woodson (Roche, 1996) wrote textbooks that deconstructed the belief—which was widespread within textbooks and the popular culture—that African Americans had not contributed significantly to the development of American history. He also founded the Association for the Study of Negro (now African American) Life and History and established Negro History Week (now African American History Month). *The Journal of Negro Education*—established in 1932 at the historically Black Howard University—published research and articles that challenged institutionalized stereotypes and misconceptions about African American students. This journal is still significant and influential today.

The problems related to curriculum invisibility and the quest for structural inclusion and self-determination by marginalized racial, ethnic, cultural, and linguistic groups that are uncovered and analyzed by Au, Brown, and Calderón are continuing, complex, and contested within mainstream schools, colleges, and universities. The discerning and comprehensive educational and curricular histories described in this book are especially timely because of the growing population of students from diverse racial, ethnic, cultural, linguistic, and religious groups who are attending schools in the United States. Although students in the United States are becoming increasingly diverse, most of the nation's teachers are White, female, and monolingual. Race and institutionalized racism are significant factors that influence and mediate the interactions of students and teachers who are from different ethnic, racial, cultural, and linguistic groups. The growing income gap between adults (Stiglitz, 2012)—as well as between youth, as described by Putnam (2015) in *Our Kids: The American Dream in Crisis*—is another significant reason why it is important to help teachers and other practicing educators to understand how factors such as race and class influence classroom interactions and student learning and to comprehend ways in which the master narrative in curriculum studies has silenced the voices and experiences of ethnic groups of color.

American classrooms are experiencing the largest influx of immigrant students since the beginning of the 20th century. Almost 14 million new immigrants—documented and undocumented—settled in the United States in the years from 2000 to 2010. Less than 10% came from nations in Europe. Most came from Mexico, nations in Asia, and nations in Latin America, the Caribbean, and Central America (Camarota, 2011). The influence of an increasingly diverse population on U.S. schools, colleges, and universities is and will continue to be enormous.

Schools in the United States are more diverse today than they have been since the early 1900s, when a multitude of immigrants entered the United States from Southern, Central, and Eastern Europe. In 2014, the National Center for Education Statistics estimated that the percentage of students from ethnic minority groups made up more than 50% of the students in prekindergarten through 12th grade in public schools, an increase from 40% in 2001 (National Center for Education Statistics, 2014). Language and religious diversity is also increasing in the U.S. student population. The 2012 American Community Survey estimated that 21% of Americans aged 5 and above (61.9 million) spoke a language other than English at home (U.S. Census Bureau, 2012). Harvard professor Diana L. Eck (2001) calls the United States the "most religiously diverse nation on earth" (p. 4). Islam is now the fastest-growing religion in the United States, as well as in several European nations such as France, the United Kingdom, and The Netherlands (Banks, 2009; O'Brien, 2016).

The major purpose of the Multicultural Education Series is to provide preservice educators, practicing educators, graduate students, scholars, and policymakers with an interrelated and comprehensive set of books that summarizes and analyzes important research, theory, and practice related to the education of ethnic, racial, cultural, and linguistic groups in the United States and the education of mainstream students about diversity. The dimensions of multicultural education, developed by Banks (2004) and described in the *Handbook of Research on Multicultural Education* and in the *Encyclopedia of Diversity in Education* (Banks, 2012), provide the conceptual framework for the development of the publications in the series. The dimensions are content integration, the knowledge construction process, prejudice reduction, equity pedagogy, and an empowering institutional culture and social structure. The books in the Multicultural Education Series provide research, theoretical, and practical knowledge about the behaviors and learning characteristics of students of color, language minority students, low-income students, and other minoritized population groups, such as LGBTQ youth (Mayo, 2014).

This informative and readable book echoes and enriches a significant theme that is described in the first book published in the Multicultural Education Series (Banks, 1996), which describes how "cultural workers and scholars have been persistent through time in developing and constructing transformative scholarship oppositional to racist and sexist mainstream scholarship institutionalized in the academic and popular worlds" (p. vii). It also extends and complements a book in the Multicultural Education Series by Lomawaima and McCarty (2006) that describes the history of American Indian education and one by Valdés, Capitelli, and Alvarez (2011) that narrates the challenges that Latino students experience learning English in public schools. This book is connected to these three books because it also describes the sobering, informative, and compelling history of how marginalized and excluded groups of color have struggled to attain structural inclusion within U. S. society while maintaining self-determination and roots within their communities. This goal is paramount because its attainment not only will benefit marginalized groups but will enrich and deepen the knowledge, perspectives, insights, and wisdom within the nation writ large.

—James A. Banks

REFERENCES

Banks, J. A. (1993). The canon debate, knowledge construction, and multicultural education. *Educational Researcher, 22*(5), 4–14.

Banks, J. A. (1996). Preface. In J. A. Banks (Ed.), *Multicultural education, transformative knowledge, and action: Historical and contemporary perspectives* (pp. vii–xi). New York, NY: Teachers College Press.

Banks, J. A. (2004). Multicultural education: Historical development, dimensions, and practice. In J. A. Banks & C. A. M. Banks (Eds.), *Handbook of research on multicultural education* (2nd ed., pp. 3–29). San Francisco, CA: Jossey-Bass.

Banks, J. A. (Ed.). (2009). *The Routledge international companion to multicultural education*. New York, NY: Routledge.

Banks, J. A. (2012). Multicultural education: Dimensions of. In J. A. Banks (Ed.), *Encyclopedia of diversity in education* (Vol. 3, pp. 1538–1547). Thousand Oaks, CA: Sage.

Camarota, S. A. (2011, October). A *record-setting decade of immigration: 2000 to 2010*. Washington, DC: Center for Immigration Studies. Retrieved from cis .org/2000-2010-record-setting-decade-of-immigration

Eck, D. L. (2001). *A new religious America: How a "Christian country" has become the world's most religiously diverse nation*. New York, NY: HarperSanFrancisco.

Lomawaima, K. T., & McCarty, T. L. (2006). *"To remain an Indian": Lessons in democracy from a century of Native American education*. New York, NY: Teachers College Press.

Mayo, C. (2014). *LGBTQ youth and education: Policies and practices*. New York, NY: Teachers College Press.

Murillo, N. (1996). George I. Sánchez and Mexican American educational practices. In J. A. Banks (Ed.), *Multicultural education, transformative knowledge, and action: Historical and contemporary perspectives* (pp. 129–140). New York, NY: Teachers College Press.

National Center for Education Statistics. (2014). *The condition of education 2014*. Retrieved from nces.ed.gov/pubs2014/2014083.pdf

O'Brien, P. (2016). *The Muslim question in Europe: Political controversies and public philosophies*. Philadelphia, PA: Temple University Press.

Putnam, R. D. (2015). *Our kids: The American dream in crisis*. New York, NY: Simon & Schuster.

Roche, A. (1996). Carter G. Woodson and the development of transformative scholarship. In J. A. Banks (Ed.), *Multicultural education, transformative knowledge, and action: Historical and contemporary perspectives* (pp. 91–114). New York, NY: Teachers College Press.

Stiglitz, J. E. (2012). *The price of inequality: How today's divided society endangers our future*. New York, NY: Norton.

U.S. Census Bureau (2012). Selected social characteristics in the United States: 2012 American Community Survey 1-year estimates. Retrieved from factfinder2.census.gov/faces/tableservices/jsf/pages/productview.xhtml ?pid=ACS_12_1YR_DP02&prodType=table

Valdés, G., Capitelli, S., & Alvarez, L. (2011). *Latino children learning English: Steps in the journey*. New York, NY: Teachers College Press.

CHAPTER 1

The Peculiar Sensation of Curriculum History

Challenging the Canon of Curriculum Studies

> It is a peculiar sensation, this double-consciousness, this sense of always looking at one's self through the eyes of others, of measuring one's soul by the tape of a world that looks on in amused contempt and pity. One ever feels his two-ness,—an American, a Negro; two souls, two thoughts, two unreconciled strivings; two warring ideals in one dark body, whose dogged strength alone keeps it from being torn asunder.
>
> —W. E. B. Du Bois, *The Souls of Black Folk,* 1903

We start *Reclaiming the Multicultural Roots of the U.S. Curriculum* with the words of Du Bois to highlight the existential experience of people of color in the United States. The experience of what Du Bois called "double consciousness" is a sense that one's experiences, culture, identity, and histories are normed in the context of ubiquitous notions of Whiteness and "Americanness." For Du Bois this double consciousness is not just an internal psychological struggle; it is a conception of self-identity mediated by multiple modes of power. Du Bois's words here highlight the pervasiveness of this phenomenon:

> The theory of human culture and its aim has worked itself through warp and woof of our daily thought with a thoroughness that few realize. Everything great, good, efficient, fair and honorable and is "white." Everything mean, bad, blundering, cheating, and dishonorable is "yellow," brown and black. The changes on this theme are continually rung in picture and story, in newspaper heading and moving picture, in sermon and school book, until, of course, the king can do no wrong—a white man is always right, and the black has no rights which a white man is bound to respect. . . . All through the world this gospel is preaching; it has its literature, it has its priests, it has its secret propaganda, and above all—it pays. (Cited in Ephraim, 2003, p. 79)

We certainly can add the histories of official school curriculum as being part of this "secret propaganda" impacting the lives of young students of color and reproducing a kind of "peculiar sensation," an inexplicable feeling that one's life and experiences, histories, and knowledge are not valued. To open the pages of textbooks and school curriculum and find out that your experiences are either nonexistent or presented in a manner that produces what Du Bois calls "amused contempt and pity" is unfortunately a perennial issue of schooling.

However, what Du Bois describes is the exact feeling or "sensation" that we, as scholars of color who studied the histories of curriculum, have experienced. Although each of us meticulously studied the trajectories of curriculum history and educational theory, even teaching and writing on the topic of curriculum in the United States, we knew all the while that something did not quite feel right about the current narrative. We each questioned why our histories and experiences were not reflected in the histories of U.S. curriculum. The ideas of progressivism, social reconstructionism, and critical theory were present in the curriculum history, but the experiences of people of color were precariously absent or, if included, presented in a way that maintained Whiteness (Brown & Au, 2014). How could a field that actively prides itself on being engaged in issues of power and difference make such an egregious error? What does it mean when a field of curriculum studies is thoroughly committed to issues of social justice while strangely missing the mark in the area of curriculum history? This unreconciled inclusion and exclusion in the field of curriculum studies gave us a Du Boisian "peculiar sensation," a feeling of alienation and not quite knowing where we fit in our very own field. This peculiar sensation was the impetus for *Reclaiming the Multicultural Roots of U.S. Curriculum: Communities of Color and Official Knowledge in Education.*

All three of the authors are scholars of color who work in the curriculum field and teach curriculum studies courses. As such, we have a particularly deep investment in these concerns. As we have taught our classes and done our curriculum work, we each have encountered and used major curriculum textbooks that have outlined a series of important figures and events—framed as foundational—that essentially gave birth to the field around, and just shortly after, the turn of the 20th century in the United States. However, when using these texts in courses, many of which we value and recognize as being of critical importance to the field (e.g., Flinders & Thornton, 2012; Kliebard, 2004; Pinar, Reynolds, Slattery, & Taubman, 1995), we have consistently been left with the nagging question, "Outside of a few references to W. E. B. Du Bois or Carter G. Woodson, where are the communities of color?" The flip side of this question might be to instead ask, "Why does the founding of curriculum studies seem to be dominated by White men in universities?" We ask these questions knowing that communities of color were substantively involved in curricular discussions at the turn of the 20th century and for several decades after. Scholars of color theorized about the meanings and purpose of curriculum, conducted research studies about curriculum and, in some cases, developed curricular materials to address the many problems in the official knowledge. Likewise, communities of color considered and struggled over just what kind of curriculum they thought was best for their children. This absence contributed to our "peculiar sensation," where the story of the origins of curriculum studies was constantly told through a gaze that distinctively was not "ours," a gaze that rendered our communities invisible.

UNDERSTANDING THE CONTEXT OF CURRICULAR SILENCE

Scholars' critique of the U.S. curriculum, however, is not new. Some of the earliest critiques focused on the limitations found in K–12 curriculum (Du Bois, 1935a; Reddick, 1934). This early scholarship critically detailed how the official school curriculum presented minorities in the curriculum, as well as how certain histories were privileged. In recent years, however, scholars have noted the kinds of exclusion found within the field of curriculum studies (Au, 2012; Brown & Brown, 2015; Gordon, 1993; Grant, Brown, & Brown, 2015). William Watkins's (1993) *Black Curriculum Orientations* was one of the first historical studies to suggest that African American scholars were engaging in both parallel and different ideological conversations about the nature of curriculum during the early 20th century. Other curriculum studies scholars have provided consistent critiques of the field in recent years, where their discontent with the field has been explicitly and implicitly expressed in three central ways (Baker, 1996; Taliaferro-Baszile, 2010).

First, scholars have noted the absent presences (Apple, 1999) of scholars and ideas in the history of curriculum scholarship (Baker, 1996; Brown, 2010; Hendry, 2011; Taliaferro-Baszile, 2010). This body of scholarship has generally noted how issues of race, class, gender, and disability, as well as other forms of difference, reside in the field of curriculum studies but in a way that still seems to marginalize some stories and ideas. An example of action corrective of such marginalization is exemplified in the edited volume *Curriculum Studies Handbook* (Malewski, 2010), which purposefully explores underaddressed areas in the field of curriculum studies. Second, critical and scholarly critiques of the field of curriculum studies have examined how issues of race were implicit in the field's ideological focus. For instance, Baker (2002), Carlson (2009), Fallace (2012), and Winfield (2007) each have argued that eugenics and discourses of racial science were not abnormalities in the field of curriculum studies but were deeply engrained in the cultural logic of curriculum during that time. Third, curriculum scholars strongly assert that our approaches to curriculum history must be entirely reconceptualized, highlighting problematic gaps in historical and epistemological knowledge within the field. In this vein, scholars such as Tuck (2011), Calderón (2011, 2014b), Paraskeva (2011), and Desai (2012) suggest that

White supremacist and colonial legacies are so deeply imbued in the field of curriculum studies that the field itself needs to be both interrupted and reconceived to attend to these issues.

THE MASTER NARRATIVE AT
THE FOUNDATION OF CURRICULUM STUDIES

Although we, as scholars of color, trust our sensory understandings of the field of curriculum studies based on our own experiences, it is important to also know that our peculiar sensations have been supported by more summative and empirical research. Indeed, two of us (Brown & Au, 2014) performed an analysis of history textbooks that were synoptic, retrospective, and synthetic and that discussed the history of the founding of the field. In that work Brown and Au surveyed more than 30 texts that focused on curriculum development, curriculum history, or the history of the field of curriculum studies itself. The findings of that study suggested that, outside of just a handful of instances (e.g., select chapters from Castenell & Pinar, 1993; Connelly, He, & Phillion, 2008; and Malewski, 2010), the history of the field of curriculum studies, at least as told by the textbooks, is mainly a story of White men in the academy. Further, the study (Brown & Au, 2014) found that, in the rare instances that they are included, the historical contributions of non-White communities to curriculum in the United States are rendered in two ways. One way is to highlight select non-White contributors (e.g., W. E. B. Du Bois or Carter G. Woodson) to the discourse of curriculum. The other way is either to silence (e.g., Flinders & Thornton, 2012) or to give explicitly limited attention to race (e.g., Baker, 2009; Schubert, Schubert, Thomas, & Carroll, 2002) across the curricular discourse. Either way, communities of color are rendered nearly invisible. This is not accidental, and the chapters that follow demonstrate that Whites actively worked to exclude communities of color within the curriculum (Gillborn, 2008).

Visible and Invisible Absences in Curricular History

Overall, there are two types of broad absences in the U.S. curriculum historical narrative. The first is the production of what we are calling the *invisible narrative*. This has to do with the glaring absence of many of the ideas, histories, and theories that were relevant to the construction of curriculum history in the United States. Here we are not talking about curricular conversations that were separate and apart from the mainstream curriculum debates of the 20th century but those that were actually part of the conversation yet never acknowledged as part of these histories. For example, although the progressive curriculum movement of the early 1900s is seen as a prominent ideological perspective in U.S. curriculum, Alain Locke, an African American philosopher and one of the leading scholars of this movement (Grant, Brown, & Brown, 2015), is rarely even mentioned in the compendium and synoptic texts. We also see this invisible narrative when alternative movements from the mainstream curriculum debates have been blatantly left out of many of the major compendia and handbooks on curriculum history. One obvious case is the near-total absence of the curricular histories of Asian Americans. Across all the curriculum histories discussed (Brown & Au, 2014), you would be hard-pressed to find any history or reference made to Chinese American or Japanese American curriculum histories, despite their fairly large presence as immigrant communities in the Western United States. This kind of invisibleness also occurred in the way certain theoretical ideas were privileged over others. Grant, Brown, and Brown (2015) argue that this kind of invisibleness is pervasive throughout the discourse on critical educational thought.

The second kind of silencing is what we call the *visibility narrative*. By *visibility narrative* we mean the process by which select narratives are included. When the contributions of non-White communities are included in the story of curriculum, such as the Booker T. Washington and W. E. B. Du Bois debates about the meaning and purpose of education for African Americans, they follow a common pattern of inclusion. Here the additive nature of inclusion still places the experiences of diverse communities as outside of the common debates and trajectories of U.S. curriculum.

The Master Narrative in Summary

Here we provide a few examples from some major curriculum texts to illustrate what Brown and Au (2014) found. In the analysis of the classic curriculum history, *The Struggle for the American Curriculum, 1893–1958* (Kliebard, 2004), the usual characters and committees are highlighted, such as the Committee of Ten, G. Stanley Hall, William Torrey Harris and the Committee of Fifteen, John Dewey, John Franklin Bobbitt, Charles Bagley, George Counts, and Jane Addams. Then in rather typical inclusion, the W. E. B. Du Bois and Booker T. Washington debate is treated as another set of interests involving the philosophical purposes of curriculum. The collection *The Curriculum Studies Reader* (Flinders & Thornton, 2012) suffers from a similar problem in that its "foundational" readings are by John Franklin Bobbitt, Maria Montessori, John Dewey, Jane Addams, George Counts, and Herbert Kliebard. Communities of color are entirely absent from the "foundational" section.

As further examples, while the synoptic curriculum studies text *Understanding Curriculum* (Pinar et al., 1995) has an entire chapter committed to the concept of curriculum as a racial text, the book repeats the same master narrative of the Committee of Ten, the Committee of Fifteen, Herbert Spencer, Charles Eliot, William Torrey Harris, E. Cubberley, Charles and Frank

McMurry, Colonel Francis Parker, John Dewey, Edward Thorndike, and John Franklin Bobbitt, among others. Again, significant scholars of color generally remain absent here. The pattern again repeated itself in Schubert's (1986) foundational text, *Curriculum: Perspective, Paradigm, and Possibility*. Although his history of curriculum provides in-depth and broad inclusion that begins with Egypt and Mesopotamia, Schubert's text locates the foundations of U.S. curriculum history mainly within the purview of White male academics. A similar account of curriculum history was found in Tanner and Tanner's (1995) *Curriculum Development*.

It is important to note, however, that Brown and Au's (2014) study did find that some of these curriculum texts addressed the histories and experiences of some communities of color, even if these treatments were never equal to the dominant narrative. For instance, portions of Pinar's (2006, 2012) work on curriculum explicitly take up race and include discussions of cultural studies and essays on lynching.[1] Unfortunately, even this work ultimately reifies the "origins" of the field by referring to "our predecessors" (e.g., Edward Thorndike, Franklin Bobbitt, W. W. Charters, Ralph Tyler, John Dewey, and William James) as a way to identify the "key" curriculum scholars of the past (Pinar, 2006). Despite a wide range of important intellectual ideas and tensions in the field of curriculum studies, the most significant voices to surface are again White male academics. Even with the presence of such inconsistent treatment of African American curriculum history in some of the texts analyzed in the study (Brown & Au, 2014), and outside of one small, but clearly important, section of a chapter on Native educational history by Deyhle, Swisher, Stevens, and Galvan (2008), there is a remarkable and nearly complete silence in the field regarding the curriculum history of Chicanos/Latinos, Asian Americans, and Native Americans during the period at the turn of the 20th century so often associated with the founding of curriculum studies.

From our research (Brown & Au, 2014) and personal experiences as teachers and scholars of curriculum and educational foundations, the kind of absences that lead to our peculiar sensations can be reduced to two words: Whiteness and silence. Whiteness scholars (Roediger, 1994; Kincheloe, Steinberg, Rodriguez, & Chennault, 2000) discuss Whiteness as both the presence of White-skin privilege and the all-encompassing constructs that normalize different social contexts (e.g., family, beauty, and housing). In the case of the current U.S. curriculum history, a subset of histories, ideas, and institutions implicitly becomes the defining historical arc of American curriculum. We argue that Whiteness is not the explicit work of White people to withhold truths and privilege certain ideas over others but more a *dysconscious* racism (King, 1991), where the story of curriculum is not explicitly a story of White American curriculum but is instead posed as a story of American curriculum that happens to be White and erases previous colonial histories. The other term that characterizes our peculiar sensations is *silence.* Trouillot (1995) defines silence as an ideological construct informed by power. In this context, silence is an act of power that imposes a historical narrative based on a corpus of knowledge, thus rendering voice for some while simultaneously establishing silence for others. In this regard, communities of color have been rendered silent in the master narrative about the discourse on the foundations of curriculum studies.

We find a troubling irony with this master narrative of the foundations of curriculum studies: that a field that has been committed to deeply theoretical and open orientations to curriculum could have such a prominent blind spot. We make this argument based on three observations about curriculum studies. The first observation is that the field of curriculum studies has a long tradition of historical introspection. Much attention has been given to what the field has meant in past years and how it has evolved and changed over time (Schubert, 1986, 2010). As Reynolds (1990) comments on the importance of history in curriculum studies:

> Historical discourse on curriculum is most important in writing synoptic texts in the field of curriculum. Synoptic texts . . . provide encyclopedic portrayals of rapidly proliferating knowledge and introduce students to a field of thought and practice, such as curriculum. . . . Historical sections have always been included in these volumes and rightly so. They help give historical perspective to the field; they help the field to develop and to move forward with the benefit of hindsight and to avoid claims that it has been ahistorical. . . . Thus, understanding curriculum discourse requires understanding past discourse. (p. 189)

However, despite Reynolds's focus on synoptic texts, his larger point, that "understanding curricular discourse requires understanding past discourse" (p. 189), applies to the curriculum field generally. So we conclude that given the significant amount of introspection within the field, scholars should have a better pulse of the kind of silences that currently exist within the field.

The second observation is that, given its location in the shifting politics and orientations found in curriculum studies over the last several decades, we think the field should have a better grasp of these kinds of exclusions. For example, in the 1970s, curriculum studies took a "critical" turn toward issues of equality and power within educational research (e.g., Apple, 1971, 2004 [first edition published in 1979]; Rosenbaum, 1976). This turn was referred to as the "reconceptualization" by some scholars in the field (Pinar, 1975, 1978; Pinar et al., 1995), although this naming was defined as a problematic category because many of the scholars Pinar identified as "reconceptualist" fundamentally rejected the term for being ahistorical and not adequately representing the full range of their work (Apple, 2010). In the subsequent decades after this critical turn, the field continued to extend its focus to include new lenses tied to social identities (e.g., race, class, gender, sexuality, ability, language), epistemologies (e.g., Marxist, neo-Marxist, feminist, postmodern, postpositivist), and politics (e.g., political economy, ecology) (Au, 2012). These inclusions, however, also helped to heighten lurking tensions within the field—with some scholars calling for a more pragmatic "return" to a perceived apolitical past (see, e.g., Wraga, 1998, 1999) and others arguing that the field is better served by a diversity of curricular scholarship (Miller, 2005). On the whole, we feel that the field has benefited from what appears to be a more expansive set of politics guiding curriclum analysis.

Brown and Au's (2014) study findings revealed a striking irony: Despite a proclivity to challenge the prevailing gender, class, culture, sexuality, disability, and race in contemporary thought, there remains an overwhelming silence and undertheorizing of race within the historical understanding of the foundations of the field of curriculum studies. We state this not to disparage the good work that has already been done in the field—noting, for instance, the strong theoretical work that challenges the role the field of curriculum studies has had in maintaining the racism of colonialism historically and contemporarily (see, e.g., Calderón, 2014b; Tuck & Gaztambide-Fernandez, 2013). We also recognize that numerous scholars have focused on race and curriculum (Gordon, 1993; McCarthy, 1988, 1990a, 1990b; Pinar, 2012). However, short of Watkins's (1993) Black curriculum orientations and Pinar's (2012) chapter on race and the textbook controversies of the 1950s, much of the work about communities' and individuals' engagement with the American curriculum has been overlooked. Thus, in summary, we argue that given the critical turn in curriculum studies, and given the expanding political commitments and analyses taking place in the field, one might think that similar expansion would have happened in the foundations of the field itself. It has not.

The third reason that the absence of the rich histories of curriculum from communities of color in the field of curriculum studies is notable is that the field has been well aware of these exclusions for some time, as William Schubert (2010) explains:

> Even if not done intentionally, exclusion is obvious in the dominant curriculum field that has been disproportionately White, male, Western European, and American. Whether this phenomenon has been derived from conscious design or whether it is a function of emergence in a slanted society, critical and contextual curriculum scholarship have clearly revealed this bias in the literature. (p. 61)

This, however, is not the only instance in which prominent members of the curriculum community conceded to the problematic rendering of American curriculum and history. For instance, Marshall et al. (Marshall, Schubert, & Sears, 2000) conceded this awareness of the absence in curriculum history:

Reflecting on the first 50 years of curriculum work finds racial, intellectual, gendered, and other voices largely invisible—a term used perceptively by the African American scholar W. E. B. Du Bois (1903). Du Bois wrote on a host of curricular topics throughout the period just discussed, yet his work is rarely cited in curriculum literature. Other African American voices (Carter G. Woodson [2000], Benjamin Mays, Horace Mann Bond) . . . [and the] voices of women and children (especially children) remain thin in this history as well. Such marginalized voices need to be excavated, studied, and integrated fully into our discourse about curriculum. These remain invisible throughout this book not because they are unimportant to the story we tell but because ours is an attempt to portray the intellectual and social history of what *has been* rather than what *might or should have been* a part of the background of contemporary curriculum studies. (p. 13, emphasis in original)

The pointedness of these comments highlights how significant figures in the field understand the shortcomings of the ways curriculum studies has developed in terms of the history of curricular ideas and experiences. However, even after coming clean, the master narrative prevailed and the authors moved forward with the same old stories of White men "struggling" for the American curriculum.

The Omissions in Summary

Given the above silences and the fact that there has been at least some metacognition of these silences within curriculum studies, we are still left wondering: How do we make sense of these omissions? Why have these voices and communities been silenced in the history of curriculum studies? Here we find Tuck and Gaztambide-Fernandez's (2013) answer particularly useful. They suggest that because the entire project of mass schooling in the United States and Canada was a project of racist, settler colonialism, then curriculum studies is merely an extension of this project, explaining that

the settler colonial curricular project of replacement seems to happen organically, without intent, even though Indigenous erasure is the arch aim of settler colonialism. It happens generally, through the commonplace tendency of appropriation and commercialization of Indigeneity, but also specifically, through the removal of Indigenous bodies and the occupation of tracts of land by settler bodies. In academe, settler colonial replacement is evident in both disciplinary structures as well as institutional practices. (p. 79)

By situating curriculum studies within the project of settler colonialism, Tuck and Gaztambide-Fernandez (2013) suggest that this exclusion occurred because those "founding fathers" fundamentally held racist views toward non-White (nonsettler) communities, which in turn barred all non-White stories, ideas, and thoughts from entering into the historical discourse of curriculum studies and history. This, however, follows Mills's (1998) discussion of the need for revisionist ontologies because racist ontologies view non-White groups as "subpersons." Tuck and Gaztambide-Fernandez's (2013) analysis also speaks to the durability of racial exclusons in the present field of curriculum studies. So despite curriculum studies' commitments to progressive politics, the erasure of communities of color from the curriculum occurred in an insidious and institutional manner, with or without explicit intent (Brown & Au, 2014).

We can offer some further explanation for these omissions. We have to remember that the period we are focusing on in this book is a moment when

- Whiteness was coalescing around definitions of nationhood in the United States.
- Mass schooling was first being implemented.
- The powers-that-be were still trying to figure out what to do with the postemancipation, postreconstruction "negro problem."
- The original captains of industry were reaping massive profits from the labor of factory workers.
- Whites were rioting against Chinese laborers (Chan, 1993; Lee, 2015).
- The U.S. government was still in the process of securing Native lands and attacking Native sovereignty (Trafzer, Keller, & Sisquoc, 2006a).

In this sense, we cannot and should not decontextualize or romanticize the founding of the field of curriculum studies, as White racism was very much encoded in mainstream thinking and policy in this country during this time.

Further, as highlighted by the research discussed here (Brown & Au, 2014), the field of curriculum studies has historically been conceptualized officially as "living" in academia and scholarly committees. This might also explain the omission of people of color from the foundations of the field for the simple fact that institutions of higher education in the United States have had ongoing and persistent issues of racial exclusion and institutional racism. Communities of color were often locked out of educational institutions, subjected to White policymakers' decisions regarding resources and curriculum, and/or forced to develop their own institutions of education. This has meant that curriculum has historically "lived" in the communities of color themselves, in community schools or in direct opposition to the racial formation of U.S. schools (e.g., segregation, resegregation, inequitable schooling policies). Thus, curriculum studies' myopic historical focus on official texts and formal institutions of education—institutions themselves constructed as of the settler colonial effort—has not only signaled to marginalized communities that "your curriculum does not live here" but has also fundamentally perpetuated the institutionalized and professional racism so present during the field's founding (Fallace, 2012).

Our discussion here is about the nexus between institutions, individuals, and the overall functioning of institutional racism. As Brown and Au (2014) have stated elsewhere, this realization about the field of curriculum studies is less about pointing a finger at individual scholars, whom we know and respect, and more about highlighting the incredible blind spot in the field that resides with the durable and complicated concept of "race" in the United States. Tuck and Gaztambide-Fernandez (2013) remind us, "One of the ways the settler-colonial state manages this covering is through the circulation of its creation story" (p. 74), and it appears the field of curriculum studies is guilty of continuing a fundamentally racist epistemology and ontology despite its contemporary commitment to a politics of equality and difference. Therefore, it falls to individuals and institutions in the field to take appropriate steps to rectify their omissions as part of a longer struggle of self-reflection and growth.

DIGGING IN THE CRATES: A GUIDING METAPHOR TO CRITICAL REVISIONIST CURRICULAR HISTORY

Given the rather astounding gaps in the field of curriculum studies, we approached this project with competing senses of optimism and concern. Our optimism was that, because of our own personal knowledge of our own community histories, all three of us came to this work with some awareness of the many histories, authors, ideas, and movements that had been left out of the typical curriculum history narrative. However, we were also concerned because we knew writing this book would be an ambitious undertaking that would require making a new way in an area of curriculum studies that had not been fully established. While in some cases we knew where to take our examination of curriculum, in other cases we were also confronted with the formidable task of exploring new areas that in many instances had not been explored in the context of curriculum history.

Therefore, from a methodological standpoint, we find that the work put into this examination was akin to what classic hip-hop deejays called "digging in the crates." The early makings of hip-hop stemmed from disc jockeys who would find break beats in songs and find ways to blend those breaks to create a new sound. However, like a researcher, the pioneering deejays producing this new sound had to engage in a meticulous process, listening to thousands of songs within different genres of music to find the next break beat or sound effect. This process of music making, known as sampling, became a staple of hip-hop production. The actual process of looking and searching for musical sounds is often referred to as "digging in the crates." The "crates" are actual milk crates where deejays and turntablists would find new records and sift through their own collections systematically looking for sounds that had not yet been discovered.

Our historical method here is analogous to digging in the crates. Each of the coauthors of *Reclaiming the Multicultural Roots of U.S. Curriculum: Communities of Color and Official Knowledge in Education* has a wealth of knowledge on the topics of this book. We possess personal collections of historical studies, memoirs, theories, biographies, and autobiographies, where different historically marginalized groups express their concerns with the social realities that define their personal and collective lives—including the meaning and purpose of education and curriculum. We delved into the educational, social, cultural, and intellectual histories of Native Americans, African Americans, Chinese and Japanese Americans, and Mexican Americans. We dug into periodicals, memoirs, biographies, articles, books, pamphlets, notes, and speeches that captured various groups' concerns with the topic of curriculum and education. Looking into what we already knew also required a thorough process of digging. For example, although Anthony has been deeply engaged in the works of W. E. B. Du Bois for more than 20 years, it took this process of sifting through these works to discover that a core concern of Du Bois was revising the school curriculum. We also "dug into the crates" to discover new "sounds" altogether—through this process, we found scholars, readings, and studies that we had not read before. For instance, although Wayne has a solid understanding of Asian American history in general, he found himself learning parts of Chinese and Japanese American educational history with which he was unfamiliar and digging through digital archives of interviews and reflections on Asian Americans from 1924 to 1925. We also found histories and perspectives that highlighted concerns that curriculum scholars and community members were grappling with in the mainstream curricular discourse, as well as concerns that were markedly different from the kind of curricular discourse in the master narrative of U.S. curriculum. Sometimes the texts we analyzed were directly tied to issues of curriculum as reflected in the mainstream discourse, but in several instances, curriculum concerns were discussed and debated within the context of groups' specific concerns or resolutions.

In the chapters that follow, we provide a foundation of what we compiled from this process of gathering and digging. Some narratives we share may speak to concerns about the intent and purpose of curriculum as much of the early curriculum history portrayed. In other instances, the narratives speak to the structural and discursive barriers that required people of color to develop spaces to critique and revise. We guess, in a sense, we were like the legendary group Soulsonic Force, who wrote a song called "Looking for the Perfect Beat." We were looking for this "perfect beat," but we were looking for the remnants of sound and voice that reflect a semblance of the contextually specific pulse of curriculum concerns of this time. In other words, like the legendary Bronx hip-hop pioneer DJ Kool Herc, we were sampling different sounds to make a new sound about the history of curriculum. We understand that there are 8 million stories of curriculum revision; our attempt for this book is to give the reader a glimpse into a period in which the official and alternative curriculum was debated and discussed in ways not often acknowledged.

THEORETICAL LENSES

The historical and conceptual work done here in *Reclaiming the Multicultural Roots of U.S. Curriculum* draws from settler colonial studies, critical theory, and cultural memory. Given that critical theory is a broad category that is influenced by various, sometimes contradictory, critical traditions (Au, 2012), here we specifically draw from critical theory to interrogate the relationships between education and power (Apple, 2012). However, to pay attention to the legacy of colonialisms at play in the United States we must understand how the dominant system of colonialism in America differentially shaped and produced educational practices (Calderón, 2008, 2014a, 2014b; Tuck & Yang 2012). Thus, we examine how settler colonialism differentially constructed Indigenous peoples and racialized groups in the United States (Byrd, 2011; Omi & Winant, 2015). We see settler colonial studies and critical theory working in tandem because both explicitly point to the ways institutional power, social context, and history both manifest and maintain unequal power relations, which thus allows us to undertake a metacritical analysis of curriculum studies itself (Au, 2012).

We also actively draw on cultural memory, a concept that refers to the discourses, texts, and artifacts that shape how we conceptualize and imagine a historical moment or a body of knowledge. The concept of cultural memory contends that implicit and explicit modes of power (discursive and material) inform the way a historical narrative is rendered (Assmann & Czaplicka, 1995; Le Goff, 1992). In the context of *Reclaiming the Multicultural Roots of U.S. Curriculum*, we use the concept of cultural memory as a guiding principle for not only our critique of the construction of the historical foundations of the field of curriculum studies but also our highlighting of the historical curricular narratives that have been left out of the canon of those foundations.

We recognize that by combining settler colonial studies, critical theory, and cultural memory as guiding theoretical frameworks, we are in many ways also addressing the use of critical race theory (CRT) in curriculum studies. Although CRT includes many elements, we find ourselves drawn to its guiding presumption that racism is an omnipresent social and institutional force in that it impacts the development of all things in the sociopolitical realm (Delgado & Stefancic, 2012)—in this case, the field of curriculum studies. This is not at odds with settler colonial studies, which examines racialization and colonization as two separate but interwoven projects (see Byrd, 2011), since the focus is on racism—a product of both. We also embrace CRT's recognition of the need for revisionist history, in that such revisionist history

> reexamines America's historical record, replacing comforting majoritarian interpretations of events with ones that square more accurately with minorities' experiences. It also offers evidence, sometimes suppressed, in that very record, to support those new interpretations. (Delgado & Stefancic, 2012, p. 20)

Similarly, settler colonial studies, informed by critical Indigenous approaches, demands that we reexamine America's historical record, exposing settler colonialism and our complicity in it, and that we replace inherently anti-Indian interpretations of events with ones that leave room for Indigenous land-based knowledges (Calderón 2014a, 2014b; Tuck & Yang, 2012). In many regards, our book takes up the task of challenging, in Delgado and Stefancic's (2012) words, "comforting majoritarian interpretations of events" within the common narrative of the founding of the field of curriculum studies.

The concept of cultural memory attends to how power is rendered through artifacts and the use of historical revisionism to reshape both the historical record and the historical narrative, which also implies the use of "revisionist ontologies" (Mills, 1998) to understand history and society. *Reclaiming the Multicultural Roots of U.S. Curriculum* thus recognizes the reality of institutionalized racism within education and the ongoing project of settler colonialism, the existence of which is built on a history of the failure to recognize some groups as fully human or, to use Mills's (1998) terminology, the tendency to treat some groups as "subpersons." Consistent with our use of settler colonial studies, critical theory, and cultural memory as our theoretic constructs, the revisionist ontology we take up within this volume not only pushes back against the predominant racist ontologies but also provides "revisionist challenges to these ontologies by the subordinated population contemptuously categorized as subpersons" (Mills, 1998, p. 113). Thus, in bringing together settler colonial studies, critical theory, and cultural memory, an act that in many ways embraces some aspects of CRT, the guiding theoretical question for this inquiry, following Apple (2000), was, "What official knowledge do curriculum studies texts present relative to the foundations of the field, and what did communities of color [and Indigenous peoples] contribute to those foundations?" In posing this question, we are essentially following Tuck and Gaztambide-Fernandez's (2013) call to "brown" curriculum studies, a process that includes "bringing attention" to the racialized and colonizing practices of the field by "interrupting the dominant narrative by rudely inserting itself, reclaiming academic space, and calling the names of those who have been replaced and forgotten" (p. 83). As such, we are explicit in our recognition that the curricular histories told here in *Reclaiming the Multicultural Roots of U.S. Curriculum* can be seen and understood only within the context of the racism, White supremacy, xenophobia, and settler colonialism that communities of color negotiated with, struggled over, and survived through the "founding" period of curriculum studies.

THE CHAPTERS

Reclaiming the Multicultural Roots of U.S. Curriculum is our attempt at addressing our nagging questions and responding to the absent presences in the field of curriculum studies. In the subsequent chapters we seek to provide historical and conceptual contexts to many of the ideas, histories, and struggles communities of color have engaged in around the issue of curriculum. We theoretically approach each chapter with the understanding that structure and agency are always at play. In a sense, the structures of race and settler colonialism have remained as durable modes of power; however, even in the midst of curricular silence and hegemony, communities have engaged in a counterhegemonic process to redress and/or slow down the effects of curricular damage.

Here in Chapter 1 we have laid the groundwork for the book, outlining how the problematic dominant narrative of the founding of curriculum studies became the impetus for this entire project. Chapter 2, "Education for Colonization or Education for Self-Determination? Early Struggles over Native American Curricular Sovereignty," focuses on Native American curricular discourse up to the 1930s. While the Indigenous peoples of what is now referred to as the United States all had their own curricular discourse predating the arrival of Europeans, the formal education of Indigenous Nations has always taken place within the context of settler colonialism. As such, a core issue for Native peoples during the founding period of curriculum studies was how to best negotiate and survive the racist, predatory U.S. government and the systems of education-for-colonization it attempted to impose on the sovereign Indigenous Nations. For instance, there were lengthy community conversations about not only what should be the "best" response to the imposition of Western culture and Christianity upon their children but also how to support their children if and when they resisted. At the root of all these conversations was the issue of curricular sovereignty for Native peoples. Chapter 2 traces the history of these issues, highlighting not only the tragic racism of official U.S. education-for-colonization but also the strength and resilience of Native Nations as they resisted and survived the inculcations of Whiteness and Christianity on their identities.

Chapter 3, "Cultural Maintenance or 'Americanization'? Transnational Curriculum and the 'Problem' of Chinese American and Japanese American Education in the Early 20th Century," focuses on early Chinese American and Japanese American curricular discourse. In this chapter we highlight the critical tensions facing both Chinese and Japanese Americans in the United States at the turn of the 20th century up until the forced removal and incarceration of the Japanese American community in 1942. As immigrant communities that are a part of the Asian diaspora, both Chinese Americans and Japanese Americans during this time period faced racism, xenophobia, and White supremacy, and the curricular discourse of both communities was in direct response to these conditions. This chapter presents examples of how both the Chinese American and Japanese American communities negotiated these conditions and took a dual approach in their curricular discourse—fighting for access to public schools as their legal right while also maintaining a separate, but parallel, system of linguistic and cultural maintenance associated with their home countries. As such, we argue that not only were these Asian Americans education activists, they also articulated a form of transnational curricular discourse.

Chapter 4, "Colonial Legacies: Shaping the Early Mexican American Discourse in Texas and New Mexico," focuses on early Mexican American curricular discourse in the Southwestern United States and the colonial histories that intimately shaped it. Focusing on New Mexico and Texas, we document the colonial histories of Mexicans in the Southwest and how U.S. expansion into these areas intimately influenced the segregation and subsequent schooling of Mexicans and Mexican Americans in the early 20th century in this region. There has been a long intellectual history of Mexican Americans struggling to revise the school curriculum, questioning the Americanization goals behind the official curriculum. Guadalupe San Miguel (1987) has thoroughly documented the persistent agitation of Mexican Americans to revise and repudiate this official curriculum. The story of Mexican Americans' confrontation with curriculum provides a powerful counternarrative showing the hidden and overt agency of activists confronting and revising the symbolic violence of curriculum, and it reminds us that to understand the curricular discourse of Mexican Americans in this particular location requires a deep understanding of the multiple colonialist projects (on the part of both Mexico and the United States) that shaped the Southwest.

Chapter 5 of *Reclaiming the Multicultural Roots of U.S. Curriculum,* "African American Curriculum History: A Revisionist Racial Project," focuses on early African American curricular discourse. In this chapter we argue that curriculum analysis for African Americans is inextricably tied to the wider freedom movement. So, in this chapter we lay out the conceptual and empirical critiques African Americans have leveled against traditional notions of curriculum found in children's literature and school textbooks.

We further argue in this chapter that the critiques of imagery of African Americans found in the official knowledge and the well-developed body of intellectual discourse that emerged from such critiques is rarely accounted for in the field of curriculum studies. Examples of this can be found in the early issues of the *Journal of Negro Education* (*JNE*). Each issue took form as a counternarrative to the pervasive racial imagery found in school texts and society. To highlight the significance of this work, we share the work of different authors and ideas across *JNE*, noting the significance of this scholarship in challenging the normative constructions of race, curriculum, and pedagogy that were pervasive during the early 20th century. The final section of this chapter reveals how scholars produced textbooks and children's literature to rethink the normatively raced ideologies found in school texts.

In the conclusion, Chapter 6, we review the broad themes of each of the chapters, seeking out parallels, congruencies, and specific differences between the various curricular discourses discussed throughout the book. We assert that, in all instances, every community discussed here must be seen as a force of early education activism for curriculum transformation and that resistance to oppression and White supremacy was consistently paramount. Finally, we conclude with an open recognition that this is an unfinished project, as there are many more curricular discourses and histories that still are yet to be told.

CHAPTER 2

Education for Colonization or Education for Self-Determination?

Early Struggles over Native American Curricular Sovereignty

> So today if I had a young mind to direct, to start on the journey of life, and I was faced with the duty of choosing between the natural way of my forefathers and that of the White man's present way of civilization, I would, for its welfare, unhesitatingly set that child's feet in the path of my forefathers. I would raise him to be an Indian!
>
> —Luther Standing Bear (whose Native name was Ote Kte, or "Plenty Kill")
> *Land of the Spotted Eagle*, 1933

Any discussion about the curricular discourse taking place in, and being enacted upon, Native American communities during the founding period of curriculum studies in the United States must be understood within the context of settler colonization characterized by the forced dispossession of tribal lands, the expansion by European immigrants (Spanish in what is today the Southwestern United States and mainly Anglo in the settling of the United States), the establishment of Western institutions and culture, and the attempted (though not wholly successful) cultural and racial genocide of Native peoples by the U.S. government (Adams, 1995; Churchill, 2004; Deyhle et al., 2008). Despite ongoing resistance by Indigenous communities, these forces had an overwhelming influence on the shape and direction of the official curriculum for Native children in the United States. Below we outline the major policies that influence the curricular history we are interested in examining here. Additionally, as we have highlighted here in this book and two of us have discussed elsewhere (Brown & Au, 2014), an analysis of this curricular history, one grounded in the field of curriculum studies, has largely been neglected and ignored in our field. Given that no history can fully be told, this chapter picks up some of the history of Native American curricular discourse absent from the founding of curriculum studies.

INDIGENOUS CURRICULUM FOR ALL OF TIME

It is critical to recognize that Indigenous peoples have always educated their communities, and this education consisted of its own curriculum, one that was shaped and controlled by their own cultures and nations that continue to this day. Given the ways that Indigenous communities are romanticized and portrayed historically and in popular culture as static and without their own development, it is important to remember that

> Native Americans had never existed in an archaic time warp. Time and travel, interaction with people, and a willingness to learn encouraged First Nations peoples to grow, adapt, adopt, and expand their ways of knowing. American Indians shared their ideas with each other and with those outside their families, clans, and tribes. Knowledge was never static. . . . Their knowledges, experiences, and educations worked for them, and for hundreds of years Indian people lived and survived without the intervention of non-Indian newcomers. (Trafzer, Keller, & Sisquoc, 2006b, p. 5)

Before the arrival of Europeans, Indigenous communities had their own complex bodies of knowledge (Trafzer et al., 2006b), highly developed cultures, and ways of educating their peoples as sovereign nations with "carefully designed educational systems" (Lomawaima & McCarty, 2006, p. 27). These systems included educating children for strength as people, educating children for gendered roles and responsibilities, educating children at specific ages, preparing children for leadership in their communities, differentiating education by clan or rank, and preparing children (and communities) for survival (Lomawaima & McCarty, 2006). Structurally, such systems of education meant children experienced a variety of teachers and pedagogies as they learned a curriculum grounded in Indigenous epistemologies (Lomawaima & McCarty, 2006) whereby "for thousands of years, American Indian people taught a variety of subjects significant to their specific needs and wishes" (Trafzer et al., 2006b, pp. 5–6). Knowledge was transmitted through oral tradition and direct instruction by elders, singers, and storytellers, and their curriculum was far-ranging and deep: mathematics, marine biology, music, botany, astronomy, dance, art, architecture, geology, cartography, language, watercraft, culture, religion, among others (Kidwell, 1985; Lomawaima & McCarty, 2006; Trafzer et al., 2006b). Tribal communities determined their own curriculum for a very long time, a fact that is important to remember as we move forward in time and analyze the impositions upon that same self-determination.

THE ADVENT OF "INDIAN EDUCATION" UNDER THE FEDERAL INDIAN POLICIES OF THE UNITED STATES

As described above, Indigenous "curriculum" has been ongoing and in process well before the first genocidal contact with Westerners and their institutions (Lomawaima, 1999). Additionally, what has come to be called "Indian education" (Lomawaima, 1999) in the United States is, in part, shaped by trust and responsibility established between the United States and individual tribes (Deyhle & Swisher, 1997). For these reasons, Dehyle and Swisher point out that "the history of Indian education is unique, complex, and not clearly understood by the majority of mainstream America" (p. 114). Part of this complexity has to do with the fact that education programs have been central tools for assimilation in the United States (Ward, 2005). Indeed, the scope and aim of Indian education is largely influenced by federal Indian policy— the policies put in place by the U.S. government in relationship to tribes, which have oscillated between conquest, assimilation, termination, and self-determination (Lomawaima & McCarty, 2006).

In fact, many observers of federal Indian policy outline seven historical policy periods that inevitably shape the curricular history we delve into here. These policy periods are

1. The formative years (1775–1820s)
2. The years of Indian removal, relocation, and establishment of reservations (1830s–1880s) (Wilkins, 2002)
3. The period of allotment, assimilation, and Americanization (1880s–1920s)
4. Limited tribal self-rule (1920s–1940s)
5. Termination and relocation (1940s–1960s) (Wilkins, 2002)
6. The federal Indian policies of self-determination (1960s–1980s) (Wilkins, 2002)
7. Tribal self-governance in an era of new federalism (1980–present) (Wilkins, 2002)

Understanding the development of Indigenous-informed curricular discourses thus requires a brief review of these policy periods, with particular attention paid to the historical span we focus on in this chapter.

First Policy Period: The Formative Years (1775–1820)

The 17th century witnessed the birth of mission schools, established by competing colonial powers in the Americas—the French, British, and Spanish. The shared educational impetus centered on civilizing and Christianizing Indigenous peoples (Grande, 2015). As the United States emerged as a new nation-state, policymakers and politicians were intent on creating and asserting a new national identity, apart from the British metropole. The education of the "Indian" was central in this project.

Second Policy Period: Indian Removal, Relocation, and Reservation (1830s–1880s)

Following the formative years period, federal Indian policy focused on Indian removal, relocation, and the establishment of reservations. Government policy was motivated by the belief that this civilizing could only be accomplished through Indian resettlement. As a result, Indian children were forcibly removed from their homes and families and taken to boarding schools far from their communities and subjected to harsh punishment (Hamme, 1995). The creation of the Indian boarding school during the early 19th century was the first phase of colonial education. In addition, these boarding schools were geographically removed from Native populations in order to encourage the breaking apart of tribal communities (Trujillo & Alston, 2005). There was also the creation of a small number of day schools near newly established reservations during the latter part of the removal policy period. The main goal of both the boarding and day schools was to "civilize" American Indians.

Third Policy Period: Allotment, Americanization, and Assimilation (1880s–1920s)

This period of Indian policy in the United States is represented by the policies of allotment, Americanization, and assimilation. In 1887 Congress passed the Allotment Act, also known as the Dawes Act, which divided up Indian land into individual lots in order to continue the goals of assimilating Indigenous peoples into U.S. society. The U.S. government continued to relocate students from diverse tribes to particular boarding schools such as Carlisle (Rosenfelt, 1973). Note that in Alaska, the passage of the 1887 Organic Act "established the first civil government in Alaska and provided the legal basis for federal provision of education," including Alaska Natives (Barnhardt, 2001, p. 16). During the early 1900s, the number of day schools established locally for tribes increased (Rosenfelt, 1973). Finally, during this time the federal government was responsible for the funding of Indian education, as Natives were not citizens of the United States and thus not eligible to enroll in public state-funded schools (Rosenfelt, 1973). As a result, in addition to boarding schools and day schools, the federal government paid the states nonresident fees in order to enroll Indian pupils in state schools (Rosenfelt, 1973). In Alaska, it was not until 1905 that a distinction was made between Alaska Natives and non-Native residents for the purposes of education (Barnhardt, 2001).

The Fourth Policy Period: Limited Tribal Self-Rule (1920s–1940s)

In the 20th century, federal Indian policy underwent a revival of "limited tribal self-rule" (1920s–1940s). This period was characterized by the report "The Problem of Indian Administration," better known as the "Meriam Report," which surveyed the failing status of the education, health, economic development, social life, and government programs of tribal peoples. It criticized boarding school education (Lomawaima & McCarty, 2006) and the impact of the previous administrations' policies such as allotment. As a result, Congress passed the 1934 Indian Reorganization Act, or Wheeler-Howard Act, which reversed the Allotment Act, restoring tribal self-governance (Wilkins, 2002). In 1934, the Johnson-O'Malley Act (JOM), a New Deal federal aid program, was enacted to subsidize states for the education and medical treatment of Indians, compelling the movement of Indian pupils from federal schools into state schools (Rosenfelt, 1973). During this time, there was also a movement by boarding schools to add high school–level grades, and some schools did in fact add up to grade 12, but by 1934 the shifting goals for boarding schools turned toward a "new" type of vocationalism that ended up bringing to a close high school accreditation (Lomawaima & McCarty, 2006).

It is within the scope of the first through fourth policy periods that we are discussing Native American curricular discourse. The policy periods that follow (the policy period of termination and relocation, 1940s–1960s; the period of tribal self-determination, 1970s–1980s; and the policy period of Tribal self-governance in an era of new federalism, 1980–present) demonstrate the instability of these policy periods. For example, during the fifth policy period of termination, federal policy swung back toward ending the tribal/federal relationship exemplified by termination and relocation policies of the time. The definitive policy statement of this period was House Concurrent Resolution 108, adopted in 1953, which authorized government termination of tribes (Rosenfelt, 1973; Wilkins, 2002). In the capacity of education, the federal government increasingly shifted its responsibility for Indian education to the states. Some federal schools operated by the Bureau of Indian Affairs (BIA) were closed (Rosenfelt, 1973), and this forced transfer of students to state schools was met with resistance by Native communities (Rosenfelt, 1973).

In the period of self-determination (1960s–1980s), beginning with the Nixon administration, federal Indian policy changed and was once more in favor of tribal self-determination, influenced by the activism of Indian peoples in the United States (Wilkins, 2002). Several important policies were enacted during this period that enabled self-determination, while some Supreme Court decisions limited it. This period witnessed the resurgence of tribally controlled schools and curriculum. However, despite the potential for greater autonomy through contract and grant schools, there were possible shortcomings of such funding because it continued to be tied to federal monies (Senese, 1991). Yet the following decades of federal Indian policies (1980–present) witnessed administrations that in name honored tribal self-determination while cutting funds for Indian programs (Wilkins, 2002). This period is represented by inconsistent policies, along with an important Indian education report, *Indian Nations at Risk: An Educational Strategy for Action* (Indian Nations at Risk Task Force, 1991), which like the *A Nation at Risk* report, gave rise to increased standardization under No Child Left Behind. Paralleling the larger educational initiatives addressing educational failure in the United States, the Indian Nations at Risk report, like the 1928 Meriam Report, outlined the problems with Indian education in the United States.

Indeed, both the historical and contemporary manifestations of Indian education have vacillated according to the political, economic, and social currents of the U.S. settler colonial context. Offering this brief review contextualizes the inconsistent policies under which Native American curricular discourse developed. As stated, in the context of *Reclaiming the Multicultural Roots of U.S. Curriculum*, we will be focusing on the second, third, and fourth policy periods, since these periods correspond to the time most strongly associated with the founding of the curriculum field and most specifically with the regional particularities of the Southeastern tribes we focus on below.

CURRICULAR GENOCIDE AND CURRICULAR SELF-DETERMINATION: THE CHALLENGES OF NATIVE CURRICULAR DISCOURSE

We recognize that Indian education in the United States was forever changed by colonization and the forced dispossession of Native lands by settlers and the U.S. government. As such, we also provide a more thorough discussion of Indian education and curriculum through the colonial period under the sweep of the policy periods we outlined above, eventually leading up to the period of focus for this chapter and book—the turn of the 20th century and the establishment of the field of curriculum studies. Using concepts of *curricular genocide* and *curricular self-determination*, we then look at the evolving curricular discourse of several Native communities during these times. Specifically, we highlight the positioning and discourse of several Tribal Nations in the Southeastern United States, many of whom established their own universities and attempted to maintain curricular self-determination as sovereign tribes seeking to prove their legitimacy to the White/Western world, which earned them the problematic label of "civilized" tribes. We then analyze the rise of off-reservation boarding schools for Native children as a central part of the "curriculum" for attempted Westernization, Christianization, and cultural assimilation of Indigenous communities. In the process we discuss various forms of curricular resistance by Indian children and their parents, and we conclude this chapter with an analysis of the shift in U.S. federal Indian policy and politics regarding Indian education that came on the heels of the Great Depression and the Progressive Era, including the influence of the progressive education movement.

Before continuing, we would like to take a moment to address some issues of language and orientation of this chapter. Here we use the words "Native," "Indian," and "Indigenous" relatively interchangeably in our discussion of Native American communities. We similarly use the terms *tribe* and *nation* interchangeably to name the affinity grouping and governmental structures associated with Native peoples. We recognize that there are complicated politics associated with names and terms and that these are contested and contestable on various grounds. Even the use of "American" in "Native American" is problematic, as this term comes from an Italian explorer, thus furthering the constructed narrative that Indigenous peoples are not "people" in their own right and thus are not worthy of existing as subjects of their own histories outside of Western contact. To put it bluntly, the English language is the colonizers' language, and in the writing of this book we are not just bound to it in various ways for historical reasons; English also carries with it the act of colonization (Ngugi, 1986) such that any discussion of Indigenous history and culture in the United States is always marred by this relationship. Although we cannot change this historical fact, we do think that we can, in English, take up a politics of exposure and critique of the power dynamics involved with the curricular discourse of Indian education during this period, and that is our intent here. Finally, before proceeding we also want to note that we take seriously Tuck and Yang's (2012) notion that "decolonization is not a metaphor." As such, despite our trenchant critique of colonization of the land now referred to as the United States of America and the relationship of that process of colonization to the curricular discourse surrounding Indian education, we do not make any loose claims to using "decolonization" as a metaphor here to understand or describe the work we do in this chapter. Rather, the critical curriculum analyses we undertake here stand more firmly on the grounds of being anti-imperialist, anti–White supremacist and against the Manifest Destiny that were all used as weapons against Indigenous peoples of the Americas.

In this chapter we make use of several concepts associated with *curriculum*, which we, as discussed in the introduction, recognize is itself a contested concept within the field. Those arguments withstanding, here we make use of the related concepts of *curricular self-determination* and *curricular genocide*. We are conceiving of *curricular self-determination* as assertions of control over the curriculum taught to their own peoples by Indigenous communities as an expression of tribal or national sovereignty. Similarly, we conceive of *curricular genocide* as the relational opposite of *curricular self-determination*. As we use it here, *curricular genocide* refers to the attempted use of curriculum, in this case by the federal government, churches, and other Western institutions in the United States, to colonize and challenge the sovereignty of Indigenous peoples. In the case of *curricular genocide*, multiple forms of sovereignty are challenged, often at once and in overlapping ways. For instance, not only does the imposition of a curriculum of colonization challenge the sovereign right of a First Nation to educate its own children, it simultaneously functions as a challenge to what we might refer to as the epistemological sovereignty of Native peoples. In addition, it functions as a challenge to what we might refer to as the cultural self-determination of Native peoples—since curriculum always carries institutional power and culture with it (Apple, 2012; Au, 2011). Further, we have purposefully chosen to name this process *curricular genocide* instead of *curricular colonization*. We feel the term *colonization* here would not be strong enough because it leaves out the purposeful intent of educational policy and curricular discourse for Native Americans: their geographic and cultural eradication from the land to make physical and cultural room for the desires of Whites (Calderón, 2014b; Tuck & Gaztambide-Fernandez, 2013).

CURRICULAR DISCOURSE DURING COLONIAL TIMES

Above we outlined the formative policy period of federal Indian policy. In this section, we spend time examining the colonial roots of the ideologies behind "Indian education." As stated, formal education for Indigenous people must always be understood within a context of colonial education (Adams, 1995; Deyhle et al., 2008), which Lomawaima (1999) defines as "the reculturing and reeducation of American Indians by secular and religious institutions of colonizing nations" (p. 3). Lomawaima goes on to explain that colonial education was based on a set of four tenets about Native Americans that were "not based on natural truths but were culturally constructed and served specific agendas of the colonizing nations" (p. 3). These tenets asserted the following:

> (1) that Native Americans were savage and had to be civilized; (2) that civilization required Christian conversion; (3) that civilization required subordination of Native communities, frequently achieved through resettlement efforts; and (4) that Native people had mental, moral, physical, or cultural deficiencies that made certain pedagogical methods necessary for their education. (p. 3)

These tenets held true from the very beginning of the colonial project to "educate" Indigenous peoples. In the 1500s, for instance, Roman Catholics established missions to convert Natives to Christianity and "civilize" them, regularly separating children from their families. Roman Catholic priests established schools within the missions to indoctrinate these children (Trafzer et al., 2006b). As early as 1665 Jesuits in New France were ordered to introduce manual labor into Indian education. Spanish missions served as models for the American Indian boarding schools established during the policy periods of the formative years and Indian removal. These schools had a curriculum of "civilizing" the "savage" Natives through teaching agricultural and domestic skills, but only at the lowest levels (Lomawaima, 1999). The English used a wide range of techniques to "educate" Native populations, and a few individuals, like Puritan missionary John Eliot, did make use of systematic Christian proselytizing. However, the English did not make use of missions in the same ways, even though they too intended to Christianize and "civilize" Native Americans, and often they combined secular academic curriculum with a curriculum of Christianization. For example, the First Continental Congress established a Committee on Indian Affairs to teach Delaware Native communities Christianity, literacy and mathematics, and vocational training (Trafzer et al., 2006b). As Trafzer et al. (2006b) explain,

> Indeed, after the United States separated from Great Britain, American education focused strongly on Christian values and vocational education so that Indian people could be "useful" to the dominant society and at the same time achieve a measure of "civilization." In addition, the government could help indirectly Christianize Indians using government policy, power, and funds. Christianization and civilization through education became the foundation of Indian education as conceived by non-Indian policy makers in the United States and Canada. (p. 8)

This mix of academic instruction, vocational training, Christianization, Westernization, and "civilization" continued to define the curricular discourse for Native communities moving forward (Cobb, 2000; Lomawaima, 1999). As we will see in the next section, even when Tribal Nations attempted to maintain sovereign control over their own curriculum in an attempt to prove their legitimacy to Whites, they still were forced to succumb to the military and institutional power asserted by both the federal government and spread of White people (and Whiteness) across the continent.

CURRICULAR SELF-DETERMINATION
IN THE CONTEXT OF COLONIZATION

There was a historical moment when several of the tribes in the Southeastern United States attempted to assert their curricular self-determination in response to pressures impinging upon them by Whites and the process of colonization. One of the assertions of Whites was that Natives were savages and not civilized in part because they maintained oral traditions, did not have their own institutions for formal schooling, and did not have systems of writing. In the context of colonization, during the period of the late 1700s and early 1800s (the formative years of federal Indian policy), the Cherokee, Chickasaw, Choctaw, Muskogee, and Seminole Nations established schools of their own. In this way, they essentially created public schools for the children of their sovereign nations where the schools and curriculum were completely governed by the tribes themselves (Trafzer et al., 2006b). The Cherokee are a good example of this, and they illustrate an attempt at Native curricular self-determination as a survival strategy in the face of ongoing encroachment by Whites and the U.S. government. In 1821 Chief Sequoyah and his daughter introduced to the tribal council a written language that he had developed for the Cherokee language (Cushman, 2011). As Cushman (2011) explains,

> For Cherokees, using this unique writing system served two purposes simultaneously. On the one hand, it offered a means for solidifying Cherokee perspectives through representation of the language in writings such as daily correspondences, traditional stories, religious practices, and legal and governmental documents. On the other hand, it symbolized their intellectual abilities and civilized culture to outsiders, acting as an important indicator of their sophistication and equality to Whites. (p. 7)

The Cherokee written language was rapidly adopted and learned by the tribe in the span of just a few years, which Perdue (1994) presents as evidence that there was widespread, grassroots support for the establishment of the language, and it allowed them to "protect, enact, and codify Cherokee knowledge and perspectives" (Cushman, 2011, pp. 9–10). In addition to starting their own newspaper printed in written Cherokee, the Cherokee published spelling, arithmetic, and other educational books for children (Cushman, 2011), which enabled children in Cherokee schools to learn to read and write in their own language (Trafzer et al., 2006b).

It is important that we recognize the double-sided politics that written language, even the Cherokee one, carries with it. In the case of Indigenous peoples, there is an inherently colonizing aspect to written language in that it represents a bending to European norms and expectations as part of a broader colonizing process. This was generally true of the Cherokee, who, in response to White and U.S. colonization, wanted to demonstrate how "civilized" they were in order to fend off physical and cultural encroachment of the White, Christian colonizers. However, the Cherokees never proved themselves "civilized" enough to satisfy land-hungry White Christians, who likely would have taken Cherokee land regardless, and ultimately did, resulting in the Trail of Tears (Zinn, 1995). There is, however, a reverse side to the development of written language as well. As Cushman (2011) points out, the creation of written Cherokee concretely created the capacity for the survival of some amount of Cherokee culture and worldview, a capacity which in itself can and should be seen as one form of resistance to colonization.

From the perspective of curriculum studies, the capacity for survival of and resistance to colonization speaks directly to the importance of the Cherokee written language, as well as the teaching and learning in Cherokee education that followed. As we highlighted above, written language allowed the Cherokee to codify their knowledge and worldview (Cushman, 2011) and pass that along to their children through instruction in Cherokee. Broadly speaking, this is "curriculum"—the combination of content, pedagogy, and curricular form (Au, 2007) structured in ways to access forms of knowledge specific to those communities (Au, 2011). In the case of the Cherokee, the formation of their own written language in the context of the establishment of their own schools represents a form of *curricular self-determination*, where the very articulation of who they are as a people can be embodied in the transmission of culture and knowledge across time and institutions.

However, the Cherokee were the exception, not the rule, and despite their articulated curricular self-determination, White government officials continued their colonizing push for more control of the education (and land) of Native Americans. Here, turning close attention to the formative years of federal Indian policy (1775–1820s) sets the stage for the U.S.-led curricular genocide. In 1818 officials began to strongly push for U.S. government control of Indian education, and by 1819 Congress passed the Indian Civilization Fund Act. This act, among other things, allowed the government to hire teachers to instruct Native communities in academics and agriculture to encourage the civilizing of tribal peoples. The Indian Civilization Act enabled Christian missionaries to be paid by the U.S. Congress to work with Native communities, and in 1820 the U.S. government started designating money to tribes for education. By 1824 Native American boarding schools served approximately 800 students, most of which had been established by Christian missionaries. These mission schools continued to entrench a curriculum of Christianity, "civilization," and vocational education, and in some cases, such as with the Methodist mission school in Kansas, they served as an institution to collect children from a variety of tribes after the U.S. government had removed them from their lands (Adams, 1995; Trafzer et al., 2006b).

It is important to highlight that, during the policy period of Indian removal, common schools were maintained by the tribes even after their forced removal to Indian Territory by the U.S. government after the Indian Removal Act of 1830 (Trafzer et al., 2006b) and that, despite ongoing U.S. government encroachment into Native lands and systems of education, in 1852 a total of 21 Native common schools existed serving 1,100 Native students being run by the tribes who had been moved to Indian Territory (Mihesuah, 1997). Indeed, as Cobb (2000) points out, even after forced removal to Indian Territory, the Chickasaw Nation, for instance, immediately set up its own day schools and boarding schools in an attempt to maintain relative control over the schooling of their own children. The Cherokee Nation reacted similarly, as Szasz (2006) explains:

> The Cherokee Nation saw school sovereignty as essential. After their prolonged pre-removal struggle to reconfirm their status as an independent nation—acknowledged by the U.S. Supreme Court but not by the U.S. president—they moved quickly toward educational control. Within three years of their arrival in Indian Territory in 1841, they had established a national school system. . . . (p. 192)

In 1842 the Choctaw Nation increased their funding for their own national school system as well, and in 1856 the Creeks used resources acquired from land sales to gain economic control of their nation's schools by opening day schools for their children that were under the direction of Indian administration (Szasz, 2006). Suffice it to say, these Tribal Nations continued to struggle to assert their educational sovereignty more generally, as well as their curricular self-determination, despite their forced removal and the decimation of their populations due to the Trail of Tears and diseases like smallpox.

FEDERAL OFF-RESERVATION BOARDING SCHOOLS

Undoubtedly the most studied and most significant influence on the curricular discourse for Native Americans was the establishment of federal, off-reservation boarding schools for Indian children (see, e.g., Adams, 1988, 1995; Child, 1998; Churchill, 2004; Cobb, 2000; Coleman, 1993; Lomawaima, 1999; Lomawaima & McCarty, 2006; Reyhner & Eder, 2004; Trafzer et al., 2006a). Although during the Civil War the U.S. government did not pay much attention to the education of Native Americans, the massive Civil War bloodshed combined with successful Native resistances against the U.S. Army in the American West pushed policymakers to consider working with tribes in other ways besides military intervention, and one of these strategies included the incorporation of language about the education of Native American children within the framing of treaties. In the 1870s the U.S. Congress began earmarking funds specifically for Indian education and began staffing small reservation schools—often using Native Americans from Christian denominations as the teachers (Trafzer et al., 2006b). As Adams (1995) explains, the turn toward education by federal policymakers makes sense:

> That reformers should turn to education . . . is not surprising. Since the days of the common school movement, the schoolhouse had come to achieve almost mythological status. Reformers viewed it as the seedbed of republican virtues and democratic freedoms, a promulgator of individual opportunity and national

prosperity, and an instrument for social progress and harmony. Moreover, because of the common schools alleged ability to assimilate, it was looked upon as an ideal instrument for absorbing those peoples and ideologies that stood in the path of the republic's millennial destiny. (p. 18)

It was during this period of Indian removal that U.S. federal policy shifted to functionally assert itself as a patriarchal power over Native peoples by defining them as "insensible wards" and giving them legal status akin to children (Lomawaima & McCarty, 2006, p. 44). Indeed, in *Cherokee Nation v. The State of Georgia*, the Supreme Court held that tribes—in this case the Cherokee—are not foreign states but rather are domestic dependent nations with a status akin to that of a ward to its guardian. This legal status also signaled that the federal government was taking parental power as wards of Indian children, which "stripped Native parents of choice in schooling their own children" (Lomawaima & McCarty, 2006, p. 44).

Within the articulation of U.S. federal supremacy over tribes, several arguments were wielded to justify education as a central policy tool for federal Indian policy, all of them based on racist, colonialist presumptions. One such justification was the presumption that Native elders could not be civilized, but the young could be "saved" and civilized. A second justification for Indian education policy was the idea that education under the control of Whites would speed up the cultural evolution of Native peoples as a whole toward being "civilized" peoples (again, obviously, by Western standards). Another justification was that education would promulgate economic self-sufficiency in Native communities, which in turn would make sure the federal government would not need to be responsible to feed and clothe them. Finally, a fourth and pragmatically racist and inhuman justification was that, according to some arguments at least, educating Indian children was seen as a less expensive solution to the "Indian problem" than the option of killing them in warfare (Adams, 1995).

From the lens of curriculum studies, there were multiple curricular aims, or even multiple intended curricula, embedded in the boarding schools. Although these intended curricula explicitly sought to teach Indian children academic knowledge and vocational training, they also clearly had the aim of cultural genocide. This curricular genocide operated on the idea that one needed to "kill the Indian" in order to "save the man" (Churchill, 2004). In the following section we will discuss not only the intended curriculum of the boarding schools but also the unintended curriculum (maybe the wrong concept). Additionally, we will address the ways that Indian children and their families resisted the curricular genocide intended by the boarding school curriculum, as well as the ways that Indigenous peoples reappropriated the academic aspects of the intended curriculum for their own purpose and agency.

CURRICULAR GENOCIDE AND THE ASSAULT ON INDIAN IDENTITY

The first federally funded, off-reservation boarding school for Indian children was established by Captain Richard Henry Pratt in an army barracks at Carlisle, Pennsylvania. Pratt continued the then well-established view that Native Americans were "savage" and "uncivilized," but unlike some others, Pratt's racism extended from his belief that their inferiority was cultural, not biological (Adams, 1995; Trafzer et al., 2006b). Indeed, the masthead of his publications read, "To civilize the Indian, get him into civilization. To keep him civilized, let him stay" (Pratt, as quoted in Trafzer et al., 2006b, p. 14). Indeed, the entire boarding school project was predicated on the idea of Native deficiency and White superiority, even at the level of emotional expression. As Lomawaima (1999) explains:

> In the federal boarding schools of the nineteenth and twentieth centuries, federal staff stereotypically expected Indian students to display a certain stoicism, and educators bent their efforts towards instilling "appropriate" forms of emotional expression. . . . Federal educators turned to stereotypes of Indian emotional and physical "deficiencies" to explain student behavior and to justify federal reshaping of Indian emotional life and expression. (p. 19)

It was also no mistake that the Carlisle boarding school was developed in an army barracks, because military regimentation, training, and uniformity lay at the heart of all the religious and federal Indian boarding schools. This style of education was seen as a way to make Native children subservient and force them to conform to non-Indian standards and ways of existing (Lomawaima, 1999), as a way to subvert their perceived, untamed "wildness" that was blocking their path to evolving into civilized peoples (Adams, 1995). Thus, while generally speaking, the official, intended academic and vocational curriculum of the boarding schools was fairly straightforward from the perspective of pure content, it was always entangled with the broader aim of the cultural genocide of Native peoples and attacks on Indigenous cultural identity.

The intended/official curriculum for Indian children in the federal boarding schools represented a linked constellation of subjects and concepts meant to surround the child in the ways of Whiteness, thereby promoting/protecting settler colonialism. On the surface there were, for instance, more-typical academic subjects being taught. Native children were taught math, science, English literacy and language, geography, astronomy, U.S. history, social studies, and physiology (Adams, 1995; Trafzer et al., 2006b). Developing fluency in spoken and written English was almost always the initial focus of the curriculum for Indian children in the boarding schools, and English-only rules were often put into place by boarding school officials, only to have those rules found to be almost impossible to enforce (Adams, 1995; Spack, 2002). As was illustrated with the example of the Cherokee writing system during the colonial era (Cushman, 2011), discussed previously in this chapter, Whites placed a high value on having an alphabet and written language and often attributed both to being representative of civilization. No doubt, in addition to daily communication, this was one of the driving reasons behind the imposition of written English upon Native children. Indeed, all of the academic subjects were tightly integrated with the view that learning such a curriculum would undo the "savagery" of Tribal Nations' cultures by cutting against all aspects of their worldviews. Physical geography challenged Indigenous knowledge systems entirely. It contradicted lessons about the cosmos and creation stories passed along by tribal elders, and it diminished the geographic and spiritual significance of major aspects of the Indian physical world (Adams, 1995). However, the cultural contradictions did not end with physical geography, and we would argue that these subjects represented an explicit curriculum of cultural genocide while also carrying with it a Western worldview that left no room for other worldviews. As Adams (1995) explains:

> Probably more significant than the specific content of the scientific curriculum was the deeper message being transmitted. Traditionally, Indian children had been taught to look upon nature in ecological and spiritual terms. To know nature was to recognize one's dependency on the earth and its creatures. . . . Whites, on the other hand, objectified nature. . . . Nature was to be controlled, conquered, and finally, exploited. (p. 145)

A similar lesson about Western knowledge was being taught with mathematics as well. In learning numbers, measurements, basic logarithms, and calculations associated with the needs of Western civilization, Native children were also learning that "the culture that was engulfing [them] placed a high priority on measuring things; space, time, goods, and money were divided and subdivided to the nearest fraction. The White man's culture was a culture of calculations" (Adams, 1995, p. 143).

The teaching of history, social studies, and citizenship was similarly implicated in the curricular genocide being enacted upon Indian children in the federal boarding schools. The concept of citizenship requires at least two things. First, it requires an allegiance to a particular nation. Second, and in turn, it requires a definition of what that allegiance means in terms of the practices of day-to-day life. In the context of Indian education during this period, one major goal of citizenship education for Native American children in the boarding schools was to attempt to get Indians to identify with the United States (as a settler colonial state) above their own identification/ allegiance to the Indigenous Nation or Tribe. This made the teaching of U.S. history, with its legacy of war and genocide against Native Americans, a curious and precarious endeavor: *curious* because citizenship education depended on the reproduction of a settler nationalism that relied on both a presence and dispossession of Indians as the predecessors of the Europeans who settled the United States (Calderón, 2014b) and *precarious* because, as Adams (1995) explains:

> Special attention also was given to instilling a heartfelt, patriotic identification with the nation engulfing them. In this connection the subject of United States history was central. But how could Indian pupils be made to identify with the "American experience" wherein Indian-White conflict and the settlement of the West were central themes in the national mythology? Frame of reference was obviously important. (p. 146)

In response to these issues, several boarding schools turned to Scudder's (1884) textbook, *A History of the United States of America*. This textbook mostly avoided discussing Native Americans, barely glossing over Indian–White conflict (little has changed to this date). In what little treatment it did give to Indians, the textbook maintained the language of them being both noble and savage, a typical narrative that continues to this day in social studies texts that fold Indigenous peoples into the fabric of the settler nation (Calderón, 2014). Even still, teachers using the text were concerned with using Scudder's text because of the negative portrayal of Indians in what little attention was given to them (Adams, 1995). At the time the Indian Office suggested fostering "a spirit of love and brotherhood in the minds of the children toward White people," focusing on the "nobility of character" of both Whites and Indians and showing "to the pupils that the guilt of the persons committing [acts of injustice] does not attach to the whole race" (as quoted in Adams, 1995, p. 147).

However, the history and citizenship curriculum was not just about trying to shift the national allegiances of Native children. It also bore the message of curricular genocide of Indian cultures necessary for the promotion of the idea of Whites as the inheritors of the original Indigenous inhabitants. Western notions of citizenship were seen as the culmination of a linear progression, one that argued that Native cultures were savage and barbarian and needed to evolve toward the Western ideal of a civilized citizen (Adams, 1995). The idea of an evolved civilized American citizen, the mantle taken up by White settlers, promoted settler futurity (Tuck & Yang, 2012). Thus, citizenship education for Indian children relied on placing Native culture on that line, labeling it as savage, pushing Native children to evolve toward being "civilized citizens," a norm that ultimately could only be possessed by White settlers, thereby protecting settler nationalism (Calderón, 2008, 2014b; Tuck & Gaztambide-Fernandez, 2013).

Still, it is important to point out that the U.S. federal government, for a variety of reasons, did not want Indians to be too educated. This can be seen in the shift in curriculum policy and focus in Indian education that took place under the leadership of Estelle Reel during the federal Indian policy characterized by the policies of allotment, assimilation, and Americanization (1880s–1920s). Reel was nominated by President William McKinley to the position of Office of Indian Affairs Superintendent of Indian Schools. She was the first woman nominated for a federal post high enough to require Senate ratification. Consistent with eugenicists of her time, Reel believed that mental capacities and intelligence were genetically bred, such that different races held biologically different (and hierarchical) intelligence. Native Americans, of course, had limited intellectual capacity by Reel's assessment, and thus should only experience the most basic curriculum possible, preferably one that trained them for manual labor. By 1918 higher-level aspects of academic learning were ejected from the curriculum for Native children altogether as "nonessential," freeing several hours a day for Native children to practice industrial work (Adams, 1995; Lomawaima & McCarty, 2006).

The idea that Indigenous peoples were inferior to settlers was not new. Indeed, these ideologies of settler superiority were foundational to the ideas expressed in key Supreme Court cases such as *Cherokee Nation v. The State of Georgia*, which established tribes as wards of the federal government. Similarly, such ideas of Indigenous inferiority were inherent in the education through citizenship curriculum discussed above. As stated, these ideologies promoted the notion that settler expansion was inevitable and indeed necessary (Moran, 2002). It is along this ideological trajectory that Reel's beliefs and the educational practices imposed on Indigenous peoples must be placed.

For instance, vocational training was always a part of the curriculum for Indigenous children in the federal boarding schools. The question, historically, was always an issue of what balance between academics and vocational training would be struck, and this balance changed depended on which administrators happened to be in charge (Adams, 1995; Lomawaima, 1999; Lomawaima & McCarty, 2006). Indian boys were given a curriculum of vocational training that included skills like farming and blacksmithing, among others; Indian girls were given a curriculum associated with domestic work that focused on skills like sewing, canning, and child care, among others. However, even vocational training carried with it the politics of curricular genocide because the work training also was aimed at the inculcation of possessive individualism among Indian children (Adams, 1995; Churchill, 2004), a cultural value associated with Western culture and capitalism that ran counter to the more collectivist cultural norms of Native Americans.

Lomawaima and McCarty (2006) make a critical point about the kind of vocational and academic curriculum and training provided to Indian children in the boarding schools: "Indian school industrial training was designed to *prevent* Native economic competition in the American workforce, just as low-level academic training precluded aspirations to professional schools or careers" (p. 49, emphasis in original). The point of Indian education was never to prepare Native children to compete on equal terms with Whites, thus protecting settler futurity. It was an education aimed at keeping Tribal Nations peoples in a racial and political underclass relative to White settlers. Indeed, Indian parents and students understood this reality and protested the low academic standards and the limitations in employment they created post schooling, but these protestations were ignored (Lomawaima & McCarty, 2006).

As we discussed in the introduction, curriculum is a varied concept that can include many things. Once such conception is that curriculum is of environmental design (Au, 2011; Huebner, 1970, 1999). To that definition, it is important to recognize that the curricular genocide was embedded in the entirety of the boarding school environment. The military-style regimentation and orderliness, for instance, was always seen as a means of "civilizing" Native children (Lomawaima, 1999). Even the design of the boarding school space itself was a part of the curriculum. As Adams (1995) explains,

> Adjusting to a new physical environment also meant adjusting to new conceptions of space and architecture. The boarding school, the new recruits quickly learned, was a world of lines, corners, and squares. Rectangular dormitories and dining rooms and square classrooms were filled with beds, tables, and desks—all carefully arranged in straight rows. Whites, Indians surmised, largely conceived of space in linear terms. (p. 113)

This regimentation and orderliness also extended to food, which became a part of curricular genocide as well. Not only were students eating new kinds of food foreign to their cultural cuisines, but, in the words of Adams (1995), they were also acquiring "the food rites of civilized society" (p. 116). From the perspective of curriculum, the dining room was a classroom where Indian students were taught about Western eating utensils, eating rituals, and the basics of the White man's conception of table manners (Adams, 1995). Indeed, this kind of regimentation extended to every aspect of the lives of Indian students in the boarding schools: eating, sleeping, working, learning, playing, singing, literally everything was placed within an ordered regimentation as part of the curricular genocide attempting to bring Western civilization to Indigenous children (Adams, 1995; Lomawaima, 1999).

However, the curricular genocide faced by Indian students in federal boarding schools went beyond the academic curriculum, the vocational curriculum, the school environment, the regimentation, and the food. Perhaps most traumatically, the curricular genocide experienced by Native children attacked their identities in physical and symbolic ways. One of the most damaging things done to Native children immediately upon entry to the boarding schools was the cutting of their hair. For Native peoples, hair often holds deep though diverse cultural meanings (Adams, 1995). The hair cutting caused trauma to Indian children, so much so that boarding school staff went to great lengths to try to hide the cutting from newcomers after having seen the outcries and occasional acts of outright physical resistance from students. Cutting the hair of Indian students was physically symbolic of curricular genocide in that it gave concrete manifestation to the schools' intent to cut away the "savage" and bring the children into "civilization" (Adams, 1995).

Akin to the process of cutting hair, Native children were given new, Judeo-Christian names and/or English names by their White schoolmasters. This is how, for instance, the noted Indian author Ota Kte (Plenty Kill) became known as Luther Standing Bear (Trafzer et al., 2006b). The White settlers believed there were practical reasons for the name changes, although the practice was nevertheless a violent act. Teachers often simply could not pronounce students' Indigenous names in their Native tongues, and some names did not translate well into English. There were also concrete, genocidal reasons for the name changes. One reason was part of the curriculum of pushing Indian children toward the White norm of possessive individuals and owning land institutionalized by the Allotment Act: Once given Western surnames, Indian property "owners" could then track ownership and inheritances and, more significantly, be taxed on those lands. Concretely, policymakers understood that the outcomes of these policies would result in the loss of Indian lands, facilitating the expansion of White settlers. Most important, name changing was an outright assault on Indian identity (Adams, 1995). As Adams (1995) explains,

> Traditional Indian names and the naming process itself were fundamentally connected to the process of cultural transmission and served a variety of educational purposes: as a stimulus to self-improvement, as a reward for a special achievement, and finally as a means of transferring traits of a revered relative or tribal figure to a member of a new generation. Because some Indian youth were sometimes given a series of names in the course of their development, and since the giving of names was frequently ritualized in elaborate ceremony, tribal naming practices were clearly central to the perpetuation of cultural outlook. (p. 111)

Names and the power they hold are critically important in all cultures, and they are used to carry tradition and express cultural worldviews and paradigms. The changing of Indigenous names to Western versions or outright White names represented a sharp assault to the very soul of Indian identity.

What we know from educational history and educational research is that, quite often, the intended curriculum, the explicit curriculum—the aims of education offered by schools, teachers, or policymakers—is not necessarily accepted by students and their communities (Apple, 2012). There is outright resistance by some children to just about anything being taught in any schools at any time, either 100 years ago or today. Whether it is the children pushing back against their schooling from their position as working-class kids (Willis, 1977) or the Pueblos of San Felipe and Santo Domingo keeping their children out of state-run public schools, we know that just because something is taught does not mean it is blindly accepted. Similarly, in addition to resisting curriculum and the inculcations of schooling, we know that students and communities reappropriate school knowledge for their own ends and purposes (Rosenfelt, 1973). Given all this, it is critical to recognize that Indian children and their communities both resisted the curricular genocide of the federal boarding schools, and they also made use of some of the very tools and experiences being wielded against them. We attend to both of these phenomena in the next sections.

REBELLING AGAINST CURRICULAR GENOCIDE

Resistance to curricular genocide of the boarding schools took many forms, large and small. Sometimes there were more day-to-day micro resistances of Indian children daring to sing songs in their native languages at night to help them sleep. Others ignored boarding school rules designed to be specifically counter to Native cultures, hid from school authorities, smuggled Indian foodstuffs from home or visitors, or stole food from the cafeteria (Adams, 1995; Trafzer et al., 2006b). In the classrooms, students and authority figures alike both figured out that

> students, not teachers, often determined the pace of classroom work. Perhaps most unnerving was the students' uncanny ability to dutifully go through the motions of compliance while inwardly resisting the teachers' efforts. When students were most obdurant [sic], teachers could only guess at the thoughts masked by expressionless faces staring back at them. (Adams, 1995, p. 231)

Native American students in the boarding schools also faked sickness, pretended not to understand instructions, created disparaging nicknames for non-Native authority figures, performed tasks poorly or incorrectly, and played pranks on school authorities (Adams, 1995; Trafzer et al., 2006b).

There were other significant forms of outright resistance as well. Some Indian children ran away from the boarding schools for short periods of time to hang out with other Indian children, speak in their Tribal languages, drum, sing, dance, tell stories, support each other, and keep cultural traditions alive. Often fleeing due to whippings, homesickness, imprisonment, and food shortages experienced at the boarding schools, many Indian children simply ran away and either returned home to their Tribes or found a place to work and live on their own (Adams, 1995; Trafzer et al., 2006b). As Child (1998) recounts:

> The explanations Native students occasionally gave for running away from boarding school illustrate the shortcomings of the Indian education system as it had developed by the early twentieth century. Isaac Plenty Hoops said he disliked the poor boarding school diet. Other children complained that they were mistreated by teachers, felt burdened by the workload, or were unhappy with the kind of work they were assigned at school. Some said they were too confined by the innumerable restrictions placed on them in boarding schools, where they also felt looked down upon as Indians. Homesickness was a persistent problem. When loneliness or tensions inevitably surfaced, the typical response of Indian students was to abandon school, usually for the security of family and tribe. (p. 88)

Some Native students would trick school authorities in ways that would end up in those authorities getting physically hurt or set fires with the specific intent of burning down buildings (Adams, 1995; Child, 1998; Trafzer et al., 2006b).

Native parents regularly subverted the curricular genocide of the boarding schools as well, either during vacations when their children returned home or by making regular visits to the schools themselves. Native parents purposefully fostered tribal languages, encouraged children to run away, encouraged children to resist completing school work, and informed children of cultural events to attend, such as tribal dances. Indian parents also found ways to resist the annual "roundup" of Indian children by federal agents intent on taking their children to the boarding schools. Some families just disappeared until the federal agents were not around to pressure them. Others tried bargaining, making arguments about space at the boarding schools and family quotas for filling that space. Once their children were in the boarding schools, Indian parents continued to resist. They withdrew their children in large organized numbers or encouraged them to simply run away from school (Adams, 1995; Child, 1998).

REAPPROPRIATION, SURVIVAL, AND
NATIONAL RESISTANCE THROUGH SCHOOLING

It is indisputable that the federal boarding schools were, on the whole, created, organized, and administered with the express intent of committing cultural genocide of the Indigenous peoples on the land officially called the United States (Adams, 1995; Churchill, 2004; Deyhle et al., 2008; Spring, 2010). Sadly, this curricular genocide was at times relatively successful, as some (not anything approaching a majority, but some) Native students internalized the curriculum, which taught them that their home cultures were savage and less advanced than that of the "civilized" Westerners (Adams, 1995). Without undermining the genocidal reality of the federal boarding schools, we do feel that it is important to recognize the various ways in which Native children and their communities reappropriated and made use of the boarding school curriculum in strategic ways. Child (1998), for instance, argues that during the Great Depression, some Native families actively saw the boarding schools as a way to use federal resources to preserve their families. Adams (1995) also highlights that some Indian students made a very strategic and pragmatic choice to go along with the boarding school program and curriculum, seeing it as a matter of national survival and not one of cultural superiority or inferiority:

> Some [Indian students] pessimistically concluded that the options facing Indians were exactly as policymakers defined them—assimilation or extinction. If the course of Indian-White history taught us anything, it was the sobering lesson that Whites would never allow Indians to live on their own terms. . . . By this line of reasoning, education was essential, not because it facilitated one's climb up the ladder of civilization, but because it ensured racial survival. (p. 257)

It is true that the boarding school curriculum did provide Native students with new skills, albeit skills aimed at negotiating the White man's world. That said, many Native peoples also used these skills to communicate their Indian identity in new and quite strong ways—including the contribution of the boarding schools to the building of a pan-Indian political identity, thus preserving some aspects of their culture with the tools meant to colonize (Cobb, 2000; Szasz, 2006; Trafzer et al., 2006a). Luther Standing Bear's (1978/1933) third book reflected on his experience at the Carlisle Indian School and discussed the fact that, despite experiencing the school's curricular genocide, he actively maintained his identity as a Lakota (Lomawaima & McCarty, 2006). Using the Chickasaw as an example, Cobb (2000) argues that this phenomenon of Native reappropriation, survival, and strategic use of skills gained through curricular genocide is particularly true with regard to the ways they made use of literacy:

> By encouraging their children to attend mission schools in their Mississippi homeland in the early 1800s, by sending their children to eastern schools while waiting for their academies to be built, by building their own academies in conjunction with missionaries after their forced removal from their homeland, the Chickasaw people proved that they saw literacy education as inherently valuable because it was useful to them, to their purposes. Literacy, for the Chickasaw Nation, was a tool, a weapon used defensively and offensively in the fight for their national survival. (p. 16)

We want to reiterate that our argument here is not meant to construe the curricular genocide of colonial education and the boarding schools as "good," per se. Rather, we want to recognize the strength, intelligence, and resilience of Indigenous peoples as they navigated the difficult cultural, political, and educational terrain of colonization and genocide. In that context, both physical survival and cultural survival are paramount, and different individuals and tribes made different decisions based on their particular situations. This meant that Indian children responded to curricular genocide in a range of ways, a range we wanted to make sure was represented in our discussion here. Surprisingly, there was also some variability in how White administrators and policymakers viewed Indian education, and this resulted in significant policy shifts in Indian education during the Progressive Era and the time of the New Deal that shaped the federal Indian policy period of reorganization or limited Tribal self-rule (1920s–1940s).

INDIAN EDUCATION AND THE PROGRESSIVE ERA OF CURRICULUM REFORM

There is also evidence that the education of Native American children within federal boarding schools in the early 1920s and 1930s was directly shaped by the larger and quite important struggles over curriculum in U.S. education so regularly addressed as a part of the history and canon of the field of curriculum studies. For instance, as progressive education began to rise to prominence as a movement in the 1920s and 1930s, there was evidence of a discernable shift in the official orientation toward the education of Native children. G. Stanley Hall, for instance, critiqued the state of Indian education and "urged teachers to build on an Indian child's natural capacities and background rather than obliterate them" (Adams, 1995, p. 313). As another example, in 1923 the Committee of One Hundred, organized by the U.S. secretary of the interior and which included several Native American leaders, produced a report calling for increased pay to attract more qualified teachers to schools for Native children, more investment in Native school facilities, more day schools for younger Native children (as opposed to boarding schools), college scholarships aimed specifically at Native children, and more Native students in existing public schools (Reyhner & Eder, 2004).

In 1928 the Institute for Government Research, under direction from Secretary of the Interior Hubert Work, produced a study titled "The Problem of Indian Administration"—also referred to as the Meriam Report after Louis Meriam, the principle investigator. The Meriam Report was critical of several aspects of federal policy toward Native communities, and it contained a section on Indian education written mainly by Dr. W. Carson Ryan Jr. and a member of the Winnebago Nation, Reverend Henry Roe Cloud.

Dr. Ryan was considered a leader in the progressive education movement and was influenced by John Dewey and others in that movement, such as G. Stanley Hall (Adams, 1995; Reyhner & Eder, 2004). The education section of the Meriam Report reflected Dr. Ryan's progressive education–influenced views, as well as Reverend Cloud's perspective as a Winnebago, in that this section critiqued the fact that the curriculum being implemented for Indian children in Indian schools was largely divorced from the experiences and needs reflected by life on the reservations. The report also recommended ending boarding schools at the elementary level, instituting more day schools, and improving the quality of food at the boarding schools. It also questioned the use of boarding school students as laborers (which often contradicted states' child labor laws). In 1929, the new commissioner of Indian Affairs, Charles Rhodes, actively supported the findings of the Meriam Report by recommending that Indians be taught using daily experiences. Rhodes also later specifically mentioned the progressive education movement in his discussion of Indian education in 1930 (Adams, 1995; Reyhner & Eder, 2004).

By 1930 Dr. Ryan became the federal director of Indian education, with the stated intent of developing community schools, developing funded programs to place Native children in existing public schools, and slowly ending boarding schools (Reyhner & Eder, 2004). Dr. Ryan even coauthored the lead article of a special issue of the journal *Progressive Education*, dedicated entirely to the topic of Native education. As Reyhner and Eder point out, however, despite the decrease in the number of Indian boarding schools during Ryan's tenure, the actual number of Native students enrolled in boarding schools increased over the same period (Reyhner & Eder, 2004). Child (1998) argues that this period of Indian education saw a critical shift, for two reasons:

> A new era in American Indian education commenced once public school education surpassed boarding schools as the foundation of U.S. Indian education, which happened in the 1930s. The smaller number of boarding schools that remained primarily existed to offset the poverty of Indian families during the Great Depression; Indian demand for the schools was so widespread in the 1930s that the decade held the highest enrollment. (p. vii)

The election of Franklin D. Roosevelt as president in 1933 continued the shift in federal policy toward Indian education. Another supporter of educational progressivism, John Collier, was appointed to be the commissioner of Indian Affairs. Once appointed, Collier continued to carry forward the recommendations of the Meriam Report, and some of his work resulted in the passing of the Indian Reorganization Act that supported some measures of Indigenous religious freedom and tribal sovereignty (Reyhner & Eder, 2004).

In many ways this Progressive Era shift in Indian education was welcome, especially relative to the genocidal curriculum being enacted on tribal children and communities through the boarding school curriculum. The progressive turn in Indian education and the intentions of giving tribes more power and connecting the curriculum more closely are important, if not symbolically, of a broader political shift happening in some sectors of federal policy more generally and in education policy more specifically. Indeed, one can see the parallel development here from within curriculum studies, where during this same period of time the more radical and populist textbooks of Harold Rugg and George S. Counts were being published and were in the much broader public debates about what children in U.S. public schools should or should not be taught (Counts, 1932; Kliebard, 2004; Rugg, 1929, 1931).

We want to be clear, however, that the progressive turn in Indian education, while certainly an improvement over the genocidal impulses of earlier education policy, was not anticolonial, anti-imperialist, or antiracist. It could be argued, in fact, that while increasing the power of some Natives over some aspects of their educational lives, progressivism also served a different kind of assimilationist curriculum, one meant to ameliorate some aspects of the mistreatment of Native communities while also creating more potential buy-in to the idea of the benevolence of the U.S. system of government. Additionally, as Adams (1995) points out, progressive education leaders like Dewey and Hall still maintained racist notions regarding the superiority of Western/White culture:

> It is important to emphasize, however, that neither Hall nor Dewey were willing to acknowledge the equality of native culture. Hall's view in this regard stemmed from two interconnected beliefs. First, Hall believed there was a direct correspondence between stages in an individual's physical-psychological development and stages in the evolution of human society. Just as children were less than psychologically mature at their present level of development, so Indian cultures were less than completely civilized. This devastating evaluation of Indian culture was followed by a second belief that mental traits were unevenly distributed across the races. Because Indians were a "lower race," Hall doubted their capacity to move much beyond their present cultural condition. . . . Dewey, on the other hand, although rejecting Hall's attribution of mental traits to race, fully subscribed to the idea of social evolution, including the distinction between savagism and civilization. (pp. 313–314)

In this regard, one could argue that the progressive education shift in Indian education was still a colonizing one. Indeed, we could not expect the curriculum for Native children under the banner of progressive education to be antiracist, anticolonial, or anti-imperialist curriculum because progressive education ideals do not necessarily seek to develop capacities and consciousness to organize against the United States' occupation of Native lands and cultures. To be clear, we would not expect any major shift in federal Indian education policy to advocate such decolonization—the system simply cannot bear that burden of its own self-destruction.

CONCLUSION

On a macro level, it is unarguable that the boarding schools were racist, colonizing institutions that sought to strip Native children of their identities as Indians—or, in the language of Pratt and other racists, change these Native children from "savage" to "civilized." Indian children did not just have their names taken away by the boarding schools; their hair was also cut, and anything that outwardly signaled an Indian or tribal identity (such as jewelry, clothing, or blankets) was often confiscated by school officials. They were forced to eat meager, non-Native foods as well, and poor nutrition contributed greatly to the disease and death of Native children (Trafzer et al., 2006b). This in itself is a curriculum of the most violent and vile sort. It is a curriculum built specifically around the aim of cultural annihilation and represents a form of *curricular genocide*, which we discussed at great length in this chapter. It was a curriculum rooted in a process of trying to get Indian children to disidentify with their "savage," Native cultural roots, while trying to simultaneously reidentify with the supposedly superior White civilization and all that designation entailed. But curricular genocide involved more than just Indian identity and culture, for as Lomawaima (1999) explains, "Historically, the goals of the colonial education of American Indians have been to transform Indian people and societies and to eradicate Indian self-government, self-determination, and self-education" (p. 5). Thus, we need to recognize that while Indian culture and identity were a central target of the curricular genocide—enacted not just through the boarding schools but also through nearly all aspects of official Indian education at the turn of the 20th century and in the centuries leading up to it—the fundamental goal undergirding the entire colonial educational project was to attack First Nation sovereignty and to dispossess Native peoples of their lands. The cultural goals of White educators and policymakers were underwritten by very concrete material goals.

Even still, as we have taken great pains to highlight here in this chapter, the relationship between curriculum, learning, and people is not a linear, mechanical one. Human beings do not robotically take in what they are presented, passively accepting the explicit or intended curriculum. In the case of the education of Native children leading up to and just after the turn of the 20th century, there were significant, ongoing, daily acts of resistance by Indian students and families, some individual and some organized, happening in every corner, classroom, and school possible during this period. Also, in keeping with Mills's notion of revisionist ontology (1998), Native American writers powerfully engaged in the use of the written word to document the context of Native American education in the United States. In this context, Native American authors employed a counterhegemonic methodology of employing "that master's tools" to revise and repudiate the experiences of Native American communities in these schooling spaces. Thus, while the guiding principles behind Indian education were genocidal—and Indian communities were indeed forced to have their own curricular conversation and dialogue within the restrictive and oppressive context of colonization, dispossession, and attacks on sovereignty—the actual educational experiences of Native children did have some variance depending on local geographic, temporal, political, and institutional contexts. As Child (1998) reminds us,

> One reason that boarding school experiences varied widely for American Indian children and youth is that their lives and ideas were significantly influenced by the times in which they attended school. Think of Luther Standing Bear, Sun Elk, Charles Eastman, and others in the first generation, arriving at Carlisle or similar institutions for haircuts and uniforms at the end of the Indian wars. Many of them . . . were from communities actively engaged in military resistance. Their experience was unique and not entirely shared by later generations. Subsequent generations of students often had already attended a mission or day school, were bilingual, or were from families who worked in the wage economy. (p. vi)

Such variance in experience meant that curricular genocide and education for colonization of Indian children and communities was both successful and wildly unsuccessful in some important ways. Yes, it transformed Indian peoples forever, and it did resounding damage to Indian culture and identity. However, despite the intended curricular genocide being enacted upon them, Indians also made active and strategic choices to co-opt and reappropriate what they were learning for their own devices and in the pursuit of national, cultural, and personal survivance (Vizenor, 1994, 2008) as Native peoples.

This variance, like the Indian educational policies and practices that oscillated between more explicitly genocidal policies and policies meant to favor tribal self-determination, must be placed within the dominant ideology of White supremacy. Lomawaima and McCarty (2006) explain that when the unique cultural and linguistic practices of Indigenous peoples threaten "shared American identity," the federal government acts in ways to curtail the threat by instituting more-repressive mechanisms against tribes. Because the interests of Indigenous peoples are perceived in varying degrees of danger to White people, federal Indian policy thus responds to this fear by Whites by expanding and constraining federal Indian policy (Lomawaima and McCarty 2006).

We see the same themes emerging in the curricular discourse of each community we engage in this book. From the status of Chinese and Japanese Americans as the perpetual foreigner in the next chapter to the ambiguous status of Mexican Americans as neither White nor Black—a unique by-product of the multiple colonialisms of the Southwest—competing visions and practices of curricular discourse created tensions that communities of color had to navigate in their respective racist, colonial, and White supremacist contexts.

CHAPTER 3

Cultural Maintenance or "Americanization"?

Transnational Curriculum and the "Problem" of Chinese American and Japanese American Education in the Early 20th Century

> I want my children to get Chinese education first; they must have Chinese custom and understand Chinese language because they always be Chinese. My son come in here under law—soon American citizen, but now I no care so much because my two last children educated here because we have good Chinese school in this city. They can go night school and Saturday and learn enough Chinese. . . . However, they don't get Chinese customs; have no idea about Chinese history and traditions. If they don't have this old country education they no good. All my children have gone to school in this country also go to Chinese school.
>
> —Seattle businessman Chin Cheung, 1924

In Chapter 2 we explored some of the early curricular discourse among First Nations peoples. For Indigenous communities, the central issues revolved around colonization, the imposition of settler culture, the forced seizure of Native lands, and the ways Native communities navigated and resisted the White supremacist agenda of the colonizers' curriculum and system of education. As such, the struggle and tension for First Nations communities was in how to respond to colonization and the educational programs and expectations being forced upon them by White Christians who in their racism viewed Native cultures and peoples as barbaric and uncivilized. In this context, the curricular discourses turned to community conversations about relative degrees of cultural maintenance (curricular sovereignty) versus degrees of acquiescence (curricular colonization)—of resistance in all its varying forms and the contradictions that arise amidst a constant White supremacist push for assimilation. However, just as we discuss in this chapter, vital to the process of conceptualizing one's place in a racialized world was to think about the importance of schooling in resisting the hegemony of race and nation during this time.

What links the early curricular discourses of Native communities and all of the communities discussed in this book is that all were engaged in a struggle over defining their humanity against the pressures of White supremacy in the United States. All of the peoples in this book were faced with answering the question posed by White America: "How does it feel to be a problem?" (Du Bois, 1994/1903, p. 3). It is a question that exists only within the context of colonization, institutionalized slavery, and the ideology of White supremacy that undergirds both; and it is a question that Du Bois answers with silence simply because any of us are only defined as a "problem" relative to the power structures that seek to define us that way.

Asian American curricular discourse must be made sense of within the context of what came to be defined as the "Asian problem," a problem whose contours were defined by the context of White supremacy in the United States. As we will see in this chapter, Asian immigrants were invited as cheap labor in an act of interest convergence with Whites (Bell, 1980). However, that invitation was revoked as soon as Asians were perceived as a threat to White resources (particularly jobs) and when Asian culture ("Orientalism") was seen as a threat to White "American" cultural hegemony (Kuo, 1998).

When thinking about early Chinese American and Japanese American curricular discourse in particular, we think it is important to understand the positioning of those communities within the context of the United States during the late 1800s through the 1930s. During this period Asian immigrant labor was

- working as cheap labor after slavery was made formally illegal on land that was originally Native and was subsequently colonized by Spain, became Mexican territory, and was then taken over by the U.S. government (Zinn, 1995);
- negotiating a dual identity as "useful labor" on the one hand (relative to the kinds of occupations they were allowed to do) while also being constantly seen as a threat to White labor on the other (Kuo, 1998);
- operating within a racialized legal context typically concerned with Blackness, Whiteness, and Native-ness, which sometimes led to legal racial ambiguity for Asian Americans (Chan, 1993; Lopez, 1996)
- racialized (Omi & Winant, 2015) in terms that were still clearly not White and not "American" (as the two are inextricably linked);
- finding themselves stuck between and, at other times, acting as agents of international relations fraught with economic competition and even war (Azuma, 2005);
- developing an identity that often started with an intention to return "home" to Asia but that, as time passed and as resources allowed,

evolved into an identity (ofttimes grudgingly) of the United States as "home" (Chan, 1993).

As we consider early Chinese American and Japanese American curricular discourse and schooling, then in many ways we have to consider what it meant to be Asian, Asian American, and/or part of the Asian diaspora in this context and its implicit political and cultural complexities. By necessity, such considerations also must include what curriculum those communities taught in light of the contextual conditions. Similar to Native communities, for Asian Americans the question of cultural maintenance was paramount, a sentiment expressed by Chin Cheung in the above epigraph. Also similar to Native communities, the answer varied based on specific historical and political contingencies. Regardless of the specific answers, Chinese Americans and Japanese Americans were viewed and treated as a "problem" to be addressed by White America, and the curricular discourse of these diasporic Asian communities illustrates how they attempted to control their own identities as they negotiated contentious national politics.

ASIAN AMERICA AND THE FOCUS OF THIS CHAPTER

We are compelled to begin this chapter with the explicit recognition that the racial category of "Asian" and its attendant term, "Asian American," are completely socially, historically, and politically constructed—even if, as will be clear later in this chapter, this racial category carried material consequences that were quite real. The continent that historically has been defined as Asia includes over 30% of the Earth's land surface, over 4 billion people, thousands of languages, dozens of sovereign nation-states, and peoples from areas as diverse as Korea, the Philippines, India, Syria, and parts of Russia (Au, 2009; Chang & Au, 2007; Goodwin, 2010). On top of that level of diversity of the category of "Asian," we have to layer on the varied conditions, historical contexts, and experiences of different "Asian American" groups once they immigrated to the United States and/or the then-territory of Hawaii. Early on, most Asian immigrants were poor and brought as laborers, but even then a fair number were from more-privileged classes. In recent decades, we have seen an increase in the number of refugees from Asia and of immigrants coming as professional and technical workers. Meanwhile, there are now Asian Americans with roots in the United States stretching back well over 100 years (for instance, the Chinese family of Wayne Au, one of the coauthors of this book, first came to Hawaii in the late 1880s, while the islands were still technically a sovereign, Indigenous Hawaiian nation and well before the illegal acquisition of Hawaii by the United States). In all cases, the "kinds" of Asian (based on nation, ethnicity, economic class, and gender, among other differences) that were allowed into the United States was largely determined by the details of U.S. immigration law—itself a product of economics, politics, and international relations (Goodwin, 2010; Lee, 2015; Takaki, 1998).

Additionally, for the purposes of this chapter, and as a general principle, we are not including Pacific Islanders in this category (as is often done under the phraseology "Asian Pacific Islander"), because we feel that this extra-broad designation functions to silence the specificities of indigeneity and colonization of Pacific Islander peoples. Further, because of the specific time period in U.S. history that we are addressing (roughly the mid-1800s to around 1940), and even though there were smaller populations of Chinese and Japanese Americans in other regions (Lai, 2004; Takaki, 1998), we are limiting our discussion in this chapter to the Chinese American and Japanese American communities largely on the West Coast of what is now the continental United States, and within that we focus mostly, but not exclusively, on California, where the largest populations lived. We want to strongly assert that this choice is not meant to silence Filipino American, Korean American, Indian American, or other Asian American diasporic communities or negate other regional histories. We emphatically recognize that there are important curricular and educational histories for these communities. However, during the time period that we focus on here, Chinese Americans and Japanese Americans were the main communities with significant populations in the United States, mostly in California. Thus, for instance, while other communities—like Filipinos—had their education directly influenced by U.S. imperialism (Maramba & Bonus, 2013), they did not have a large population of school-age children in their U.S. communities at this time. We also explicitly recognize that the term "Asian American" is an identity grouping that was constructed out of the ethnic studies, Asian American studies, Black and Brown power, women's rights, and lesbian, gay, bisexual, transgender, queer (LGBQT) movements of the 1960s and 1970s (Lee, 2015). As such, various Asian diasporic communities in the United States during the early 1900s did not identify as "Asian American," per se, but rather more strongly identified along ethnic and nationalist groupings associated with their countries (and regions) of origin (Takaki, 1998).

HISTORICAL CONTEXT FOR CHINESE AND JAPANESE AMERICAN CURRICULAR DISCOURSE

We also need to explicitly recognize that the intent of this chapter, as with all the chapters of this book, is not to present a discussion of Asian American curricular discourse across the entire history of the United States. Rather, we are focused here on the Chinese American and Japanese American curricular discourse during what is loosely defined and canonized as the founding period in curriculum studies, which is a period that encompasses the turn of the 20th century and continues into the 1930s or so (Brown & Au, 2014). This particular time frame has two broad implications for understanding Asian American curricular discourse. First, it means that compared to contemporary times, there were relatively few Asian American communities established in the United States. By 1930 there were only four main Asian immigrant groups in the United States: Chinese American, Japanese American, Indian American, and Korean American. Of these, the numbers of Indian and Korean American immigrants in the country were still quite small (less than 10,000 total each). By that same year, there had been over 375,000 Chinese immigrants since 1820 and over 275,000 Japanese immigrants to the United States since 1860 (Weinberg, 1997). Second, this particular time period for Asian Americans was deeply impacted by ongoing racism against Asians and Asian Americans in the United States. Such racism shaped both U.S. immigration policy (thereby limiting who and how many were allowed to immigrate) and the educational experiences of and curricular discourses in Asian American communities (Chan, 1993; Daniels, 1988). Indeed, this period of time was a height of the idea of the "yellow peril" in the United States, where White Americans feared that "Oriental" hordes (first Chinese, then Japanese) were descending on the United States and threatening to wipe out "American" identity, the White race, and Western civilization (Kawai, 2005; Shim, 1998).

The Du Boisian "peculiar sensation" for Chinese American and Japanese American curricular discourse during this time period was produced by the contradictory tensions created by the racism and politics of White "American" national identity and yellow peril fears. As has been the case for so many other groups, at the heart of this tension was a consideration about how Asian Americans "fit" into the cultural, political, and economic fabric of the United States, a country that invited Chinese and Japanese labor when it suited the needs of capital but also (and often simultaneously) eschewed the Chinese and Japanese on cultural and racial grounds such that White Americans would seek to get rid of them once they were perceived as a potential threat (Lee, 2015; Takaki, 1998). As such, Chinese American and Japanese American curricular discourse can and should be viewed as attempts by these communities to negotiate and respond to the peculiar sensation of being immigrants from Asia, attempting to navigate White racism and yellow peril backlash, and figuring out just how they fit (if at all) into the cultural and educational narrative of the United States.

In asking the question, "What kind of education would best serve our children?" the curriculum conversations that took place within the Chinese American and Japanese American communities came down along two broad questions. One question was, "If our children and families were going to stay in the United States and settle, then shouldn't they have access to the existing public school system and, in part, be taught how to survive there?" This question raised the dual specters of Americanization and assimilation, as well as the cultural angst inherent when Americanization and assimilation meant moving toward Whiteness. The other question, which often, but not always, contradicted the first, asked, "Shouldn't the education of our children include cultural and linguistic maintenance so that their cultural heritage and tools for survival in their home communities would not be lost?" As will be discussed later in this chapter, sometimes this second question sprang from a want to return to Asian homelands, but other times this question surfaced from an understanding of the need for strong cultural and community identity to survive the White supremacist norms embedded in the culture and politics of the United States. These questions speak to the historic transnational character of Asian Americans, which is characterized by ongoing immigration to the United States since colonial times, the continued ties to countries of origin, and the maintenance of culture and language in the United States. The transnational character of Asian Americans describes the realities of Asian Americans as communities negotiating multiple nation-states while intimately being shaped by the policies of statism (Lee & Shibusawa, 2005).

The curricular discourse of both the Chinese American and Japanese American communities is thus the story of these cultural and national tensions, where the conversation moved (sometimes simultaneously) between legal access to the U.S. public schools and maintaining independent community-funded language and cultural schools. Early Chinese American and Japanese American curricular discourse, therefore, might best be understood as an expression of *transnational curricular discourse* that necessarily embraced the wide range of complexities of cultural maintenance associated with countries and cultures of origin while also negotiating survival within the context of racism and White supremacy of the United States. In what follows, we trace the histories of Chinese American and Japanese American educational and curricular discourse as these communities contended with their racist contexts and contemplated just what kind of education they wanted for their children. We begin here chronologically with a discussion of Chinese American curricular discourse and follow with that of Japanese American curricular discourse. Each of these broad sections will themselves be split into two so that we can address each of the struggles over access to public education and the struggles surrounding the Chinese American and Japanese American independent language schools.

EARLY CHINESE AMERICAN TRANSNATIONAL CURRICULAR DISCOURSE

The Context of Early Chinese American Transnational Curricular Discourse

Substantive Chinese immigration into the United States started in the late 1840s, with economic dislocation from China (largely caused by Western imperialism) and the California gold rush serving as push and pull factors, respectively (Chen, 2002). The trajectory of the early Chinese American community was also shaped greatly by racist anti-Chinese laws and the White supremacist fears of yellow peril. Chronologically, the 1882 Chinese Exclusion Act banned Chinese workers from entering the United States until 1892; the 1888 Scott Act was aimed at keeping Chinese workers who had returned to China for visits from reentering the United States; the 1892 Geary Act continued the barring of Chinese workers from the United States for an additional 10 years; and in 1904 the Chinese Exclusion Act was extended indefinitely (Chen, 2002; Lee, 2015).

These restrictive and racist laws also corresponded with significant racist violent attacks on Chinese Americans, mostly by White workers. The earliest documented violence against the Chinese took place in Los Angeles in 1871, where, after a dispute internal to the Chinese American community there spilled out to the broader community and triggered the involvement of local police, men with guns tracked down fleeing Chinese and murdered them. Chinese workers were attacked in Chico, CA, in 1877, and in 1885 in Rock Springs, Wyoming Territory, White railroad workers surrounded and fired upon the 600 Chinese railroad workers—killing 28 and wounding 15. Between the autumn of 1885 and winter of 1886, Chinese workers were also attacked in the Washington Territory. The Anti-Chinese Congress gathered in Seattle in the fall of 1885, demanding that all Chinese leave Tacoma and Seattle—even forming committees to go house to house, telling the Chinese to leave by November 1. The deadline passed and no action was taken, but on November 3, 1885, six hundred Chinese were forcibly removed from Tacoma and left at a station for the Northern Pacific Railroad (where some died of exposure during the night). Then in Seattle on February 7, 1886, a mob of anti-Chinese protestors went to Seattle's Chinatown and forcibly put 350 Chinese into wagons with the intent of loading them onto a steamship—a plan that ultimately failed (Chan, 1993). While the incidents in the Wyoming and Washington territories remain the most well documented, there were also dozens of acts of anti-Chinese violence that took place all over the West at that time (Chan, 1993; Lee, 2015). Between these exclusionary immigration laws, pressures from White labor unions (who were against the use of "cheap" Chinese labor), anti-Chinese violence, and the general economic depression in the United States at this time (from 1890 to 1910), the Chinese American population fell from a little over 107,000 to just over 71,000 in 20 years (Chen, 2002).

It is critically important to note that the anti-Chinese laws and exclusions were largely aimed at Chinese laborers, specifically, and that Chinese professionals and small businesspeople were part of an exempt class of Chinese immigrants. This meant that upward of 40% of the 71,000 Chinese in the United States in 1910 were from these more moneyed and professional classes and were not classified as laborers. Further, it is important to note that because of the discriminatory exclusion laws, which also generally barred Chinese women from entering the country, as of 1910 there were only 4,675 Chinese American women (or 6.5% of the total Chinese American population) in the United States (Chen, 2002). By 1920, some 29% (or about 18,000) of the 62,000 Chinese in the United States had citizenship, mostly by birthright, and by 1940 the number of Chinese in the United States with U.S. citizenship outnumbered those Chinese in the United States born in China (Chan, 1998).

Accessing the U.S. Curriculum and Education

> Very few Chinese go to public school. Chinese at that time have cue [braided pony-tail]. Boys make fun them. Make lots of fun. No like to go public school.
>
> —Chin Cheung, 1924

There were essentially two parallel educational paths undertaken by early Chinese Americans: demanding access to existing public schools and establishing their own privately funded Chinese language schools. These two paths were not necessarily mutually exclusive, and they both represent early Chinese American curricular discourse because at the heart of the matter was a curricular question of what Chinese American children should learn. Gaining access to existing public schools undoubtedly raised the Du Boisian peculiar sensation of Chinese Americans being viewed as a "problem" for White folks. Attending public schools meant attending schools that were predominantly White and generally being taught by White teachers. It also meant integrating these schools, with all of the political and racial implications such integration carried with it. The White community generally did not want Chinese children attending school with their own, and it was not even clear that Chinese parents necessarily wanted their children to be educated in these predominantly White institutional and cultural spaces. However, as immigrants to the United States and its Western territories, sometimes with U.S.-born children (naturalized citizens), Chinese Americans also raised the issue of the right of their children to be educated, regardless of immigration status.

Requests by Chinese community leaders for their children to have access to public schools began in the 1850s and were regularly met with resistance from racist White school officials. For instance, in 1857 the San Francisco School Board flat-out rejected a request by Chinese American community leaders to allow their children to attend public schools. Then, in 1858, as they were trying to solve the Chinese educational "problem," the San Francisco School Board suggested that Chinese American students attend the segregated African American school there instead (Weinberg, 1997).

Chinese leaders refused this suggestion, explaining that they would choose not to send their children to a public school, "unless it were either integrated or segregated for the Chinese" (as quoted in Weinberg, 1997, p. 18).

The White rejection of integrated schools for the Chinese was steeped in deep-seated racism. As one San Francisco newspaper wrote in 1858, segregation laws

> let us keep our public schools free from the intrusion of the inferior races. If we are compelled to have Negroes and Chinamen among us, it is better, of course, that they should be educated. But teach them separately from our own children. Let us preserve our Caucasian blood pure. We want no mongrel race of moral and mental hybrids to people the mountains and valleys of California. (Kuo, 1998, p. 190)

The San Francisco School Board agreed, and in 1859 school board members were overheard grouping the Chinese as being in the same class of animals as monkeys and baboons; one superintendent said that integrating Chinese into schools there would demoralize the higher races (Weinberg, 1997). To deal with this issue, the San Francisco School Board created the first Chinese Public School in 1859 (Morimoto, 1997; Tom, 1944). This school was poorly attended and closed after being open 4 months—when protests by White parents forced the San Francisco School Board to open it once again. The San Francisco superintendent of schools blamed the low attendance on his own view that the Chinese were simply not interested in learning, a justification that was used to close the Chinese Public School a second time. The school was reopened after the Chinese community and advocates protested. Low attendance at the Chinese Public School was more likely due to constant struggles for control over the choice of teachers, curriculum, and location—the school was relocated to a White neighborhood, outside of Chinatown, creating a problem of transportation through areas often openly racist against the Chinese (Kuo, 1998; Wollenberg, 1976).

In 1860, shortly after the establishment of the Chinese Public School, the California School Law passed, forbidding African American, Chinese American, and Native American children from attending public school alongside White children there. Under the Burlingame Treaty of 1868, both China and the United States were supposed to respect the public educational rights of citizens living in each other's country, but the United States did not enforce this part of the treaty (Kuo, 1998; Morimoto, 1997; Wollenberg, 1976). California state officials led a campaign against the inclusion of Chinese American children in public education such that, with the closing of the Chinese Public School in San Francisco in 1871 (Morimoto, 1997; Tom, 1944), Chinese American children had no legal right to public education of any kind from 1871 to 1884 (Kuo, 1998; Morimoto, 1997; Wollenberg, 1976).

As Kuo (1998) notes, the Chinese American community was left with three choices regarding their children's education at this time. One option, as discussed later in this chapter, was to send their children to community-run Chinese-language schools. Another option was to send their children to schools run by Christian missionaries. While these missionary schools were sites for learning the English language, such schools were established with the main purpose of converting Chinese away from their traditional religion and cultural beliefs and into Christianity. However, as a third option, there were substantial numbers of Chinese Americans who actively fought the racist and discriminatory educational laws during the period by pushing the San Francisco School Board and the California State Legislature to give Chinese American children access to public schools. For instance, a year after the Chinese Public School was closed, parents unsuccessfully petitioned the school board to open a night school for Chinese children. Later, in 1878, a group of businessmen again petitioned the school board for the right of Chinese American children to gain access to public schools. This petition was sent to a judicial committee for a legal ruling, but instead of waiting for the ruling, the Chinese community gathered 13,000 signatures and presented them to the state legislature. Further, as Kuo (1998) explains, this petition spoke to the kind of education that Chinese Americans felt compelled to ask for within the context of anti-Chinese racism:

> This petition also revealed that integration was not necessarily a priority for all Chinese American parents struggling to gain access to the public school system. By stating that they preferred to have a separate school for their children, these parents revealed their opinion that segregation was perhaps more desirable than integration. Facing discrimination and racism to such a potent degree in the late 1800s, Chinese Americans may have recognized that "Separate but Equal" facilities would benefit them more than suffering through the violence and prejudices of the other Americans in the same school. (p. 195)

Although this petition was rejected, it demonstrates that even amidst enduring and sharp anti-Chinese racism and hostility, the Chinese American community continued to advocate for their children's educational rights. As such, this early, community-based educational activism helped pave the way for later access to public school for Chinese American children (Kuo, 1998).

Mamie Tape and the "Oriental School"

In 1874, in *Ward v. Flood*, the Supreme Court of California ruled that the state legislature could not use race as a factor to exclude children from access to the public school system, under the rights guaranteed by the Fourteenth Amendment's Equal Protection Clause. To be in compliance with this ruling, in 1880 the word *White* was removed from the California school law, thus giving African American and Native American children access to public schools there—even if it was segregated schooling. However, regardless of the changes to the California school law and the Supreme Court of California's ruling, Chinese children were still excluded from public schooling in California. It wasn't until 1885, when the case of *Tape v. Hurley* was brought to court, that this would change (Kuo, 1998; Morimoto, 1997; Wollenberg, 1976).

Mamie Tape was born to a Chinese American father and a White mother. In 1885, when she was 8 years old, Mamie Tape was denied access to public schools in San Francisco. Her family then contacted the Chinese consulate, who in turn sent a letter to the superintendent of San Francisco schools, Andrew Moulder, in which the consulate requested school access for Mamie. In his turn, Moulder contacted State Superintendent William Welcher, seeking support for his decision to deny Mamie Tape access to public school. Stating that public education should only be granted to "citizens," Welcher obliged Moulder and rejected the request of the Chinese consulate (Kuo, 1998).

In response to the San Francisco School Board's decision, Mamie's White mother penned an angry letter to the board:

> Dear sirs, Will you please tell me! Is it a disgrace to be Born a Chinese? Didn't God make us all!!! What right! . . . You had better come and see for yourselves. See if the Tape's is not the same as other Caucasians, except in features. It seems no matter how a Chinese may live and dress so long as you know they Chinese. Then they are hated as one. There is not any right or justice for them . . . . Mamie Tape will never attend any of the Chinese schools of your making. Never!!! I will let the world see sir What justice there is When it is govern by the Race prejudice men! . . . Just because she is descended of Chinese parents I guess she is more of a American than a good many of you that is going to prewent [*sic*] her being Educated. (As quoted in Weinberg, 1997, p. 19)

The Tapes then took the issue to court in 1878, and in *Tape v. Hurley* the San Francisco Superior Court ruled in the Tapes' favor (Kuo, 1998; Morimoto, 1997; Wollenberg, 1976), stating,

> To deny a child, born of Chinese parents in this State, entrance to the public schools would be a violation of the law of the State and the Constitution of the United States. It would, moreover, be unjust to levy a forced tax upon Chinese residents to help maintain our schools, and yet prohibit their children born here from education in those schools. (As quoted in Kuo, 1998, p. 197)

This decision was later upheld by the California Supreme Court. Using the equal treatment provision of the Fourteenth Amendment, Judge James Maguire highlighted the fact that Chinese Americans were required to pay a public school tax and were thus being denied benefits they were due. This ruling ended the legal exclusion of Chinese American children from access to public schools in California, even though the court upheld that the state could still provide for segregated, public schooling (Kuo, 1998; Morimoto, 1997; Wollenberg, 1976)—a decision to uphold "separate but equal" schooling for Chinese Americans that the Northern Circuit Court of California later affirmed in 1902 (Kuo, 1998). Thus in order to comply with the ruling, rather than enroll Mamie Tape in a regular school, the San Francisco School Board created a racially segregated school, the "Oriental School," for her and other Chinese American children (Kuo, 1998; Morimoto, 1997; Wollenberg, 1976).

Upon its opening in 1885, the Oriental School had an enrollment of 24 students, likely because Chinese parents were suspicious of the school's intentions. Enrollment climbed to 130 by 1900 and to 695 by 1916, with a new building opening in 1915 to meet the growing demand (Weinberg, 1997). By 1923 over 900 students attended the school (Kuo, 1998). In 1925 the Oriental School was renamed the Commodore Stockton School, perhaps signaling the end of the assigning of schools based on Chinese American ethnicity, and the population of Chinese American students had grown so large in San Francisco that the school board had no choice but to let Chinese American children attend surrounding schools (Weinberg, 1997).

In his 1924 interview, eventual Chinese Vice Consul of Seattle David Young (1924) provides a good example of a relatively privileged Chinese American child trying to attend school in San Francisco. After returning to the United States from a 1901 missionary visit to China (his parents were Chinese Christian missionaries), a teacher from the Chinese Baptist Mission tried to enroll him in grammar school, but, as Young recounts:

> They refused to take me in because I was a Chinese. Finally we went in one day and went to see the principal, and I think she must have taken me for a Filipino or something and I entered the fourth grade . . . A month before I graduated from the grammar school, during lunch, I was talking to the other Chinese boy. We both had been taken for Japanese or Filipino, so the American boys went and reported us to the principal. I was called up to his office and asked if I were Chinese. Naturally, I told him yes, and he said I would have to leave the school, as there was a school for Orientals in Chinatown and I must go back there. (p. 2)

Young (1924) continues by explaining how, when the principal of the Oriental School left for Philadelphia to get married, he took advantage of the change in administration and went to a White, public elementary, called Washington Grammar School. The principal at Washington welcomed Young and let him into the 6th grade. When the new principal at the Oriental School found out, he complained to the superintendent of San Francisco public schools, who went to Washington Grammar School and attempted to return Young to the Oriental School. The principal at Washington defended

Young, citing his good performance and the fact that he was now in the 6th grade (keeping in mind that the Oriental School only went up to 5th grade), and the superintendent let Young stay put. Young eventually went to high school for a few months in San Francisco before returning to China.

What Kind of Oriental School Curriculum?

Even though the San Francisco School Board provided the segregated Oriental School for its Chinese American students, it does not mean that the quality of education given these children met their cultural needs. The first Chinese-speaking teacher was not hired until 1926, with one more hired in 1928 and another in 1930. That first teacher was Alice Fong Yu. She recalls that she was specifically told not to speak Chinese in the classroom. Victor Low described the teachers in the Chinese schools as "either old timers set in their culturally biased ways or . . . ineffective teachers shunted to their assignment of last resort" (as quoted in Weinberg, 1997, p. 20). The public schools in San Francisco Chinatown "paid little heed to traditional Chinese culture. Denigration rather than celebration marked their efforts" (as quoted in Weinberg, 1997, p. 21). The Oriental School was an English-only space, with no Chinese language allowed.

The racism against Chinese found in textbooks and curriculum and among classroom peers also made things difficult for the few Chinese American students attending predominantly White schools in areas outside of San Francisco. Despite feelings of having a generally favorable educational experience, in a 1925 interview one Chinese American student recounted:

> In grade school I was fairly successful in being admitted to the "inner circles," as it were. . . . It was only during geography and history that I became in a way race-conscious. When we came to the study of China, the other children would turn and stare at me as though I were Exhibit A of the lesson. . . . I remember one particularly terrible ancient history lesson; it told in awful detail about "queer little Chinamen, with pigtails and slanting eyes"—and went on to describe the people as though they were inhuman, and at best, uncivilized. Even I, young as I was, resented these gross exaggerations which were considered the gospel truth by other pupils. I meditated on ways and means of absenting myself from class that day. (Interview with a Chinese student, 1925, pp. 2–3)

Socially, Chinese American students in predominantly White schools often faced increasing alienation as they moved through school. In interviews from 1924, Lillie Leung tells the story of her growing alienation as she made her way from elementary through high school:

> We have never lived in Chinatown, but have always lived in an American neighborhood. I have always had a number of American friends. I mingled with all

the children quite freely, but when I was about twelve years old they began to turn away from me and I felt this keenly. Up to that time I never realized that I was in any way different, but then I began to think about it . . . . In high school I did not enter into the different activities because I felt that I was not wanted and I was quite sensitive. (Leung, 1924, p. 2)

Thus, as Chan (1998) notes, Chinese American young people were also segregated within many aspects of recreation in addition to school, including being forced to sit only in certain sections of theaters and being excluded from using public swimming pools out of public fears of contamination.

"Colored" or Not? Chinese American Students in the Mississippi Delta

While in this chapter we mostly focus on California for our discussion of the transnational curriculum aspirations of the early Chinese American community, the experiences of the Chinese in the Mississippi delta are important to note here. After the Civil War ended in 1865, planters in the Southern United States started recruiting Chinese laborers from Cuba and China. Later, once the transcontinental railroad was finished in 1869, a pool of Chinese labor became available as well. As Lim de Sanchez (2003) explains,

> Cotton plantation owners initially hoped that Chinese "coolie" workers would help replace the loss of African-American slave labor and that competition between the two groups would compel former slaves to resume their submissive status on plantations. This experiment proved to be an unmitigated failure. African Americans sought independence from White supervision and authority. And, Chinese immigrant workers proved to be more expensive and less dependable than African-American slave labor. (p. 74)

Instead of remaining as laborers or sharecroppers, many of these Chinese opened small stores in African American communities, with many marrying African American women (Lim de Sanchez, 2003). Mississippi law forbade Chinese families from attending public schools, but occasionally White schools would admit one or two Chinese students if the White community did not object. However, like those in San Francisco, Chinese parents generally did not want their children to attend the Black schools in the South (Lim de Sanchez, 2003; Weinberg, 1997).

Both the 1925 Mississippi Supreme Court and the subsequent U.S. Supreme Court decisions in the case of *Gong Lum v. Rice* offer an important landmark in educational law and in the racialization of Chinese Americans historically (Kuo, 1998; Lim de Sanchez, 2003; Weinberg, 1997). The lawsuit originated in the shifting racial educational politics of Rosedale, Mississippi. Up until the mid-1920s Rosedale was fairly tolerant of the small Chinese American community there, even allowing Chinese children to attend the White public schools. However, the towns and counties surrounding Rosedale excluded Chinese American children from public schools. In response, Chinese parents began moving to Rosedale or sending their children to live with other Chinese families in Rosedale in order for their children to have access to Rosedale public schools. This increase in Chinese students attending Rosedale schools upset the White community there, and in a typically racist response, Chinese American students were officially and systematically barred from attending Rosedale public schools (Lim de Sanchez, 2003).

Martha Lum, daughter of the plaintiff in *Gong Lum v. Rice* and a U.S. citizen by birthright, was thus denied entry into the Mississippi public schools in Rosedale. In 1924, Gong Lum sued the Rosedale schools for excluding his daughter. In his lawsuit he argued that "Chinese" was different from "colored," and thus the Chinese should not be treated as "colored" in the eyes of the law. Judge William A. Alcorn of the Mississippi Circuit Court ruled that the Chinese were in fact "Mongolian" in race and not "Negro" and as such could not be denied access to schools (Kuo, 1998; Lim de Sanchez, 2003).

Mississippi law was built around separate-but-equal doctrine and decreed that separate schools be maintained for White and "colored" children. Within this framework, the question was raised as to whether citizens of Chinese descent were legally considered "colored." Using Mississippi's 1890 constitutional language as a basis, which held that the "Caucasian" race had the right to stop racial mixing, and basing its arguments on the idea that the Chinese were of the "Mongolian" and not "Caucasian" race, the Mississippi Supreme Court ruled that Chinese children were "colored" and therefore legally not allowed to attend White schools. When the case was taken to the U.S. Supreme Court, the court ruled that "yellow" was in fact a color—and certainly not "White"—and thus fell into the established interpretation of the law that separate schools for Whites and "colored races." Citing *Plessy v. Ferguson*, the U.S. Supreme Court thus argued that the Chinese could attend "separate but equal" colored schools and Mississippi would not be in violation of the Equal Protection clause of the Fourteenth Amendment (Kuo, 1998; Lim de Sanchez, 2003). This ruling was consistent with previous Supreme Court cases such as *Ozawa v. United States*, which in 1922 decreed that the "white" skin of the Japanese did not make them White in the eyes of the law, and *United States v. Thind*, which in 1923 decided that, even though people from India are technically "Caucasian," they still were not White in the eyes of the law and had no rights to U.S. citizenship (Lopez, 1996).

Schooling on the Edge of Immigration and Xenophobia

As this portion of the early Chinese American experience indicates, the Chinese community was continually interested in seeking access to public education for their children, and they were continually confronted with the realities of racism, nativism, and White supremacy. While sometimes tolerated (and most times not), the Chinese were never fully accepted within the identity of "American"—they were a "problem" for the White power structure—left with no choice but to try to educate their children by any means necessary and in preparation for an immediate future of existence as a transnational community. This tension was reflected in the attempts of the Chinese community to access public education and the curriculum therein. Although there most certainly was a pragmatism of the needs and rights to have their children attend school, there was also a clear expression of a need to prepare their children to survive in the United States. However, there was also clearly a curricular commitment to cultural maintenance, holding onto Chinese culture and varying degrees of identification with China as a community home. This curricular commitment to cultural maintenance was also shaped by the context of White supremacy and anti-Chinese racism, for Chinese families had to constantly contend with being forced to return to China. As Chen (2002) reminds us,

> Despite the growing number of families established in the United States, American Chinese were under constant threat of having to go back to China. The 1912 congressional attempt to deport wives and children of deceased merchants, the fact that some came into the country on purchased papers and therefore lived in precarious legal status, and other legislative or administrative proposals further regulating Chinese immigration and residence served as sources of fear. (pp. 120–121)

Chen goes on to tell the story of Thomas Chinn, whose parents moved from Oregon to San Francisco in 1919, just so he and his family could have access to a Chinese school. Chinn's parents wanted their children to learn Chinese culture and language because they "always felt . . . that they may be forced to go back to China, not by choice but because they were kicked out" (as quoted in Chen, 2002, p. 121). Thus, in part because of exclusion and in part because of a cultural investment in their children, the Chinese also developed and maintained a system of Chinese language and cultural schools that existed parallel to the public school system.

Chinese-Language Schools

In beginning this section, there are two important things to highlight before discussing the Chinese-language schools. First, while there were other Chinese schools outside of the San Francisco Bay Area, specifically, and California more generally—in major cities like Detroit, New York, Chicago, Boston, and Cleveland, as well as smaller towns like Astoria, Oregon, and McGehee, Arkansas (Lai, 2004)—by far the largest population of Chinese

Americans was in San Francisco (Kuo, 1998). Therefore, much of the history of Chinese-language school education and curricular discourse we recount here focuses on this area. Second, it is important that we remember that this entire period of Chinese American education takes place during anti-Chinese exclusion laws. The racism, White supremacy, xenophobia, and discrimination associated with the yellow peril helped enforce a "sojourner" orientation among Chinese immigrants, which meant maintaining strong ties to China while negotiating the possibility of making a life in the United States (Chen, 2002; Kuo, 1998).

Private Chinese schools appeared first in San Francisco around the 1870s. Just after the Chinese Exclusion Act of 1882 was passed, representatives from China in Washington, DC, pushed the Chinese Consolidated Benevolent Association (CCBA) to prepare a school that would teach Western and Chinese subject matter. However, the process unfolded slowly because of a lack of resources and community fears of anti-Chinese racism. In 1888 the CCBA was ready to open the school, called Daqing Shuyan, but by that time San Francisco was legally forced to open the segregated public "Oriental School" for Chinese children in 1885. Following educational reforms in China, the CCBA created the Daqing Qiaomin Xuetang (Great Qing Overseas Chinese School) in 1909 (Lai, 2005). Later renamed the Zhunghua Qiaomin Gongli Xuexiao (Chinese Public School), the school did not allow the enrollment of girls until 1920 (Lai, 2005). Several other schools were opened during this time period. The Morning Bell School was started in 1919 using monies raised from performances by the Morning Bell Theatrical Society. Morning Bell was coeducational from its beginnings, and it stayed open until 1925. In 1920 business leaders in Nam Hoy Fook Yum Tong founded Nam Kue School, and in 1922 the Yeong Wo Association founded the Yeong Wo School, which operated 3 hours a day, 6 days a week. In 1929 the Zhunghua Qiaomin Gongli Xuexiao (Chinese Public School) became the Chinese Central High School, and it was the first Chinese school in the United States to offer a high school–level curriculum. In the 1930s St. Mary's and Hip Wo Chinese schools also added high school levels. It is important to note that during this entire period, anti-Chinese immigration laws restricted the numbers of teachers available to Chinese schools (Lai, 2004, 2005).

Chinese-Language School Curricular Discourse

The Chinese-language schools and their curriculum played an important role in the Chinese American community in helping Chinese children develop and maintain strong identities. As Chinese scholar Kim-Fong Tom (1941) elaborates,

> Chinatown has been described by some American writers as a place of opium dens and gambling houses. The pulp magazines and some motion pictures have

served to keep this illusion alive. Even today, many Americans still have the notion that [Chinese] people are inferior and backward. Living in a country where the Chinese have been looked down upon and ill-treated, it is easy for them to develop inferiority complexes. To prevent the children from falling into conviction, it is necessary for them to have a correct knowledge of China and the Chinese civilization. (p. 559)

Tom's observations highlight the point that Chinese-language schools helped to develop in their students a positive appreciation of Chinese culture and identity. Tom argues further that Chinese-language schools helped students negotiate their racial identities within the cultural context of being both Chinese and American. There was a functional pragmatism at play here as well, where the Chinese-language schools also prepared their children to "function in a Chinese-speaking environment without too much difficulty either in the Chinatowns of America or in China" (Lai, 2005, p. 194).

Chinese-language schools mostly used traditional textbooks published and used in China. The population of children enrolled in these schools was so small that the market was not large enough to warrant Chinese American populations creating their own textbooks. Chinese schools in the United States thus made use of national language readers and other history, geography, civics, and "common knowledge" texts from China. Some language schools, like the Daqing Qiaomin Xuetang (Great Qing Overseas Chinese School) operated for 5 hours a day, 6 days a week, and students studied calligraphy, Confucian philosophy, classical Chinese literature, Chinese history and geography, military band, and choir. Other schools, like the Daqing Shuyan, focused on Chinese literature, writing, and use of the abacus, or those like Morning Bell taught letter writing, drawing, Chinese history and geography, calisthenics, morality, and public speaking on political issues (Lai, 2004, 2005).

Scholar Him Mark Lai (2005) attended the Nam Kue School, and his parents had purchased some typical Chinese texts for use in the home. As Lai recounts of the texts:

Each reader included sixty lessons. In the second reader the bulk of the lessons dwelled on topics in daily life such as the first day of school, writing implements, articles of clothing, cooking utensils, the mid-autumn festival . . . and so forth. Characteristically many lessons also introduced what the editors considered correct habits, attitudes, and standards of conduct for Chinese students. . . . One lesson that aimed to teach diligence told the tale of a slow-witted student who managed to place first in examinations by studying harder than his classmates. . . . Other readings variously encouraged the pursuit of education, pointed out the folly of telling lies, and counseled against avarice. Anecdotes such as that of Kong Rong voluntarily taking the smallest pear because he was the youngest sibling in the family, and the obedient filial son Huang, who cared for and served his old father while studying hard at school, were presented as correct ethical and moral behavior. (pp. 206–207)

Lai (2004, 2005) also recounts how national awareness and pride in China were taught through Chinese geography and history, highlighting the 5,000-year history, military successes, mistreatment by European colonial powers, and biographies of great Chinese leaders, among other information. Pedagogically speaking, these texts were taught by reading passages aloud in unison, with the teachers offering explanations of the text. Students would then be tested on their ability to cite or write information from memory. The objectives, he says,

> were to teach Chinese Americans the mechanics of the Chinese language, help them understand the world from a Chinese perspective, instill a sense of morality and responsibility to society according to Chinese moral standards, cultivate respect of and pride in China, a nation with ancient traditions and history, and sensitize students to foreign aggressions that had infringed on China's territorial integrity and sovereignty. The contents in the textbooks were often nationalistic in tone and many teachers had strong nationalist feelings. (Lai, 2005, p. 208)

Tom (1941) offers that the purposes of the Chinese-language school curriculum were four-fold and mainly addressed "family adjustment, cultural diffusion, social and recreational functions, and vocational preparation" (p. 557).

Even if, as Tom (1941) suggests, the Chinese-language school curriculum served to support Chinese student identity as a bulwark against racism and the issues facing various Chinatowns in the Western United States, the question remains as to their outcomes. As an answer, Lai (2005) explains that in many ways we can see a level of bifurcation that we would argue encapsulates the transnational identities of Chinese American curricular discourse. On the one hand, racism against Chinese Americans sometimes matched well with the Chinese nationalist curriculum taught in the schools, encouraging some Chinese Americans to become strong Chinese nationalists themselves without necessarily having ever been in China. On the other hand, under the influences of public schools and Christian institutions, Chinese American children were still learning English, becoming Americanized, and at times learning the barest minimum of Chinese culture and language. Still, the Chinese-language schools played a critical role as one articulation of early Chinese American curricular discourse. As we recount in the next section, early Japanese immigrants and Japanese Americans faced similar dilemmas, and their answers to those dilemmas both paralleled and departed from those of the Chinese American community.

EARLY JAPANESE AMERICAN TRANSNATIONAL
CURRICULAR DISCOURSE

Before discussing the early Japanese American curricular discourse, it is important that we clarify some specific terminology we use here. There are three important terms to understand within the current context: "Issei" is the term used to describe Japanese immigrants to the United States—representing the first generation. "Nisei" is the term used to describe the children of the Issei—those born in the United States, representing the second generation. "Nikkei" is a broader term used to refer to the Japanese American community in general (Asato, 2006). Throughout the following section we will be using these terms to refer to specific sections of the Japanese American community, and we will be using "Nikkei" and "Japanese American" interchangeably as well.

The Context of Early Japanese American Curricular Discourse

The first Japanese immigrants to the continental United States arrived in 1869, and the first Japanese consulate was created in San Francisco in 1870. By 1890 there were just over 2,000 Japanese in the United States, over half of whom were in California, mainly San Francisco. The restriction on Chinese immigration through the 1882 Chinese Exclusion Act depleted the pool of available immigrant labor, and so U.S. capitalists turned toward Japanese labor as a viable alternative. By 1910, at just over 72,000 people, the Japanese American population in the United States just barely exceeded the Chinese American population (Harris, 1914), and by 1920 the Japanese American population in the United States rose to over 110,000 people, whereas the Chinese American population fell to just over 61,000 people (U.S. Department of Commerce, 1921). However, anti-Japanese sentiment began to increase on the heels of World War I, with groups like the Japanese Exclusion League being formed with the support of the American Legion and the Native Sons and Native Daughters of the Golden West. By 1924, Congress had prohibited all immigration from Japan (Wollenberg, 1976).

On June 10, 1893, the San Francisco School Board passed a resolution requiring all Japanese American children to attend the Oriental School already established for the Chinese Americans. In response, Japanese Consul General Sutemi Chinda wrote a letter to the local press highlighting how few Japanese American students there were (40–50 total in the San Francisco school system) and made a plea that these students be allowed to attend any school in the area. Under California state law at the time, local school boards were given discretion to establish separate schools for children of "Chinese or Mongolian" heritage and if separate schools existed for these children, then they were not allowed to attend other, regular San Francisco public schools. This set up a school board policy question as to whether or not Japanese American children were to be considered "Chinese or Mongolian," with the San Francisco board voting 7 to 2, overturning their previous resolution and allowing Japanese American children to attend any public school there (Daniels, 1988; Weinberg, 1997).

However, pressure against Japanese American students attending the regular public schools continued to build. In 1901 the Union Labor Party of California suggested that Japanese students be segregated, and in 1905 there was a movement to exclude Japanese children from public schools in Berkeley, California, but neither campaign was successful. In 1905 the San Francisco School Board passed a similar resolution supporting the exclusion (in principle, not in policy) and did not overturn it despite continued protestations of the Japanese consul (Morimoto, 1997; Weinberg, 1997; Wollenberg, 1976).

In 1906 the San Francisco School Board passed a resolution requiring that all Chinese, Japanese, and Korean children attend the Oriental School. While attendance at this school was already mandated for Chinese American students, this new resolution forced San Francisco's 93 Japanese American students, many of whom were attending the regular public schools, to join them at the segregated school. The Japanese in Japan and Japanese Americans united in their opposition to the discrimination against Japanese American students. Most of the Japanese parents resisted the school board resolution, with all but two Japanese American children staying home from school—and one of those two withdrew after their family talked to the Japanese consul. The secretary of the Japanese Association testified against the resolution at the San Francisco School Board. Two Methodist missionaries presented the school board with a resolution, passed by the Interdenominational Mission Congress, opposing the discriminatory policy, with one of the missionaries calling the segregation order "un-Christianlike." The Japanese consul penned a letter of protest, and Japanese American leaders contacted Japanese newspapers, who subsequently expressed outrage over the discriminatory practices affecting Japanese immigrant communities in the United States. In effect, the San Francisco School Board's resolution discriminating against the Japanese American students developed into an international incident, with the U.S. ambassador in Tokyo eventually contacting Washington with a message that a crisis was brewing (Asato, 2006; Kuo, 1998; Wollenberg, 1976).

President Theodore Roosevelt expressed concern over the international tensions created by the forced segregation of Japanese American students in the Oriental school, and some politicians began advocating for the integration of Japanese Americans into the public school system generally. In a December 4, 1906, speech, President Roosevelt was moved to remark that keeping the Japanese American children out of public schools was a "wicked absurdity" (as quoted in Wollenberg, 1976, p. 60), condemning the poor treatment of the Japanese American children and pushing Congress to allow Japanese immigrants to become naturalized citizens in the process. He then ordered the attorney general of the United States to take legal action (*Aoki v. Deane*) against the San Francisco School Board. The legal process was long and drawn out, and instead of a judicial ruling, President Roosevelt sought to reach a "gentleman's agreement" with the San Francisco School Board, who agreed to allow Japanese American students back into the public schools in exchange for increased limits on Japanese immigration to the United States (Kuo, 1998; Weinberg, 1997; Wollenberg, 1976).

This incident with Japanese Americans and the Oriental School in San Francisco highlights a key difference between the transnational identities of the early Chinese Americans and the early Japanese Americans and their experiences with education in the United States: In terms of international power and standing, at that time the Chinese government was relatively weak and the Japanese government was relatively strong. As such, the Japanese government was powerful enough to compel politicians to consider the implications of local policies affecting Japanese immigrants out of fear of destabilizing international relations (Asato, 2006; Kuo, 1998). Furthermore, this incident highlights the transnational nature of the Japanese American community at that time, who despite their own wishes, were often caught between two empires (Azuma, 2005). So while the dilemmas facing the Japanese American community were in some ways the same as those facing the Chinese American community, particularly in terms of how they fit into the identity of "America" and how they had to navigate racism, xenophobia, and White supremacy at every turn, the historical and political context of the Japanese Americans in the United States and relative to international relations (including the run-up to World War II) gave their curricular discourse a different trajectory—for the Japanese government at times attempted to treat the Nikkei community as a political tool.

However, the international strength of the Imperial Japanese government was not something that deterred anti-Japanese racism in the United States (indeed, it likely exacerbated it). For instance, in the midst of ongoing anti-Japanese racism, in 1909 the California State Assembly passed a bill to segregate the Japanese American students, but then reconsidered and defeated the bill once again under pressure from the federal government (Weinberg, 1997; Wollenberg, 1976). Then in 1921 the California legislature amended existing state law to include Japanese as a group qualified for school segregation. Only four small Sacramento County school districts (Florin, Walnut Grove, Courtland, and Isleton) made use of this legal shift by establishing separate "Oriental Schools" for Japanese American students. Tellingly, in all four of these districts, Japanese Americans constituted a numerical majority of the students enrolled in the schools (Wollenberg, 1976). In Florin, for instance, Japanese American students, who were 76% of the 225 students, were officially listed as "Orientals" (Weinberg, 1997). Despite community concerns about the poor performance of Japanese American students there (Morimoto, 1997), Florin was used as an example of racial harmony and the Americanization of Japanese immigrant communities, where English-language instruction was even added for Japanese American kindergartners (Weinberg, 1997). However, as one White resident of Florin explained regarding the perceived need for segregated schools,

> That's easy. Race prejudice. It got so my daughters went mostly with Japanese girls. The principal was letting Japs crowd our boys off the grammar school team just because they could play better baseball. The town around us began to razz our kids because of that. . . . Well we couldn't stand for it any longer, so we separated our schools. (As quoted in Wollenberg, 1976, pp. 72–73)

Whites in Florin decided to build separate schools for White and Japanese American children in 1923 (Weinberg, 1997). However, the segregated schools of Florin, Isleton, Courtland, and Walnut Grove served only 575 Japanese American students, whereas almost 30,000 Nisei children attended public schools alongside White children at that time (Wollenberg, 1976). This would remain the general pattern for Japanese American public schooling until all Japanese Americans on the U.S. West Coast were forcibly removed and incarcerated by the federal government during World War II.

Similar to the Chinese Americans, Japanese Americans were committed to access to public education for their children, and, also like the Chinese American community, Japanese Americans were educational activists willing to go to court and confront those in power when they felt they were being discriminated against. However, as noted previously, unlike the Chinese American community, the imperial power of Japan made politicians more cautious in their legal and extralegal discrimination of Japanese American children—in stark contrast to the treatment of Chinese Americans, who didn't have a powerful Chinese government to intervene internationally. Despite all the international and domestic political machinations associated with access to public schools for Japanese American students, like the Chinese American community, Japanese Americans were also interested in cultural maintenance for their children, and they ultimately developed extensive networks of Japanese-language schools to serve this purpose. However, as we take it up in the next section of this chapter, the curricular discourse of the Japanese American–language schools was fraught, for they too were negotiating transnational community identity in the midst of the racist, White supremacist, and xenophobic power structure at the time.

The Transnational Curricular Discourse of Japanese-Language Schools

It is critical to recognize that the early curricular discourse of the Japanese-language schools cannot be understood without also understanding the viciousness of the racism, White supremacy, and xenophobia of the anti-Japanese movement in California. To put it bluntly, anti-Japanese activists in California wanted to dispossess Japanese Americans of land. While anti-Japanese racism had been building for decades, the post-WWI Japanese exclusion movement in California officially started in 1919 when the California Oriental Exclusion League was founded by leaders of the Native Sons of the Golden West, the State Grange, the California State Federation of Labor, the Native Daughters of the Golden West, and the American Legion. The California Oriental Exclusion League wanted to end the gentlemen's agreement with Japan and end Japanese immigration entirely. The League also pushed for a constitutional amendment to strip the Nisei of their citizenship—thereby taking away their rights to own land in California (Asato, 2006).

California and the Oriental, a report published by the California State Board of Control in 1920, was used to study Japanese landholdings. In the preface to the report, then-governor William D. Stephens lamented that Californian children were forced to attend schools "crowded with other children of a different race" (as quoted in Asato, 2006, p. 51), that Japanese immigrants had been circumventing the 1913 Alien Land Law by purchasing land in the name of their U.S.-born children, and that the Japanese-language schools were primarily maintaining the traditions and morals of Japan (Asato, 2006).

In 1920 the U.S. House of Representatives Committee on Immigration and Naturalization held a hearing on Japanese immigration. In this hearing, Valentine S. McClatchy, a member of the Native Sons of the Golden West and former publisher of the *Sacramento Bee* newspaper, drew heavily upon the racist fears of the yellow peril to argue that Japanese immigrants were unassimilable and still loyal to the Japanese emperor and only sought citizenship as a means to serve the aims of the Japanese government. McClatchy also argued that Japanese-language schools should be abolished, made false claims about the number of Nisei children who had returned to Japan to attend schools there, and relied on an entirely false story from *The Northman*, a Swedish publication from Portland, Oregon, to supposedly illustrate the kinds of indoctrination the Nisei children were receiving while in Japan. The House Committee visited Japanese-language schools in Florin and Peryn, California, taking textbooks to examine. Soon after, Japanese-language schools became a specific point of negotiation between the U.S. and Japanese ambassadors (Asato, 2006).

In an attempt to position themselves to lead a nationwide anti-Japanese movement, the Japanese Exclusion League of California reorganized itself and began a campaign to deny citizenship to all "Asiatics" (Asato, 2006, p. 65). The Native Sons and Native Daughters of the Golden West then also began pushing forcefully against the Japanese-language schools, echoing McClatchy's arguments that Issei and Nisei represented a Japanese invasion and colonization of the United States in the pages of their newspaper, the *Grizzly Bear*. One editorial argued,

> [In] Jap schools . . . their children born upon our soil are instructed in the language, government and traditions of Japan, to realize the conquest of California . . . for the glory and expansion of the Yamato race. . . . A Jap is always a Jap at heart . . . his allegiance is everlastingly pledged to Japan, and though born upon American soil he is always a subject of Japan. (As quoted in Asato, 2006, p. 56)

These are the people, politics, and forces that the Nikkei had to negotiate as they considered what curriculum was best for their children and community.

Japanese-language schools arose out of the desires of Issei parents to pass on Japanese language and culture to their children, out of consideration of the possible future education of their children in Japan and potential job opportunities within their community, and to serve as a bridge between Japan and the United States (Asato, 2006). Japanese-language schools also were important for other reasons. As Asato (2006) explains:

> Japanese language schools often played another indispensable role for immigrant parents as mediator between public school teachers and parents. Since most Issei did not speak English well, it was hard for them to communicate with their children's public school teachers, so Japanese language school teachers often went as their representatives. (p. 44)

Japanese American supporters of the language schools saw them as sites of cultural maintenance, resistance to the anti-Asian racism surrounding them, and as a way to combat the deculturalization they saw happening to their U.S.-born children (Morimoto, 1997).

The first Japanese-language school in California, Nihon Shogakko (Japanese Elementary School) was founded in 1902 in San Francisco by a Japanese American Christian couple, and Meiji Shogakko was started in April 1903 by the San Francisco Buddhist Church of Honpa Honganji Bukkyodan. In November 1903, the Sacramento Buddhist Church established its own Japanese-language school, Sakura Gakuen. The San Francisco schools were destroyed in the 1906 earthquake and fire but were later rebuilt. In total 18 Japanese-language schools started in California between 1903 and 1912, nine of which were connected to Buddhist churches and three affiliated with local Japanese associations (Asato, 2006; Morimoto, 1997). By 1914 there were 31 Japanese language schools, employing 52 teachers; by 1920 there were 40 language schools, employing 81 teachers; and by 1933 there were 220 Japanese-language schools in California, serving an estimated 65% of the Nisei population (Morimoto, 1997; Wollenberg, 1976).

The curriculum of the Japanese-language schools varied. The early Japanese-language schools were largely independent and as such had relatively independent curriculums. Some focused on Japanese education as primary to the U.S. public education of Nisei, whereas others saw the Japanese-language schools as mainly supporting the U.S. education. Japanese history and geography were taught using the Imperial Japanese Monbushō curriculum; others focused on moral education, drawing, and mathematics in Japanese; and others focused primarily on the Japanese language (Asato, 2006; Morimoto, 1997). This variation in the Japanese-language school curriculum is important because it reflects the Japanese American community engagement in deep, substantive discussions about just what they wanted their children to learn, and within the context of White supremacy and U.S. racism, significant contention existed within the community itself. At the crux of these community conversations was a question about the purpose and aims of the Japanese-language school curriculum. However, because curriculum is an expression of identity and social location (Au, 2011), at the heart of this question was yet another question about the "problem" of how to fit (or not fit) into the racial and cultural fabric of mainstream American society and culture. In what follows, we track this community conversation about the Japanese-language school curriculum through the public exchanges and reporting in the Japanese American newspapers, through the decisions made in the well-developed networks of professional organizations associated with the language schools, and in the shifting struggles over the content of the language school textbooks.

Facing Racism, White Supremacy, and Yellow Peril: What Should the Japanese-Language Schools Teach?

There was an immense amount of community conversation and dialogue surrounding the curricular shape and trajectory of the Japanese-language schools, and much of this conversation happened publicly in the media and in official meetings of various Nikkei community educational groups. A May 1908 editorial published in the *Shin Sekai* (New World), a daily community newspaper published in San Francisco, provoked this Japanese American–community curricular discourse by raising significant questions about the role of Japanese schools for Japanese American children born with U.S. citizenship and attending public schools. This editorial sparked a community discussion on the nature of the education of Nisei children, which led to a survey of Nisei children by the Japanese Association of America. The survey results spurred some Issei leaders in 1909 to form the Mokuyobi Kai, or the Thursday Club, as a space to discuss the present and future of Nisei education. At their 1910 meeting, the Thursday Club recommended an education of Americanization accompanied by Japanese-language maintenance, stating that "the cardinal principle . . . must be principally the assimilation of American customs and manners, supplemented by education in other essential ideas so that they will not forget the motherland" (as quoted in

Morimoto, 1997, p. 28). The Thursday Club established the Golden Gate Institute (Kinmon Gakuen) in San Francisco in 1911 to operate as a model for their vision of education (Asato, 2006; Ichioka, 1988; Morimoto, 1997).

In an attempt to unify the Japanese language schools in California, in 1912 the Japanese Association held a meeting for Japanese teachers in the state. There, 34 leaders of the Japanese Association and teachers affirmed that Japanese-language schools should "educate permanent residents of the United States," and "provide . . . instruction in Japanese and education about Japan" as a supplement to the education Nisei were getting in public school, which was seen as primary (as quoted in Asato, 2006, p. 48). They also decided that moral education would generally follow the Kyoiku Chokugo, or the Japanese Imperial Rescript on Education (Asato, 2006; Morimoto, 1997).

Japanese-language school teachers met again in 1913 and established the Japanese Teachers Association of America (Zaibei Nihonjin Kyoiku Kai), which decided to abandon the specific teaching of moral education explicitly, functionally ignoring the Kyoiku Chokugo in their statement of purpose of the curriculum and instead teaching it as embedded in Japanese language, geography, and history (Asato, 2006; Morimoto, 1997). Their reasoning for this decision was that "the goal to be attained in our education is to bring up children who will live and die in America, and as such, the whole education system must be founded upon the spirit of the public instruction in America" (as quoted in Morimoto, 1997, p. 28). However, as a 1918 survey showed, 5 years later, over half of the Japanese-language schools were still specifically teaching moral education (Asato, 2006).

The Pacific Coast Japanese Association Deliberative Council (PCJADC) was established in 1918 to also study and guide Nisei education. This council was made up of the four Japanese associations on the West Coast: the Central Japanese Association of Southern California (Los Angeles), the Japanese Association of America (San Francisco), the Japanese Association of Oregon (Portland), and the Northwest American Japanese Association (Seattle). At their 1918 meeting in Seattle, representatives of the Japanese Association of America suggested the creation of Kyoiku Chosa-kai (the Education Survey Committee) as part of the PCJADC, with the expressed purpose of shifting Japanese-language schools to be more palatable to White Americans. The PCJADC met again in February 1920 to discuss the future of the Japanese-language schools. Representatives from the Japanese Association of Oregon argued for the abolition of the Japanese-language schools as being a barrier to Americanization. Some members of the council believed that the language schools put Nisei children at increased risk of political attack by racists who were already advocating that all American-born, second-generation immigrants be stripped of their citizenship. Others believed that poor performance of Japanese American students in some public schools was a result of Japanese-language education negatively impacting their education. For instance, the Nikkei community temporarily shut down its school in Florin, in part because of the racist atmosphere and in part because 70% of the Nisei students failed their English exams and would not matriculate to the next grade—a failure that many Nikkei parents blamed directly on the Japanese-language schools (Asato, 2006; Morimoto, 1997).

Again, in response to anti-Japanese racism in California, in October 1920 the Japanese Teachers Association met for their ninth annual conference and moved to shift the mission of Japanese-language schools to be "supplementary to effect the education of good citizenship of the American-born Japanese based upon the spirit of the public school instruction in the United States of America" (as quoted in Asato, 2006, p. 63). The teachers also moved to change the names of their "elementary schools" to "institutes" in order to disassociate themselves from the idea of schooling (e.g., the organization named the Japanese Language Schools of Northern California became the Japanese Language Institutes of Northern California) and agreed to teach only enough Japanese language to allow the children to communicate with parents. The teachers also agreed to speed up the compilation of new Japanese-language school textbooks—with content from both Japanese and U.S. texts—as another means of deflecting anti-Japanese racism. These policy declarations were translated and delivered to the California state superintendent of public instruction, Will C. Wood, who promptly suggested that a law be created banning language schools associated with those loyal to foreign nations and requiring all private school teachers to pledge their loyalty to the United States (Asato, 2006).

Wood's suggestion became law in 1921, when the Private School Control Law was enacted in California to specifically stop the growth of language schools, generally, and Japanese-language schools specifically. The law required (1) that all administrators and teachers at foreign language schools obtain official licenses from the superintendent of public instruction, (2) that teachers at language schools be required to know U.S. history and the English language (proven through examinations), and (3) that language schools not teach before public school hours or exceed more than 1 hour a day, 6 days in a week, or 38 weeks in a year. Additionally, the superintendent of public instruction was given power to monitor the Japanese-language schools and approve curriculum and textbooks used in language schools. The 1921 law also required language school applicants to sign affidavits stating their intent to Americanize students (Asato, 2006; Morimoto, 1997).

This law had an immediate effect on the Japanese-language school teachers. For instance, the U.S. history and civics testing requirement served to keep some Japanese-language school teachers out of the classroom. In preparation for the requirement that Nikkei teachers pass state exams in U.S. history and civics, in 1921 2 week long workshops took place each in Los Angeles, San Francisco, and Fresno. A total of 131 San Francisco teachers took the test and only 108 passed. In Fresno, 25 took the test and 17 passed (Asato, 2006). Additionally, the Private School Control Law also impacted Japanese-language school teachers' practices. Teacher Yusen Kawamura suggested that, in his experience, the law pushed teachers toward patriotic Americanism as they prepared for the examinations; kept schools from hiring Japanese teachers who could not understand English; moved the Association of Japanese Language Schools toward using more-Americanized textbooks; shrank the time of Japanese language instruction, hampering its effectiveness; and increased financial difficulties in some Japanese-language schools (Morimoto, 1997).

The Nikkei Community Struggle Over Japanese-Language School Textbooks

The politics, tensions, and difficulties found in the early Japanese American transnational curricular discourse is perhaps best embodied by the community conversations regarding which textbooks and which specific textbook content should be used within the Japanese-language schools. Generally speaking, the textbooks created and edited in Japan were incongruent with the Nisei experience in the United States, and this incongruence was illustrated in the efforts by Japanese-language school educators to adopt new textbooks, develop their own, or revise existing texts. For instance, in June 1913 at the founding meeting of the Japanese Teachers of America in San Francisco, the agenda included items about developing new textbooks. This need for new textbooks was later rearticulated at a meeting of the PCJADC, at which representatives highlighted the need for Japanese-language instruction and maintenance but also expressed that the Japanese texts placed too much emphasis on developing loyalty and patriotism toward the Japanese emperor, which in turn could spark a stronger push from mainstream and White officials to further Americanize Nisei children. A resolution to publish special textbooks was passed by the Conference of the Japanese Association on the Pacific Coast, and educators at the Issei educators meeting of 1915 in Southern California passed resolutions in support of (1) positioning Japanese education as being "supplementary" to public education in the United States, (2) limiting the curriculum to the teaching of Japanese language, (3) enforcing the idea that all children attending Japanese schools also attend regular public schools, (4) making sure that anything that might be interpreted as anti-American be changed in Japanese school textbooks, (5) publishing Japanese school textbooks aligned with what was perceived as "Americanism," and (6) creating a Committee on Americanization (Morimoto, 1997).

In 1919, the eighth annual Japanese Language School Association Conference specifically discussed the inappropriateness of textbooks from Japan. There were also arguments about whether it was best to just teach the Japanese language or support teaching the spirit of Yamato Minzoku (the Japanese race) and whether or not to submit all new Japanese school textbooks for approval by the California State Board of Education. At a 1920 meeting of the Japanese Language Institutes of Northern California in Fresno (keeping in mind that in 1918, in response to increasing racism against their schools, Nikkei educators made a conscious decision to change their names to "institutes" from "schools"), participants passed resolutions affirming that the language institutes would be supplementary to public education in California and instruction would align with public school instruction, prioritizing the goal of helping Nisei children become good citizens. Meeting attendees also resolved that (1) Japanese and White American teachers be used in early childhood education in order to support their successful entry into public schools, (2) Japanese-language instruction be limited to 30–60 minutes a day, (3) the language institutes offer playgrounds for children to keep them out of trouble and to support physical health, and (4) the institutes establish a committee to review and revise their Japanese textbooks to be more appropriate for the needs of U.S.-born, Nisei children (Morimoto, 1997).

The textbook revision for grades K–6 was to be completed within a year by a representative each from the Japanese Teachers Association of America, the Japanese Teachers Association of Northern California, and the Japanese Teachers Association of Southern California. The language institutes also established a headquarters for textbook revision and compiling in San Francisco and committed to getting feedback from teachers and advisement from the California State Board of Education. After the 1921 passage of the Foreign Language School Control Law in California, discussed previously, Japanese-language teachers translated the older, Japanese Monbushō textbooks and submitted them to the California State Board of Education for review and official approval. The board allowed the schools to continue to use the older textbooks while the newer textbooks were being developed, but in order to use the Monbushō texts, several stories that the board thought supported Japanese nationalism were required to be removed. In August 1923 the California State Board of Education approved the *Beikoku Kashu Kyoiku-kyoku Kentei, Nihongo Tokuhon* [The *Japanese Reader*, approved by the California State Board of Education], which was officially published in 1924. The state board decreed that all Japanese-language schools in California use these new texts, which was the case until the California Language School Control Law was rejected by the U. S. Supreme Court (Morimoto, 1997).

The new *Japanese Reader* was still contentious within the Nikkei community. Several leaders pointed out the misprints and typos contained in the *Japanese Reader*, suggesting that the old Monbushō texts were better and cheaper and could either be edited to allay the concerns of U.S. officials or be interpreted in ways that substitute U.S. patriotism for Japanese nationalism. According to Morimoto (1997), others, like Kando Ikeda, publisher of *Hokubei Hyoron*, contended that there was no need to compile new textbooks, considering that the other ethnic minority groups such as Italians and Chinese used textbooks edited in their own countries. He was especially critical of what he considered to be the accommodating attitude of Japanese educators who volunteered to edit the alternative textbooks. . . . He considered *Nihongo Tokuhon* to be less than satisfactory (p. 46)

In 1931 a survey conducted by the Association of Japanese Language Schools in California found that 22 schools used the older Monbushō textbooks and 17 used the *Japanese Reader* exclusively. Eleven used both textbooks and two used neither. The Central California Japanese Language School Association struggled over developing a policy on textbook use in 1931, and at the 1936 conference of the Japanese Language School Association in Fresno, 23 representatives were chosen to revise the *Japanese Reader* and produce 16 volumes. To raise money for the textbook revision, the Southern California Japanese Language Association held an athletic competition in the Los Angeles Coliseum for all the Japanese-language schools. The event drew 10,000 participants and raised enough money to pay for the new textbooks (Morimoto, 1997).

The prospectus for the new/revised textbooks, likely written after the 1936 conference in Fresno, still spoke to the educational and curricular positioning of the Nikkei within the racist context of the time:

> *Nihongo Tokuhon* is the textbook for Japanese children born in the United States, based on the premise that the Japanese-language school is a supplementary institution, but which follows the spirit of American education for the sake of educating good and useful citizens. With this premise, the textbook aims at providing Japanese-American children with necessary linguistic and cultural education for their present and future lives. (As quoted in Morimoto, 1997, p. 48)

The prospectus goes on to explain that there were two main reasons for the textbook revision. One was that the previous textbooks created in California and Washington were outdated. More important, the prospectus points out that the earlier textbooks were produced during a period of time when the Japanese American community was decidedly split about whether the education of Japanese American children should focus on Japan or on the United States. Thus, the prospectus argued, new Japanese-language textbooks were needed in order to address the experiences and futures of the current generation of school-going Japanese Americans, the majority of whom were born in the United States (Morimoto, 1997).

We have to note here that, while the focus of our analysis and narrative of the Japanese-language schools in this chapter was on California, Washington State (with schools mainly in Seattle and Tacoma) followed a similar trajectory. Indeed, the first Japanese-language school on the North American continent was started in Seattle in 1902. The Nikkei community in Washington State faced similar anti-Japanese racism, which included (1) the formation of the anti-Japanese League, (2) White politicians and community members pushing legally and publicly to close the Japanese-language schools, (3) state bills to deny citizenship to Japanese immigrants (and others), and (4) an attempt to pass Washington State's own version of a language-school control law in 1921. For a more detailed discussion of Washington State's history in this regard, we recommend reading Chapter 4 of Asato's (2006) *Teaching Mikadoism: The Attack on Japanese Language Schools in Hawaii, California, and Washington, 1919–1927*, an excellent text that we relied on heavily for portions of this chapter (see also Asato, 2005).

CONCLUSION

In this chapter we have only begun to tell the story of early Asian American curricular discourse in the United States, outlining the contextual conditions of racism, xenophobia, White supremacy, and yellow peril backlash faced by Chinese Americans and Japanese Americans and how these conditions mediated the educational strategies undertaken by these communities at the time. We have also suggested that, through their legal fights, petitions, and public protests, members of these communities were also ardent educational activists on behalf of their children. Further, we have argued that both Chinese Americans and the Nikkei community expressed an early form of transnational curricular discourse as they simultaneously sought to access the mainstream "American" public school system and developed and maintained language and cultural schools of their own.

We find it important to recognize that the transnational curricular discourse for early Chinese American and Japanese American communities was always imbued with community-based and government-based considerations of domestic and international politics. For instance, as we discussed previously, during this time period the Chinese government was not very powerful internationally, and consequently the U.S. government did not consider any potential foreign relations implications in developing racist, anti-Chinese policies and laws (Asato, 2006; Kuo, 1998). Further, it seemed that Chinese Americans faced violence, with little reprisal or justice coming from local, state, or federal law enforcement. So while initially welcomed as a labor pool as part of an interest convergence (Bell, 1980) with White capital, Chinese Americans quickly became targets for a fairly widespread anti-Chinese movement that itself was an expression of a broader construction of the yellow peril (Kawai, 2005; Shim, 1998). For Chinese American families raising their children in the United States, this context presented formidable educational issues generally, and curricular issues specifically. In a most basic sense, early Chinese American curricular discourse was always done under constant threat and fear of forced removal—either by White mob rule or through officially sanctioned government policy (Chan, 1993; Chen, 2002; Lee, 2015).

Early Chinese American curricular discourse paralleled these political realities. On the one hand, Chinese Americans were concerned with making sure their children developed skills to survive in America (and we use "America" here specifically as a term that connotes culture and race in ways that "United States" does not), and on the other hand they wanted to make sure that their children could also survive in the Chinese dominant cultural and linguistic contexts of U.S.-based Chinatowns and China itself. However, Chinese American curricular discourse was not purely defensive against White racism and yellow peril stereotypes, either. It also represented a community commitment to cultural maintenance that likely would have existed regardless of the social, cultural, and political context of the United States at the time.

As noted above, the Japanese American community articulated its curricular discourse in much the same way as Chinese Americans. However, there were two key differences, also noted above. One difference was that the Japanese Imperial government was powerful enough to give U.S. politicians and policymakers pause when making decisions that might impact the educational experiences of the Nikkei community in the United States, out of fear of offsetting a delicate foreign relations balance. This meant, for instance, that the Nikkei struggle over access to public schools more than once triggered federal intervention into the politics of segregation in California (Asato, 2006). The other difference for Japanese Americans was that, while there clearly was a Nikkei curricular discourse surrounding cultural maintenance and the negotiation of the racism of yellow peril backlash, xenophobia, and White supremacy, the Japanese American orientation was more toward staying in the United States and intentionally establishing a community there, as opposed to returning to Japan (Asato, 2006; Morimoto, 1997). This shifting orientation toward staying in the United States contributed greatly to the Nikkei curricular discourse both in terms of access to public schools and the focus and content of the Japanese-language schools. Of course, once WWII started and the United States and Japan went to war with each other, the international positioning and political capital lent by the Japanese government evaporated, the questions of Japanese American integration and "fit" into mainstream cultural and political constructions of "America" were settled by racism, and the Nikkei community on the West Coast of the United States faced the horrendous experiences of forced removal and imprisonment. This in many ways echoed the mobs of angry Whites chasing the Chinese out of multiple cities some 60 years earlier and continued a pattern of relative Asian American "acceptance," perhaps in a moment of interest convergence (Bell, 1980), until such acceptance is revoked by physical, cultural, or policy violence once a threat is perceived.

Combined, these histories, policies, and contexts define the early transnational curricular discourse for both the Chinese American and Japanese American communities: never fully welcomed, often shunned; trying to make a home; trying to survive racism, White supremacy, xenophobia, and the notion of the yellow peril; not fitting into the cultural, linguistic, and racial fabric of mainstream "American" culture; working to maintain cultural heritage, linguistic heritage, and a community identity that was decidedly not White. In this sense, we might say that the early transnational curricular discourse for both the Chinese American and Nikkei communities was also a curriculum of purgatory, of in between, of unsureness of place despite sureness of survival. Their transnational curricular discourse was shaped both by force and by choice, and in the midst of both, the Chinese American and Japanese American communities were education activists and curriculum activists, struggling against a "curriculum of colonization" (Goodwin, 2010), asserting the need for self-definition, and fighting for the kinds of education they wanted for their children.

CHAPTER 4

Colonial Legacies

Shaping the Early Mexican American Discourse in Texas and New Mexico

A discussion of curricular discourse and Mexican Americans during the foundational period of curriculum studies in the United States, like the discussion of Native American curricular discourse, must be understood within the specific context of the colonization processes that characterized the dispossession of Mexicans in the Southwest, the Anglo expansion into what is now Texas and New Mexico, the subsequent establishment of White institutions and culture, and the attempted cultural exclusion and assimilation of Mexican peoples by Anglo state leaders in the Southwest (Estrada, Garcia, Flores Macias, & Maldonado, 1981). Mexicans were then and continue to be settlers in the context of the Southwest (Sánchez and Pita, 2014), and this informs the *peculiar sensation* of Mexican American curricular discourse shaped by the unique history of segregation policies and structural racism that targeted Mexican Americans.[1] On the one hand, Mexican Americans were subjected to racism through the mechanisms of segregation, lynching, and land dispossession, yet they were also considered what legal scholar Laura Gomez (2005) refers to as "off-white . . . an ambivalent racial niche, being neither black nor white" (p. 9).

This racial niche, or racially ambivalent status, formed in the 19th century in the Southwest, became a central point of contention in the early-20th-century civil rights fights surrounding the segregation of Mexican Americans in schools (Gomez, 2005). Therefore, in this chapter, guided by Gomez's claims, we argue that understanding Mexican American curricular discourse in the early to mid-20th century (1900s–1950s) requires a study of these colonial origins to understand the dominant curriculum of segregation applied to Mexicans and Mexican Americans in New Mexico and Texas in the early 20th century. Such an understanding also informs how these origins continue to play out in the Southwest. This allows us to (1) situate Mexican American curricular discourse as a response to *off-white* status, (2) understand the coexistence of assimilatory and oppositional positions within Mexican American curricular discourse, (3) explore curriculum as an extension of segregation in the Southwest, and (4) examine how this history shaped the lives and work of key figures in the development of Mexican American curricular discourse.

Accordingly, this treatment is both distinctive from and similar to the experiences of Native Americans, African Americans, and Asian Americans whom we document in the other chapters of this volume. Like Asian Americans, Mexicans and Mexican Americans were targets of Americanization through education programs. Mexicans and Mexican Americans were also simultaneously perceived and treated as culturally and intellectually incapable of acquiring the full benefits of such Americanization projects due to their supposed inferiority and thus deemed to be suited only for manual labor (San Miguel, 1987). Like African Americans, Mexicans and Mexican Americans were the targets of educational segregation, but unlike African Americans, they were not restricted by official policy or de facto segregation (Donato & Hanson, 2012; Godfrey, 2008).

These experiences of Mexicans and Mexican Americans in the context of early U.S. schooling had their origins in the same context as Native Americans and involved territory, or land, and their dispossession of it (Gomez, 2005); yet Mexicans and Mexican Americans, unlike Native Americans, were in a favored racial position vis-à-vis Indigenous peoples in the Southwest (Mexicans also dispossessed American Indians of their lands). Also, Mexican Americans came into the United States under the legal category of citizenship (Menchaca, 2001) and were not members of sovereign Tribal Nations that had the legal capacity to pursue educational self-determination in the same ways as American Indians—self-determination that has proven to be key (along with Indigenous knowledge systems) to Native American curricular discourse (Wilkins & Stark, 2010). Like the African American and Asian American experiences we document in this book, Mexican Americans during this time period both desired to be part of the fabric of the United States and to reap the full benefits of U.S. citizenship while maintaining Mexican cultural integrity and the Spanish language.

Despite the ongoing resistance and adaptation by Mexican American communities so fundamentally shaped by colonial origins, these forces had an overwhelming influence on the shape and direction of the official curriculum for Mexican American children in the United States that maintained segregation. Below we outline the major ideologies and policies that influence the curricular history we are interested in examining here. Additionally, as we have highlighted here in this book and elsewhere (Brown & Au, 2014), an analysis of this curricular history, one grounded in the field of curriculum studies, has largely been neglected and ignored in our field. Given that no history can fully be told, this chapter picks up some of the history of Mexican American curricular discourse absent from the founding of curriculum studies.

Therefore, to flesh out this complexity, we examine Mexican American curricular discourse in the context of the Southwest, paying attention to the impact of Spanish colonialism, the Mexican nation, and Anglo expansionism in New Mexico and Texas. As a result, the history of Mexican

American curricular discourse is caught up in a complicated history that oscillates between assimilatory or conciliatory approaches to the White-dominant curriculum exemplified at times by political organizations such as the League of United Latin American Citizens (LULAC) and the work of George I. Sánchez, an educational scholar and activist who fought to dismantle segregation and the accompanying deficit perspectives institution-alized against Mexicans and Mexican Americans in the early 20th century (Blanton, 2003).

The contributions of educator and activist Dr. George I. Sánchez played a key role in early Mexican American curricular discourse, particularly the manner in which the discourses he favored rejected the idea that Mexicans and Mexican Americans were inferior to Whites and advocated for equal and integrated schooling. Hence, we strive to situate his fight against the segregation of Mexican Americans in schools in the early part of the 20th century within a nuanced understanding of differing colonial projects that shaped New Mexico and Texas, two of the states that figure prominently in this history of Sánchez. Gilbert Gonzalez (1985), an expert on Mexi-can American educational history, correctly claims that "the segregation of Mexican children can be studied as part of a continuing pattern of domina-tion established after the Mexican-American War" (p. 56).

Furthermore, understanding the coexistence of assimilatory goals and resistance, which characterized Mexican American curricular discourse in the early 20th century, requires us to look at how the unique racial status of Mexican and Mexican Americans in the Southwest led to both accom-modationist and resistant stances exemplified by the different positions of LULAC and Sánchez. Sánchez's life and the experiences of Mexicans and Mexican Americans thus embody the *peculiar sensation* that Du Bois identified. To understand the contours of the peculiar sensation developed in this context, we first examine the role of the 1848 Treaty of Guadalupe Hidalgo in shaping the complex racial status of Mexicans and Mexican Americans. Accordingly, we scrutinize the caste system put in place in the Southwest that operated post 1848, how it produced the ambivalent White status of Mexican Americans in the Southwest, and how it played out dif-ferently in places like Texas and New Mexico, echoing though not ap-proximating the double consciousness Du Bois so prophetically identified.

We then examine how schooling was shaped by this complicated co-lonial process in the Southwest, tracing how race influenced the advent of schools following the 1848 Treaty of Guadalupe Hidalgo and into the turn of the 20th century. Establishing this important context, we turn our atten-tion to schooling and the Mexican American experience in the early 20th century, from 1900 to 1940. Through the life and work of George Sánchez during the early to mid-20th century, we trace how his life and work in New Mexico and Texas were also in conversation with African American civil rights movements. Thus, Mexican and Mexican American curricular discourse did not occur in a vacuum but rather was keenly aware of the larger national racial logics of the time as well as the complex history that preceded it in the Southwest. Indeed, the story of George Sánchez is a testament to the enduring legacy of the racial politics informed by the complicated histories of New Mexico and Texas.

As stated, this history of Mexican American curriculum did not occur in a vacuum. Indeed, the history of key figures and organizations in the development of Mexican American curricular discourse, such as Sánchez and LULAC, was shaped by the regional histories that were so important to Mexican American history in the early 20th century (Menchaca, 2001; Valencia, 2005). Moreover, while Mexican American history tends to be depicted as insular, it developed in conversation with the larger historical movements of the time, such as the African American civil rights movement (Blanton, 2003), the regional racial and colonial regimes that intimately shaped the status of Mexican Americans in the Southwest, and the commitment by Whites to maintain the segregation of Mexicans and Mexican Americans.

MEXICAN AMERICANS AND THE FOCUS OF THIS CHAPTER

In this chapter we use the terms *Mexican* and *Mexican American* to denote that, though differently labeled, these communities coexist within the politics of "the other" in the context of U.S. society and are thus social constructs that imply both assimilation and exclusion. One term denotes a national identity (Mexican), whereas the other is a racialized identity (Mexican American), yet both function in the context of Mexican American curricular discourse to demarcate how citizenship, language, and identity materially reproduced the conditions of the Mexican and Mexican American experience. Also, we use the term *Anglo* interchangeably with *White* since people in the Southwest explicitly applied the term Anglo to refer to Whites during much of the time period we examine. Furthermore, many of the authors we draw from use the term *Anglo* and thus, for continuity with these authors' work, we use *Anglo* when drawing from their work (Gomez, 2005, 2007; Horsman, 1981).

Additionally, we are limiting our discussion of this chapter on Mexicans and Mexican Americans to the region of the Southwest, particularly New Mexico and Texas. While we know that the presence of Mexicans in the United States preceded the formation of states such as Arizona, California, Colorado, Nevada, and Utah, we choose to focus on New Mexico and Texas because of our biographical engagement with George I. Sánchez, who was born in New Mexico and spent his formative educational years in New Mexico and Texas. Also compelling is the fact that both New Mexico and Texas offer clear examples of how the regional differences in Anglo expansionism shaped racial identity and politics in each state in relation to the presence of Mexicans that preceded statehood. (For instance, the Pueblo and Mexican ancestors of the author Dolores Calderón reflect this history. Her settler ancestors had been in New Mexico since the 1600s, and her Pueblo ancestors and family have been in southern New Mexico since time immemorial and in Texas post 1680.) Finally, because of the general time period we cover in this chapter (approximately 1848–1940), we focus on Mexicans and Mexican Americans as they were the largest ethnic origin group of what we call today Latinos in the United States during this time period.

COLONIAL ORIGINS OF MEXICAN AMERICAN CURRICULAR DISCOURSE

In this section, we detail the starkly different colonization processes that shaped New Mexico and Texas. In agreement with Gomez (2005, 2007), understanding Mexican American curricular discourse of the early 20th century requires an examination of how colonization informed the contours of Mexican American curricular discourse, a necessary approach when drawing from settler colonial theorizing (see Byrd, 2011; Tuck & Yang, 2012). We do this for several reasons. The differing histories of New Mexico and Texas offer a portrait of the complicated ways that Mexicanness and thus Mexican American identity and subsequent access to power were shaped. Legal scholar Laura Gomez (2005) writes that the racial ambivalence of Mexican Americans considered in mid-20th-century civil rights litigation such as *Hernandez v. Texas* in U.S. jurisprudence has "its origins . . . by virtue of American occupation of Mexico's northern territories" (p. 10). She describes how these racial origins have much to do with the transition from "Spanish-Mexican to Anglo-American control of the Southwest" (p. 11) exemplified by the Treaty of Guadalupe Hidalgo of 1848. It is these histories and tensions that directly shaped the de facto status of Mexican American school segregation in the early part of the 20th century, a central preoccupation of Mexican American curricular discourse.

Indeed, the Treaty of Guadalupe Hidalgo, signed between Mexico and the United States in 1848, which ended the Mexican–American War, represents a landmark moment in this history of Mexicans in the United States (Menchaca, 2001; Padilla, 1980). However, examining the impact of this treaty ahistorically (Ledesma, 2013), as a point of departure to dig into the history of Mexican American curricular discourse in the Southwest, fails the goals of our theoretical framework if we do not examine the regional colonial regimes in place that characterized the racialized nature of Mexican Americaness in their regional specificity, which was fundamental to Mexican American curricular discourse (Acuña, 1988; Cotera & Saldaña-Portillo, 2014; Duncan-Andrade, 2005). Certainly, if we look at the history of New Mexico and Texas, the nuances that shaped each state's racial and territorial dynamics depict important differences, demonstrating the flexibility and accommodation embodied by Anglo settler colonialism in the Southwest that adapted Spanish and subsequent Mexican colonial regimes (Acuña, 1988; Cotero & Saldaña-Portillo, 2014; Gomez, 2005, 2007; Menchaca, 1993; 2001).

THE CONTEXT OF NEW MEXICO

Land distribution and the status of the Mexican population at the time of the treaty in 1848 was shaped by the early-17th-century land-grant patterns established by the Spanish. In northern New Mexico, one of the more precarious outposts of the Spanish empire was settled as communal land grants that established the smaller, communal landholdings and practices that have come to shape northern New Mexico (Alaniz & Cornish, 1983, 2008). In the southern part of New Mexico, land grants were given to a few Spanish and *Criollos* (the social class that existed below Spanish that allowed for some Indigenous ancestry but retained largely European heritage). These haciendas employed the labor of Indigenous and mestizo populations, though these landholding patterns broke down following the Reconquista (reconquest) following the Pueblo Revolts of 1682. Land tenure in New Mexico (and Texas) was pivotal in shaping Mexican and Mexican American identity and politics. Certainly, the life of George I. Sánchez, as we examine later, was influenced by land tenure in the Southwest (Blanton, 2015).

By the time of the Mexican–American War, the land tenure system that the United States encountered in New Mexico was complex (Dunbar-Ortiz, 2007). The Treaty of Guadalupe Hidalgo, signed in 1848, officially ended the war. Article IX of the treaty was included to deal with the status of Mexicans in U.S. territory. As a result of the Treaty of Guadalupe Hidalgo, Mexicans now in the United States found themselves with a choice: stay in what was now the United States or relocate south beyond the new borders that divided Mexico and the United States—a choice that for many was influenced by a complex set of circumstances, the most important of which was the potential for having communal or individual landholdings (Cotero and Saldaña-Portillo, 2014). Thus, one of the dilemmas posed to Mexicans during this time period was whether they wanted to remain Mexican citizens or claim U.S. citizenship. In truth, for many Mexicans or communities living in these regions, the dilemma was multifaceted, characterized by where one stood in relationship to Mexican citizenship (Indian, mestizo, genizaro, Spanish, African, etc.) (Cotero and Saldaña-Portillo, 2014).

However, a claim to federal citizenship offered to Mexicans (in all the former Mexican territories) who chose to remain in the United States was not all that it appeared to be. In this time period, federal citizenship was not the dominant form of citizenship through which the day-to-day rights of citizens were exercised. Instead, it was the citizenship offered through individual states that granted these rights and privileges (Perea, 2001). Thus, in New Mexico, following the Treaty of Guadalupe Hidalgo, Mexicans found that while the treaty granted Mexicans federal citizenship, it did not guarantee the same rights offered under state citizenship in New Mexico. Constructing such a type of caste citizenship was done purposefully and reflective of the type of political power states of the border region required for managing racial and national populations in the colonial context of the Southwest (Acuña, 1988; Cotero & Saldaña-Portillo, 2014; Gomez, 2005; Menchaca, 2001; Perea, 2001). This predicament of citizenship would be repeated in the early 20th century when the question of segregation in schools and the racial status of Mexican Americans became the focus of Mexican American curricular discourse.

To make matters more complicated, the status of Mexican Americans was also grafted onto the Spanish colonial system. Gomez (2005) explains the quandary of Mexican status in New Mexico: "The U.S. colonization of the nineteenth-century was grafted onto a previous European colonization of the region—the Spanish colonization of the seventeenth and nineteenth centuries" (p. 14). In New Mexico, Anglos, Gomez (2005) continues, "encountered a fully developed Spanish-Mexican legal system, as well as an entrenched system of canon law in the Catholic Church" (p. 14). This system had produced a malleable racial caste system that determined political and economic rights as well as social status according to whether one was Spanish, Mexican, or Indian (or one of many variations in between), where money and access to political power allowed mobility and a "whitening" of racial status (Gomez, 2005; Menchaca, 2001). The category of Indian was further stratified between *Indios bárbaros*, referring to seminomadic and nomadic Indians, and *Indios civilizados*—civilized Indians. For example, the numerous Pueblos were not considered *Indios bárbaros*; rather, they were categorized as civilized Indians due to their permanent village settlements and agricultural practices (Gomez, 2007). In New Mexico this caste system was not fixed. Indeed, mestizos found that they could, as Gomez (2005) illuminates, transform themselves "into civilized persons in the context of a presumed uncivilized, majority Indian region" (p. 16). Arguably it is these origins, also shaped by Anglo settler colonialism, that later came to define what Gomez (2005, 2007) refers to as the off-white status of Mexican Americans in the early 20th century.

Despite the scientific racism relied on in the United States to justify the logics of White supremacy applied in both New Mexico and Texas (Gomez 2005), Anglo settlers and their governance mechanisms were unsure where Mexicans would fit within the context of White supremacy (Gomez, 2005; 2007). Anglo settler colonialism, in the context of New Mexico, was thus layered onto these caste dynamics, relying on—when necessary—the cultural and racial logics that facilitated the territorial dispossession of American Indians (Sánchez & Pita, 2014; Wilkins, 2010; Williams, 1990), the enslavement of Blacks, and the intermediary yet subordinate status of Mexicans (Gomez, 2007). Thus, tied to the question of citizenship was land. Hence, it was this flexibility of caste and racial identity that came into play in later civil rights initiatives on behalf of Mexican Americans due to the characterization of Mexicans and Mexican Americans as off-white.

Certainly, at the core of Anglo desires and the Treaty of Guadalupe Hidalgo was territorial acquisition. As with Indigenous communities, the individuals behind U.S. expansion in the Southwest were mainly interested in acquiring these territories with as little Mexican presence as possible (Acuña, 1988; Gomez, 2005; Menchaca, 2001), a key policy of Anglo settler colonialism (Wolfe, 2006; Byrd, 2011) that was imposed on the communities encountered through westward U.S. expansion (Cotero & Saldaña-Portillo, 2014; Menchaca, 2001). Thus, as Gomez (2005) explains, Mexicans in New Mexico were not granted full rights to citizenship under the treaty, as they were not accorded state citizenship, which "within the context of the meaning of citizenship in the mid-nineteenth-century" gave them "a kind of second-class citizenship" (p. 21). They were nevertheless granted greater political and social standing than Indigenous tribes (Sánchez & Pita, 2014).

Unlike Texas, which at the time of the Texas Revolution had about 4,000 Mexican citizens (compared to 30,000 Anglos and a small number of American Indians), New Mexico had 60,000 Mexicans, a much larger number of American Indians (75,000), and a very small number of Europeans (1,000), leading to a different dynamic of racial and cultural demographics (Alaniz & Cornish, 1983, 2008; Gomez, 2007). Additionally, there was a large population of *Genízaros*, captive Indians sold into slavery to Mexican and Pueblo communities in New Mexico, which added complexity to the racial landscape of New Mexico and would come to shape the life of Mexican American educator George Sánchez. Certainly, this political landscape is one characteristic of a caste system of colonialism brought by the Spanish into the Americas and maintained into the late 19th and early 20th century in places like New Mexico that had large numbers of Indigenous people and Mexicans. All this was set against the historical backdrop of Spanish entry into the region in the 17th century (Sánchez & Pita, 2014), which meant that there had existed an almost 250-year period for the establishment and maintenance of Spanish and Mexican governance and institutions.

As a result, Mexicans found themselves in an interesting position, entering the categorical logics of settler colonialism, between Anglos on the one hand and Indigenous tribes on the other (Cotero & Saldaña-Portillo, 2014; Menchaca, 1993, 2001). As Gomez (2005) clarifies, no longer were Mexicans the settlers or "subjects of the colonial project" (p. 24); they became "natives" or "objects of the colonial project" (pp. 24–25). Subsequently, U.S. interests acted to co-opt Mexicans (specifically Mexican elites) so they would not continue an alliance with local tribes, particularly Pueblo Indians, as had occurred in northern New Mexico during the initial years of Anglo occupation (Gomez, 2005). This was done by allowing Mexicans (and not Indians) to adopt some of the benefits of White status socially and structurally.[2] Thus, according to Gomez, Mexicans' off-white legal status was used as a wedge to drive apart Mexican and Pueblo peoples, which was adopted and put into practice by the elite Mexican class and further aided the disenfranchisement of Pueblo men. We see this same approach by Mexican American elites repeated throughout the brief time period covered in this chapter, which served to shape the differing curricular discourse adopted by Mexican Americans. The fragile, liminal status of Mexicans, between Whites and Indigenous peoples, resulted in Mexicans, on the one hand, accessing power because of Spanish ancestry while, on the other hand, being disenfranchised for their Indigenous ancestry (Cotero & Saldaña-Portillo, 2014; Gomez, 2005; Menchaca, 1993, 2001). The hierarchy of caste in New Mexico put those with the purest European ancestry at the top and those with the least pure toward the bottom, a system that inevitably shaped George Sánchez's life in New Mexico.

This history of New Mexico demonstrates that Mexicans and Mexican Americans operated at times within racially ambiguous categories whereby Whiteness was used as a tool to, as Gomez (2005) states, "negotiate their position in the new, post-occupation racial order" (p. 34).[3] Considering that Mexican American identity is fraught with the peculiar sensations identified by Du Bois, we do not dismiss the consequences of identity informed by this colonial context, which came at the expense of other caste groups (Menchaca, 1993; Sánchez & Pita, 2014). Applying a settler colonial framework also necessitates that we examine how land was used to facilitate Anglo settler governance and its impact on Mexicans and Mexican Americans. We thus consider that land figures prominently in the ideological and political makings of community, particularly that of Mexican Americans in the Southwest. Certainly, as a result of the larger populations of Mexicans and Indians, large-scale dispossession of lands in New Mexico took place in a later time period (mid-1870s) than in Texas (Estrada et al., 1981). It was finally the U.S. military that facilitated access to lands in New Mexico, but instead of integrating into the existing caste system in New Mexico, Anglos partnered with the army to impose military order (Dunbar-Ortiz, 2007; Estrada et al., 1981) and the logics of settler colonialism (nevertheless informed by the preexisting Spanish caste system) (Sánchez & Pita, 2014). Additionally, by the late 19th century, the boom in railroad construction facilitated economic development and the penetration of Anglo interests into New Mexico, resulting in larger numbers of Anglos entering the New Mexico territory. With this population increase came a greater demand for land by Anglos, which sped up the territorial dispossession of both Indians and Mexicans (Estrada et al., 1981).

One of the main mechanisms put in place to speed up the disenfranchisement of Mexican landholdings specifically was through taxation.

Estrada et al. (1981) tell us that "the Spanish-Mexican traditional practice had been to tax the products of the land. Under the new Anglo regime, land itself was taxed" (p. 106). Because taxes no longer depended on what the land produced, farmers with less access to capital were unable to meet the new increased taxes, causing many to lose their land (Estrada et al., 1981). This taxation scheme was in some ways similar to the Allotment Act (also known as the Dawes Act) of 1887, which shifted communal tribal land holdings into private, individual parcels, the result of which was the inability of individual tribal members to pay taxes on lands, thus paving the way for the purchasing of these lands by Whites. We do not believe that the similarities are a coincidence (Simmons, 1977); rather, they are part of a sustained ideological and policy practice put in place by Whites to gain territory (Calderón, 2014a), inexorably tying the experiences of Mexican Americans in the Southwest to land dispossession.

Indeed, the end of the 19th century in New Mexico marked a rapid dispossession of lands from Mexicans (and tribes who were impacted to a much larger degree), created in part by the growing number of Anglo settlers coming into New Mexico (Gomez, 2007). Federal agencies operated boldly to compel this dispossession that would come to shape the segregation of Mexican communities in New Mexico and thus schooling. The U.S. settler colonialist legal mechanisms of territorial acquisition allowed for federal oversight and management of lands that were transitioned into the public domain in places like New Mexico. However, such transfer necessitated the settlement of claims against such lands (Gomez, 2007). No longer were Spanish customs used to adjudicate or even inform such transfer. Instead, the Anglo settler colonial jurisdictional system was put into place, which ensured that no Mexican voices would inform the process of facilitating the transfer of lands into Anglo hands (Estrada et al., 1981; Gomez, 2007).

There was a similar process to Mexican land dispossession in Texas. And like in Texas, Mexican elites in New Mexico were convinced to join in the Anglo system that unfairly took lands away from non-elite Mexicans, and most certainly Indigenous tribes. For Mexicans this marked a merger between class and ethnicity that would come to shape the segregation policies of the late 19th century and early 20th century (Estrada et al., 1981). It was this demarcation of Mexicans in New Mexico—as in Texas, as we examine later—that influenced the different approaches that would spring up at later times in the history of Mexican American curricular discourse.

THE CONTEXT OF TEXAS

Much of what we share in the previous section on New Mexico resembles the context of Texas. On the other hand, in Texas, the racial dynamics were shaped by a different historical regional politics and demographics and the later entry of Spanish and Mexicans into the state during the 18th century (Sánchez & Pita, 2014), though the initial settling of Texas by the Spanish did begin in the 17th century through land grants given to a few Spanish and mestizo (mixed) men of high ranking. These lands were exploited through a debt peonage system that consisted of communities further down the caste system: Indigenous groups and mestizos of more-suspect heritage and class status (Alaniz & Cornish, 1983, 2008). Following independence from Spain, Mexico found some of its northern territory with small numbers of people, and thus in 1819 it encouraged and allowed immigrants from the United States to settle in what is now Texas (Estrada et al., 1981). In order to satisfy the increased demand for cotton in industrial England, Whites illegally flooded into Texas in search of new (and cheaper) land for cotton cultivation, resulting in Anglos outnumbering Mexicans (Alaniz & Cornish, 1983; Gomez, 2007). As a result of conflicts between the northern Mexican territory and the centralized Mexican government, which desired a more federalist union, war broke out between Anglo settlers and the Mexican government.

The early Mexican Republic called for the end of slavery in 1829, including in its northern territories. This decree was, in fact, a major impetus for the Texas Revolution of 1835–1836 (Godfrey, 2008; Gomez, 2005), and thus the institution of slavery and its accompanying racial, economic, political, and social structures had a lasting impact on the legal status and treatment of Mexicans in Texas (Godfrey, 2008; Perea, 2003). Estrada et al. (1981) explain,

> A constellation of factors—attitudes of racial superiority, anger over Mexico's abolition of slavery, defiance of initially agreed-upon conditions for settlement, and an increasing number of immigrants who pressed for independence from Mexico—strained an already difficult political situation. Direct and indirect diplomatic efforts at negotiation failed. The result was the Texas Revolt of 1835-36, which created for Anglo-Texans and dissident Mexicans the so called independent Texas Republic, which was to exist until 1845. This republic, while never recognized by the Mexican government, provided the pretext for further U.S. territorial expansion and set the stage for the war between Mexico and the United States (1846-48) (p. 104).

When Texas joined the Union, the merger was arguably less challenging than that of New Mexico because of the large numbers of Anglos present in Texas (Menchaca, 2001).

In Texas, Mexicans fared worse than their counterparts in New Mexico due to their smaller numbers, the type of White supremacy instituted, and the intensive military campaign carried out against them by the Texas Rangers (Alaniz & Cornish, 1983, 2008; Sánchez & Pita, 2014), a fact that explains the more intensely segregated schools in Texas. Estrada et al. (1981) explain that "the social and economic displacement of Mexicans and their reduction to the status of a colonized group proceeded rapidly, in clear violation of the civil and property rights guaranteed both by treaty and protocol" (p. 105). Unlike in New Mexico, there was a large and rapid transfer of land from Mexican to Anglo ownership (Estrada et al., 1981) that happened early on. Because of their smaller numbers, Mexicans were at a legal disadvantage compared to their more entrenched counterparts in New Mexico. Even in turning to Anglo courts to protect their settled lands, Mexicans and Mexican Americans were met with yet more forms of dispossession. Estrada et al. (1981) describe that, like in New Mexico,

> Mexican landowners, often robbed by force, intimidation, or fraud, could defend their holdings through litigation, but this generally led to heavy indebtedness, with many forced to sell their holdings to meet necessary legal expenses. With depressing regularity Anglos generally ended up with Mexican holdings, acquired at prices far below their real value. (p. 105)

Furthermore, in Texas, the cattle and sheep industries (which Mexican settlers were already engaged in) as well as the production of cotton were encroached upon and expanded by the larger Anglo populace, creating a type of mercantile cotton industry (Estrada et al., 1981) that allowed for a deep and quick penetration of U.S. forms of capital (Dunbar-Ortiz, 2007), ultimately replacing the Mexican feudal caste system (Gonzalez, 2013). In particular, the growth of the cotton industry "helped create and develop the mercantile towns that soon became conspicuous features on the Texas landscape. Mexicans, instead of reaping the economic rewards of ownership, found themselves only contributing their labor" (Estrada et al., 1981, p. 106). This also shifted the racial dynamics in Texas as enslaved Blacks were brought in larger numbers into Texas. As described, Mexicans in Texas were disenfranchised quickly (in contrast to New Mexico), moving from being owners to laborers in a short time period, which had a profound impact on their social identity due to the discrimination they encountered and the violence enacted on them (Estrada et al., 1981; Sánchez & Pita, 2014). Yet Mexicans were positioned above Blacks, a material fact that intimately shaped Mexican American curricular discourse in the early 20th century. Finally, in Texas, because of the Anglo majority and their dominant ideology around Indianness (Klos, 1994), there was no differentiation of tribal groups as was the case in New Mexico, where some were given more citizenship rights as civilized tribes (Klos, 1994). In Texas, all tribes were perceived to be uncivilized according to the racial Anglo Saxon ideologies that informed White expansionism, thus becoming targets of violent expulsion, like Mexican Americans, following the Treaty of Guadalupe Hidalgo.

Unlike in New Mexico, the racial logics that informed Texas institutions more explicitly relied on the White supremacy of Anglo expansionism, itself characteristic of the settler colonialism of the United States more generally. Yet Mexicans had to be accounted for in ways that racial Anglo Saxonism did not account for, and that was through Article IX of the Treaty of Guadalupe Hidalgo. Together, these factors shaped the type of segregated curriculum implemented in the Southwest in the early to mid-20th century.

We recognize that the racial ordering that placed Mexicans and Mexican Americans above Indigenous peoples and Blacks along with the dispossessions of Mexican lands shaped the ideological contours of Mexican American curricular discourse that came later. Some of the origins of the accommodationist views of Mexican American educators can be traced back to this early history of caste strategies employed by Southwestern states.

MEXICAN AMERICAN RACIAL AMBIGUITY
AND THE IMPACT ON SCHOOLING

Citizenship following the 1848 Treaty of Guadalupe Hidalgo created an ambiguous status for Mexicans in the new U.S. territories of New Mexico and Texas. Moreover, the unique racial politics and practices of New Mexico and Texas facilitated a racial ambiguity whereby Mexicans occupied a middle ground between Whites (or Anglos) on the one hand and American Indians and Blacks on the other. As argued earlier, these racial logics informed the early-20th-century status of Mexican Americans and, in turn, Mexican American curricular discourse. However, these racial logics were not initially used to inform the legal remedies adopted by the United States when adjudicating and legislating around issues of state-sponsored racial segregation. The uneven application of law to Mexican Americans created the peculiar condition of being treated as White, to a degree (Donato & Hanson, 2012). Such a racial status was also used to discredit Mexican claims of racial discrimination because of this off-white status (Donato & Hanson, 2012). Ironically a successful strategy to maintain the segregation of Mexicans and Mexican Americans was therefore the argument that because they were considered White, Mexican Americans were not discriminated against, leaving schooling conditions and larger patterns of segregation unchanged (Bowman, 2001; Donato & Hanson, 2012; Gross, 2003).

To understand this racial ambivalence, or what Laura Gomez (2005) refers to as Mexican Americans' off-white status, we took a step back to examine the colonial histories of the Southwest to understand the origins of these practices. As Powers (2008) points out, "The racialization of Mexican Americans in the Southwestern United States had deep roots in what Horsman (1981) described as the racial Anglo Saxonism that fueled Manifest Destiny in the mid-nineteenth century" (p. 468) and even further back to the Spanish caste system (Gomez, 2005). But this "racial Anglo

Saxonism" was not uniformly applied, as the examples of New Mexico and Texas demonstrate, because this regime had to account for the existing colonial contexts.

Nevertheless, Mexicans and Mexican Americans found themselves having to adjust to the dominant racial, social, political, and economic ordering of racial Anglo Saxonism, in many cases going from landowners to laborers. One such practice imposed on Mexicans and Mexican Americans was segregation in schools and elsewhere that maintained the labor status of Mexicans and Mexican Americans at the service of the new mercantile-driven economy in Texas. Drawing upon the work of Gonzalez (1985) and San Miguel (1986), Menchaca and Valencia (1990) explain that one major goal of school segregation in Texas was the creation and maintenance of cheap labor.

In both Texas and New Mexico, before they became United States' territories, there had been schools, particularly those run by religious orders (mainly Catholic), and after the 1848 Treaty of Guadalupe Hidalgo, other religious denominations opened schools. These included Protestant schools that had the curricular goal of Americanization, a project with colonial roots. Yet following the treaty, it was the Catholics who opened the largest numbers of schools to reassert Catholic authority in the region. Public schools that opened in the Southwest following the treaty were mainly for Anglo students; however, by the late 19th century the number of public schools serving Mexican Americans increased dramatically (San Miguel & Valencia, 1998). Of course, the public schools that opened continued with a pattern of segregation common in the United States, but they accommodated the specific context of the Southwest. In New Mexico, for instance, San Miguel and Valencia (1998) write that schools began to segregate between Whites and Mexicans as early as 1872 and that by the 1880s over half of New Mexico's children were school age, with most being Mexican and enrolled in segregated schools. Similarly, in Texas, segregated schools for Mexicans were created (San Miguel & Valencia, 1998). During the same time period in Texas, segregated schools were opened for Mexican children of working-class backgrounds to maintain a large labor pool for the rural ranches and prevent Mexican students from attending schools with Whites (Valencia, 2005).

It is important to emphasize how schools played an important role in the reproduction of certain forms of labor such as menial and vocational types that were not limited to the Mexican and Mexican American experience. In fact, we would argue that the history of Mexican and Mexican American students that we are highlighting should be read in a similar and overlapping light as the Du Bois/Washington debate, which focused on the question of whether vocational or broad-based liberal forms of education were appropriate for African American students. As Du Bois's analysis of industrial capitalism and schooling in the United States shows, White industrial philanthropists and Southern aristocrats agreed on what type of education African American students were best suited for: vocational and service-based curriculum (Du Bois, 1920, 1935/1998).

The key difference between Texas and New Mexico regarding the advent and maintenance of public schools during the 19th century was that Texas schools implemented more intense deficit-curriculum approaches to Americanization designed to remove those qualities and cultural practices deemed Mexican. In New Mexico this process happened more slowly for the demographic and political reasons (San Miguel & Valencia, 1998) illustrated in the previous section. Another key difference between Texas and New Mexico emerges when we examine how Spanish and Mexican culture were handled within each state's approach to school curriculum. In Texas, laws mandating English as the main language in schools while limiting the use of Spanish in schools were passed as early as the 1850s and reaffirmed in the 1870s. In New Mexico, a similar law was proposed, but the political power and number of Mexicans and Mexican Americans in New Mexico prevented its passing. It wasn't until 1891 that an English-only law was passed in New Mexico. Similarly, Mexican culture and history within the school curriculum were done away with more quickly in Texas because of the smaller number of Mexicans and Mexican Americans and the relatively small presence of Catholicism as an institution. This was not the case in New Mexico during the same time period, but similar curricular inclusions of Spanish and Mexican culture were also done away with in New Mexico toward the end of the 19th century (San Miguel & Valencia, 1998). In both states, the English-only politics and policies of the Anglo segregationist curriculum were met with much resistance by the Mexican and Mexican American communities.

During this period of rapid westward expansion by the United States, with its accompanying ideologies of Manifest Destiny and White supremacy, schooling in the Southwest embraced the racist tools of Americanization that deemed Mexicans as inferior to and incapable of equality with Whites. This shaped the segregationist curriculum (Rosiek & Kinslow, 2016) of the Southwest that removed anything Mexican from the schools and imposed curriculums aimed at Americanizing Mexicans and Mexican Americans. As a result, Spanish and any signs of Mexican culture were removed from the schools. Another approach adopted by the segregationist Anglo populations was the delinking of schools from religious orders that favored Mexican identity. Mexican American and Catholic school officials—who had supported the creation of public school systems in the Southwest—were removed by Anglo or White officials (Ruiz, 2001). The increased secularization of schools was seen as an affront by Mexicans, many of whom had sent their children to Catholic schools and valued the curriculum, which taught Spanish and Mexican histories (Ruiz, 2001).

In spite of all the changes imposed by the Americanization policies implemented by the United States, a close examination of the history of Mexican American schooling demonstrates that these communities were also actively resisting (Barrera, 2006). Like American Indians, Mexicans and Mexican Americans were schooled in the 19th century by religious orders such as the Catholics and the Methodists in Texas and, increasingly, by public schools in the early 20th century (Barrera, 2006). Unlike American Indians, however, schooling was not necessarily a requirement for school children. Subsequently, the common belief of the time regarding Mexican Americans and schooling in places such as Texas in the early 20th century focused more on how Mexicans were not interested in schooling their children, choosing instead to send children to work (Barrera, 2006; San Miguel, 1987). Yet researchers of early-20th-century Mexican and Mexican American schooling challenge this view that Mexicans did not value education, documenting how communities from Texas (Barrera, 2006; Gonzalez, 1982) to New Mexico organized, resisted, and worked for schooling opportunities for young people and curriculums that celebrated their heritage.

Certainly, Mexican and Mexican American communities did not stand idly by. In Texas, schools called *escuelitas*, or little schools, were created in the 19th and 20th centuries by local communities that wanted to maintain Spanish and Mexican culture (Barrera, 2006; Gonzalez, 1982; San Miguel, 1987). Following the treaty, some of these *escuelitas*, such as the Aoy Mexican School started in 1887 in El Paso, Texas, began teaching English to prepare students to enter U.S. public schools (Barrera, 2006; San Miguel, 1987), a key moment signaling how later Mexican American curricular discourse would treat language in relation to curriculum. Some of these schools celebrated the racial caste ordering of the Spanish and colonial times, celebrating Mexican land tenure histories. Additionally, schooling in many communities was increasingly tied to property and class. In Texas, for instance, many middle-class Mexican and Mexican American families from rural communities purchased land and built homes in towns so that their children could go to better schools (Barrera, 2006; Gonzalez, 1982), a reality that most Mexicans and Mexican Americans could not achieve. Yet the ability of this small class of Mexican Americans to purchase land reveals the capacity of Mexican Americans to use their off-white status for educational access.

The histories of the 19th century fundamentally shaped the contours of Texan and New Mexican lives and the schooling of Mexican American children. At the turn of the century, Mexican Americans numbers were buttressed by the growing number of immigrants coming from Mexico (Ruiz, 2001). In the 20th century both the economic upheaval of industrialization and the Mexican Revolution shifted the immigration patterns in the U.S. Southwest (Powers, 2008). These immigration patterns led to a complexity of racial and ethnic identity within the Mexican and Mexican American community, which included long-time Mexicans or Hispanos whose connections could be traced back to the 18th century alongside recent immigrants (Ruiz, 2001). This demographic growth and complexity also shaped the production of Mexican American curricular discourse in the early 20th century that was fundamentally shaped by White supremacy and the institutionalization of curriculums that were central to segregation (Rosiek & Kinslow, 2016).

Subsequently, the different events that unfolded in what are now New Mexico and Texas were inevitably shaped by these differing histories and the colonizing and racializing projects they invoked. Moreover, Mexicanness, being Mexican-American or Hispanic, was shaped in part by these different territorial histories. While in New Mexico there existed the Spanish caste system of race and in Texas the Anglo North American racial order dominated (Gomez, 2005), it was clear that the "ambiguity of Mexicans' racial status . . . positioned them to play a role as off-white or intermediate white group in the context of the Southwest" (Gomez, 2005, p. 18). Herein lies the tension in historical Mexican American curricular discourse.

Thus the histories of Texas and New Mexico, the territorial dispossession of Mexicans and their shifting position into labor, and the differing racial logics in place led to a territorial reconfiguration that produced segregation, which was exacerbated by the increase in Mexican immigration at the turn of the 20th century (Gomez, 2007; Ruiz, 2001). Schooling tied to segregation patterns deeply influenced Mexican American curricular discourse in the early 20th century that positioned itself against the deficit perspective of the dominant Anglo segregationist curriculum while seeking the integration of Mexican American students into American life through schooling. The segregation of Mexican and Mexican American students was deliberate, facilitated by the historical context laid out above. Indeed, as Valencia (2005) argues, "[b]y the beginning of the 1930s, the educational template for Mexican American students—one of forced, widespread segregation, and inferior schooling—was formed" (p. 395). As Gonzalez (1985) argues, "The segregation of Mexican children can be studied as part of a continuing pattern of domination established after the Mexican-American War" (p. 56), indicating that Mexican Americans' off-white status was more than a parallel universe of Whiteness (Foley, 1997).

FROM COLONIZATION TO SEGREGATION IN SCHOOLS: TWO SIDES OF THE SAME COIN

Studies examining segregation of Mexican Americans across the Southwest in states such as Arizona, California, Colorado, New Mexico, and Texas all find that segregation—whether residential, political, social, or educational—was a common practice in these regions (e.g., Arriola, 1995; Donato,

1997, 2003; Foley, 1997; Gonzalez, 1990; Menchaca & Valencia, 1990; Montejano, 1987; Powers, 2008; San Miguel, 1987; Wollenberg, 1976). In the mid-1930s, segregation of Mexican and Mexican Americans in the Southwest was rampant, with one study finding that 85% of the districts surveyed were segregated in various forms—including some being segregated through the 5th grade and others through high school (Gonzalez, 2013). In Texas and New Mexico, which had relatively large Mexican and Mexican-American populations, these percentages were even higher (Donato & Hanson, 2012; Montejano, 1987). These historical patterns set the stage for the continuance of inferior schooling for Mexicans and Mexican Americans and the commitment to the racist practices of Americanization through schooling (Gonzalez, 2013; San Miguel & Valencia, 1998).

School segregation in the Southwest, which was widespread in the early 20th century, also served the interest of capital. Donato and Hanson (2012) clarify that "the various aspects of segregated schooling—Americanization, testing, tracking, industrial education, and migrant education—were parts of a single system that was designed to process Mexican children as a source of cheap labor and that such segregation perpetuated the low status of the Mexican community within the larger political economy (Gonzalez, 1990)" (p. 204). In fact, segregation persisted into the late 20th century as evidenced by *Alvarado v. El Paso Independent School District* (1979), a class action suit brought by parents on behalf of their children in the border city of El Paso, Texas. Like African Americans, Mexicans and Mexican Americans were impacted by the goals of Jim Crow, such as exclusion of non-Whites from public places and political participation (Donato & Hanson, 2012; Montejano, 1987; Valencia, 2008), the racialized violence against them (Carrigan, 2004), and the early Anglo legal regimes put in place to disenfranchise Mexican Americans, described above. The impact of White supremacy on schooling resulted in segregationist curriculum that was imbued with both deficit and Americanization characteristics while systematically segregating Mexican Americans (Nieto, 2007) through a variety of means including testing, which we describe in the next section.

Yet, unlike the segregation that faced African Americans in the South during this same time period, the segregation imposed on Mexicans and Mexican Americans was not official policy, or de jure, but was accomplished largely through curricular justifications based on the perception of the linguistic needs of Mexican American students as well as their supposed intellectual incapacities (San Miguel, 1987). Also, unlike the more centralized efforts of African Americans against segregation, San Miguel (1983) explains that in the early 20th century (1900–1929) Mexicans in Texas were not well organized and lacked spokespeople, which prevented them from effectively challenging school segregation, especially in public schools.

San Miguel points out that there were multiple reasons for this lack of organizing. First and most important, "There was no statewide organization of Mexican Americans to articulate the group's interests, develop collective positions on important issues confronting the community, or bring pressure on local and state school officials" (p. 344). Second, because Mexican American communities had regional differences, cross-regional organizing was more challenging. Though there were Mexican organizations, they were mostly mutual-benefit associations, or *mutualistas,* which many times consisted of immigrants who had fled the Mexican revolution and believed theirs was only a temporary stay in the United States (Garcia, 1984). Also, "the Mexican community had not been integrated into the American system; that is, it had not yet been socialized into accepting the legitimacy of American social, economic, and political institutions, including public schools" (San Miguel, 1983, p. 344). Exacerbating the isolation and lack of integration of Mexicans into American society was language. Most Mexicans spoke only Spanish, and because of the long-established history of Mexican communities in states such as New Mexico and Texas, many in the Mexican community showed little interest in integrating into U.S. Anglo institutions and culture, especially in the early part of the 20th century.

It wasn't until the 1920s that a "fundamental shift in ideological and organizational orientation occurred within the Mexican communities of south Texas [and elsewhere] which significantly affected the social and cultural development of the overall Mexican population" (San Miguel, 1983, p. 345). Mexican Americans who came of age knowing nothing but the United States as their country responded to the economic and social crises, rooted in racism against Mexicans, facing their communities (Garcia, 1984; San Miguel, 1983). The organizations they created were reflective of their middle-class positions, adopting integrationist approaches that sought to incorporate Mexicans into U.S. society (Garcia, 1984; San Miguel, 1983), as opposed to the more regional and land-based organizations of their parents' generation. One of the organizations that adopted the ideals of Americanization and assimilation (Ruiz, 2001) was the League of United Latin American Citizens (LULAC), formed in 1929. LULAC and other similar organizations were different from the earlier *mutualista* organizations formed by Mexicans to assist the Mexican community.

> [T]he Constitution of LULAC illustrated [a] fundamental transformation. According to the Constitution, one of the central aims of the organization was "to develop within the members of our race, the best, purest, and most perfect type of a true and loyal citizen of the United States of America." The making of citizens itself was not a major concern for the middle class Mexican Americans since over half of the Mexican population living in South Texas were already citizens. Rather, from their rhetoric and based on their actual behavior it appears that they were more concerned with the making of active citizens who would practice their citizenship by participating in the dominant political, economic, and social institutions of the land. (San Miguel, 1983, p. 345)

Additionally, to be a member of LULAC one needed to be a U.S. citizen, something that had not been a condition of membership for Mexican and Mexican American organizations previously. Many Mexican American leaders emerging at the time believed that it was through the exercise of citizenship rights that they could address the poverty in the Mexican American community (San Miguel, 1983), and more importantly, LULAC relied on the off-white status of Mexican Americans to challenge educational segregation of Mexican American students.

Mirroring the ambiguous status of Mexicans following the Treaty of Guadalupe Hidalgo, however, many of the Mexican American organizations of the time (such as LULAC) were "not calling for the total assimilation of the Mexican population into Anglo cultural society"; rather, they were seeking selective "integration into Anglo-American political and social life" (San Miguel, 1983, p. 346). Yet the initial history and influence of the *mutualista* organizations did not lessen. Researchers argue that, in fact, these earlier organizations that promoted Spanish-language education and the retention of Mexican culture "contributed to an ongoing activism designed to further the education of Mexican Americans in Texas" (Barrera, 2006, p. 37), directly shaping Mexican American curricular discourse that sought both integration and the maintenance of Mexican American culture and language that was uniquely shaped by the de facto segregation faced by Mexicans and Mexican Americans.

During the early to mid-20th century, challenges to the segregation of Mexican American students in schools from Mexican community leaders and organizations such as LULAC could not be made on the grounds of de jure segregation. Godfrey (2008) explains:

> The legal classification of Mexicans and Mexican Americans as "white" in a nation founded on white supremacy, placed them in a highly controversial and complex position within the racial hierarchy. As a result, their segregation in Texas was never de jure since the Texas constitution declared school segregation as being only for "colored children" [citation omitted]. (p. 247)

However, to understand the segregation fashioned by structures of White supremacy in the Southwest and the marginalization of Mexican Americans, we must move beyond the question of whether Mexican American segregation was de facto or de jure, as this does not fully capture the colonial mechanisms that preceded statehood. What should be focused on is how colonial practices were deployed in the early period of statehood through the early 20th century, which shaped and concretized segregation in the Southwest in important ways. In Texas, the reduction of Mexicans and Mexican Americans to laborers, for instance, cemented their status as inferior to Whites, though not in the same sense as enslaved African Americans and their freed descendants (Godfrey, 2008). Indeed, as Donato and Hanson (2012) explain:

> Unlike the de jure segregation African Americans experienced in the American South before *Brown*, the segregation of Mexican Americans has been framed by scholars as de facto because it was the product of local custom and because state governments in the Southwest never sanctioned it. (p. 203)

But while there were not statutes in place in the Southwest legally enforcing Mexican segregation, to characterize it as only de facto does not acknowledge the policies and practices of White school administrators and boards of education that enforced segregation of Mexicans and Mexican Americans (Alemán & Luna, 2013; Donato & Hanson, 2012; Gonzalez, 1990). Besides, as shown in the previous section, it was indeed government policy—through colonial territorial reconfiguration and legal mechanisms—that led to the widespread dispossession of Mexican Americans. In Texas, this is more heavily influenced by the role of slavery in that state's ideological, political, and social context (Godfrey, 2008).

The schooling history of Mexicans and Mexican Americans in the Southwest offers a provocative counterpoint to using legal metrics instituted by courts to measure racial disparities as official and unofficial, reminding us of the works of critical race scholars that challenge us to consider how civil rights language and historical assessment of race, racism, and territory fail to capture the complex ways U.S. settler colonial projects unfolded differently for different groups—in this case, for Mexican and Mexican Americans. As Ian Haney Lopez (1994) reminds us, U.S. law plays a powerful role "in reifying racial identities" (p. 3), and in the context of Texas and New Mexico, so do these earlier colonial configurations and dispossessions around land. The racial status of Mexican Americans developed in Texas alongside the central role of states in being able to define and order their own racial logics, as codified in *Plessy v. Ferguson* (1896) (Menchaca, 1993). In Texas and New Mexico, Whites used other mechanisms to disenfranchise Mexicans and Mexican Americans in spite of the earlier federal ruling in Texas, *In re Rodriguez* (1897), which held that Mexicans had the right to become U.S. citizens. This ruling mattered little in the fight for integration because *Plessy* had earlier established the separate-but-equal doctrine (Godfrey, 2008; Menchaca, 1993). Schools in places like Texas thus maintained the segregation of Mexicans and Mexican Americans on the basis of both ideology and structure through school curriculum that was rooted in the colonial and labor needs of the country (Godfrey, 2008). For example, in the 1930 case *Del Rio Independent School District v. Salvatierra*, the Texas state court held that Mexican students were not segregated on a racial basis but on a curricular basis, and thus the segregation was deemed permissible (Godfrey, 2008; San Miguel, 1987). Interestingly, in this case, lawyers for the Mexican American students argued that, as Whites, Mexican American students should not be segregated from Whites. However, the court instead focused on both the supposed linguistic needs and labor status of Mexican and Mexican American students to justify the separate curriculums. Indeed, the curricular basis for separation was due to the differing enrollment patterns that resulted from Mexicans and Mexican American migratory work as well as their language needs, which the district superintendent argued demanded different curriculum (Godfrey 2008). However, neither the court nor the district actually required mechanisms to be put in place to find out whether students of Mexican ancestry were actually migrants and what their English proficiency was, thereby relying on deficit views of Mexican American students (Romo, 1983).

In agreement with Donato and Hanson (2015), we contend that the historic, consistent, and pervasive practices that brought about the segregation of Mexican and Mexican Americans in the Southwest should be recognized as official policy. However, it is interesting to note that the legal constructs of de jure and de facto directly influenced the manner in which Mexican American curricular discourse developed, particularly around a series of antisegregation cases we examine below. Furthermore, we contend that segregation must also be understood within the regional specificities of New Mexico and Texas. Certainly, the racial ambiguity, or off-white status, of Mexican Americans in the Southwest is part of the reason why segregation practices against Mexicans and Mexican Americans were characterized as de facto in the Southwest. We argue that the de facto nature of segregation is best understood when the historical colonial regimes of the Southwest are made explicit, thereby demonstrating that perhaps such labels used retroactively and uncritically do little to offer context to the institutionalized segregation of Mexicans and Mexican Americans in the Southwest. Much of Mexican American curricular discourse in the early 20th century was shaped by this dilemma, embedded in the legal ordering of race in the United States and the Southwest. Certainly, the off-white status of Mexican Americans complicated the community's legal fight against segregation (Donato & Hanson, 2012). Hence, understanding this complex and liminal position occupied by Mexicans and Mexican Americans since the mid-19th century offers a context to the historical reasons for how and why Mexican American curricular discourse was at once assimilatory in nature while at the same time rejecting the view of Mexican inferiority. This complexity is also reflected in the activism of Mexican and Mexican American communities.

We have analyzed features of the curricular discourse around the education of Mexican and Mexican American students through the lens of colonial and legal structures in the Southwest. The most salient of these features we want to emphasize is the impact of the off-white status of Mexican Americans on shaping educational segregation. While Mexican Americans attempted to use their White status to dispute segregation, school officials made arguments that segregation was necessary based on the language skills and aptitudes of Mexicans and Mexican Americans. In the next section, we examine the interrelated use of testing based on eugenics ideology to maintain the curricular segregation of Mexican American students and how Mexican Americans mobilized around this specific issue.

EUGENICS, IQ TESTING, AND THE SEGREGATION
OF MEXICANS AND MEXICAN AMERICANS

A bifurcated curriculum developed in Anglo-run schools, with one curriculum for Mexicans and Mexican Americans and another for Whites. This system was driven by the belief that Mexicans were inherently less intelligent than Whites and thus required a separate curriculum. Gonzalez (1985) explains that the driving ideology and practice in these schools "held that children were distributed along a continuum in intelligence, interests, abilities, and industriousness and that the curriculum must be adjusted 'to fit the child'; thus tracking and curriculum differentiation were to meet the range of intelligence, ability, etc., in any population" (p. 59). These beliefs directly shaped the curriculum of segregation, which withstood repeated court challenges by Mexican Americans, allowing for what Donato and Hanson (2012) call an "easy dismissal of the impact and intentionality of policy decisions made at the local level . . . [that] can hide the deliberate and racial nature of the segregation Mexican Americans experienced" (p. 205). In both New Mexico and Texas, as well as in other Southwestern states (such as Arizona and California), testing was one such deliberate mechanism, used to segregate Mexican Americans in schools during the early 20th century (Blanton, 2003; Gonzalez, 1974, 1978, 1979, 1982, 1990; San Miguel, 1987; Valencia, 2005).

In Texas, because the state constitution established that school segregation applied to "colored children," the White power structure relied on testing to do the de facto work of segregating Mexicans and Mexican Americans in Texas schools (Godfrey, 2008; San Miguel, 1987). This allowed for the institutionalization of a curriculum of segregation to be put in place across the Southwest that relied on the ideologies of White supremacy and the racial inferiority of Mexican Americans. During the 1920s, support for eugenics was widely spread, influencing not only educational practice and policy but national policy as well. An example is the Immigration Act of 1924, which favored Northern European immigrants and limited immigration from supposedly inferior Southern European countries and excluded other groups such as Asians entirely. Certainly in the late 19th and early 20th century Mexican Americans were perceived to be intellectually and culturally deficient, but by the 1920s eugenicists began focusing on the environmental and cultural aspects of the deficiency of particular groups, including Mexicans and Mexican Americans (Blanton, 2003; Valencia, 2005). Despite the arguments for the role of environment, other social scientists continued to argue that minorities were biologically inferior to Whites (Menchaca &Valencia, 1990). In Texas and New Mexico, prominent eugenicists William Sheldon at the University of Texas at Austin and Thomas Garth at the University of Denver administered tests to Mexican American pupils. The poor results, they argued, demonstrated the intellectual inferiority of Mexican Americans (Menchaca & Valencia 1990; Wollenberg, 1976).

Influencing William Sheldon was the work of Lewis Terman of Stanford University, who developed national IQ testing used to measure so-called intelligence. Terman believed in the inferiority of races and believed his tests proved this (Blanton, 2003; Gould, 1996). Regarding Mexicans and Mexican Americans, Blanton (2003) offers this revealing history: "Terman claimed that such alleged feeblemindedness was 'very, very common among Spanish-Indian and Mexican families of the Southwest and also among negroes [sic]'" (p. 43). More important in the context of Mexican American curricular discourse, Terman believed testing should be used to segregate Mexicans and Mexican Americans. Blanton (2003) continues, "Regarding school policy, Terman recommended that 'Children of this group should be segregated in special classes and be given instruction that is practical'" (p. 43). As a result of this research, school boards in places like New Mexico and Texas used tests to justify the institutional and curricular segregation of Mexicans and Mexican Americans (Menchaca & Valencia, 1990), in turn shaping Mexican American curricular discourse of the time. Menchaca and Valencia (1990) explain, "Because it was common for Mexican students to score considerably lower than their white peers, school boards used test results, in part, to separate Mexican and Anglo students" (p. 231). Much of the same reasoning we see today for gifted programs was used to justify the separation of students by race and ethnicity: "It was rationalized that Anglo students must be instructed in separate schools in order to prevent them from getting behind. Mexican students were identified as slow learners needing special instruction in separate schools" (Menchaca & Valencia, 1990, p. 231). Thus, segregation in places like New Mexico created not only separate classrooms and curriculums for Mexicans but also separate schools (Gonzalez, 1985). In Texas during the 1920s, IQ tests were used to accomplish just what the Anglo population wanted: to keep Mexicans and Mexican Americans segregated (Blanton, 2003; Hendrick, 1977; Wollenberg, 1976). By the late 1950s, only 25% of Mexican American students in Texas reached the 8th grade, and of those who went on to high school, only 8.5% reached the 12th grade (Blanton, 2015). It is no surprise that an integrationist-oriented discourse around curriculum and schooling emerged during the early to mid-20th century in the Southwest among Mexican Americans.

CHALLENGING AND RESISTING SEGREGATED SCHOOLING

The more I think about it the more I believe that the time has come to go after the segregated school. . . . I think this is the biggest single contribution that anyone can make in this entire field. I can think of no more important a service to our people and our country than to have this issue settled once and for all (George I. Sánchez, quoted in Blanton, 2015, p. 164)

The development and articulation of a racial caste system that placed Mexicans in an ambiguous middle position, at times between Anglos on one side and Indigenous tribes and Blacks on the other, produced the off-white status of Mexican Americans (Gomez, 2005). Yet, despite this status Mexicans and Mexican Americans were dispossessed of the lands they occupied in the Southwest, becoming laborers exploited by the Anglo settler populations. This history came to shape the unique context of Mexican Americans in the Southwest and specifically the racial segregation of Mexican Americans in schools in the early to mid-20th century. It was this context that shaped the life and work of George I. Sánchez, a leader in the field of Mexican American curricular discourse.

Concluding with the figure of Sánchez in this chapter allows us to trace how this history informed the creation of Mexican American curricular discourse in educational research and activism and the influence of Mexican Americans' off-white status, particularly around the issue of school segregation in the production of curricular discourse. Although there were a multitude of organizations and figures that shaped Mexican American curricular discourse, we focus on Sánchez, in part, because his legacy throughout the Southwest is so large, intersecting with organizations such as LULAC, the NAACP, and the ACLU. We also highlight the life of Sánchez because so little has been written about his work and influence (see Blanton, 2012, 2015). His life offers a glimpse into the complexity of Mexican American curricular discourse, allowing us to identify the representative moments and movements that were more critical of segregation and White policies that maintained it.

EARLY LIFE AND EDUCATIONAL TRAJECTORY OF GEORGE I. SÁNCHEZ

George I. Sánchez was born in Albuquerque, New Mexico, on October 4, 1906, during the territorial era of New Mexico, which ended in 1912 when New Mexico gained statehood. His early identity was indubitably shaped by the Hispano narratives of Spanish colonization and the caste system so dominant in New Mexico (Blanton, 2015). Indeed, a part of his anger at being denied access to equitable education and having his academic abilities questioned later in life came from his reliance on narratives of being descended from "centuries-old aristocratic Spanish families that had, by his own time fallen into dire straits" (Blanton, 2015, p. 14). These claims on his part are not out of the ordinary, particularly within the complicated caste system that shaped identity in the New Mexican territory, which in turn influenced Sánchez. However, Blanton (2015) points out that Sánchez also presented his identity more fluidly—as Spanish to Whites, at times as a *mestizo* to Mexican audiences—and by the 1940s, he was also challenging the celebration and romanticization of Spanishness common in the Southwest. Sánchez's life and shifting and flexible identity can arguably be attributed to the fluidity of identity created by the caste system in New Mexico (Blanton,

2015; Gomez, 2005; Nieto-Phillips, 2008). Moreover, it offers a regionally specific sense of what identity was like for many Mexican Americans in New Mexico that we cannot confuse with a type of Indigeneity as we look back on his life and work (Sánchez & Pita, 2014). Nevertheless, his early life in Jerome, Arizona—particularly his experiences as the son of a miner and staunch unionist—definitively shaped the political consciousness and activism that he would take with him as a faculty member and educational activist in Texas (Blanton, 2015; Duran, 2013; Romo, 1983).

His own schooling experiences attending small, integrated public schools in Arizona and New Mexico facilitated his learning of English. After returning to New Mexico from Arizona, Sánchez graduated in 1923 from Albuquerque High School at 16, moving on to work in menial labor jobs, play music, and box (Blanton, 2015). His first job in education was as a teacher in a one-room segregated school in the rural village of Yrisarri where he discovered the deep inequities that plagued New Mexican schools (Blanton, 2015; Romo, 1983). Yrisarri was a typical village that reflected the patterns of Spanish and later Mexican settlement: it was established by a Spanish loyalist who was driven out of Mexico and settled in New Mexico. Later, Sánchez taught at a school in El Ojo Hedondio near the Navajo reservation, a more rural and remote location than Yrisarri. Both of these schools made Sánchez realize that, though he had had a tough upbringing, conditions in these schools and communities were far worse (Blanton, 2015; Romo, 1983).

In 1925, Sánchez was once again moved, this time to a school closer to Albuquerque in Los Padillas (Blanton, 2015), a village that was originally a land grant given to Diego de Padilla (a Spanish settler) in 1718 (Sisneros, n.d.).[4] Here he was appointed principal, which Sánchez attributed to his marriage to Virginia Romero, daughter of a landowning and well-connected and well-regarded Hispano family. Indeed, his marriage to Virginia arguably contributed to his ability to move up quickly, coupled with his talents. By 1930, Sánchez was also a county supervisor for the local school district, where he began enacting progressive educational policies and pedagogies (Blanton, 2015). During this time Sánchez also went to school at the University of New Mexico, graduating in 1930, and earning his master's in education from the University of Texas at Austin a year later, where he focused on testing (Blanton, 2015; Romo, 1993). It was in Texas that Sánchez rallied around the issue of IQ testing as a mechanism to segregate Mexican and Mexican American students, challenging the notion that IQ tests were objective (Romo, 1993). Sánchez's work against testing earned him a lot of enemies in both New Mexico and Texas (Blanton, 2015).

After graduating, he returned to New Mexico for a short period to work for the New Mexico Department of Education (NMDE). Sánchez then went back to school to get his doctorate in educational administration from the University of California, Berkeley. He finished in 1934 and returned to work in the NMDE (Blanton, 2015; Romo, 1993). During his time in

New Mexico, Sánchez made many political enemies while also retaining the important support of the Rockefeller-funded General Education Board that funded his master's and doctoral work (Blanton, 2015). Later as president of the New Mexico Education Association, Sánchez once again embarked on a series of bold progressive educational programs of equalization for Mexicans and Mexican Americans, though his role in the passage of the Equalization Act in school funding resulted in his position being cut (Blanton, 2015). In 1935–1940, Sánchez left the New Mexico State Department of Education and became "an employee of major national foundations [such as the GEB and the Julius Rosenwald Fund out of Chicago] and then an educational administrator in a foreign county, and [he] reemerged in New Mexico as an adjunct, nontenured professor" (Blanton, 2015, p. 46). Again, though, his involvement in the passage of the Equalization Act resulted in a tenure track position at the University of New Mexico being withheld. In 1940, Sánchez took a faculty position at the University of Texas at Austin (Blanton, 2015).

Certainly, Sánchez's trajectory reflected a rapid climb through the ranks of the academic world, but what is more interesting about the life and work of George I. Sánchez is that it reflects the larger structure of Mexican American curricular discourse in the early 20th century. That is, the Mexican American community and its leaders did not operate in a vacuum. Rather, they were keenly aware of the racial logics that ordered life around them, exemplified by the way Sánchez spoke about his racial identity in different ways to different groups. Indeed, Sánchez's life and views on race are representative of the manner in which Mexican Americans' off-white status allowed for such fluidity, something we do not see in the African American experience, for instance, because of the inherent anti-Blackness of Anglo racialism that characterizes settler colonialism (King, 2014). Accordingly, the socially progressive programs of the New Deal (1933, 1938) emboldened the already activist and progressive work of people in the Mexican and Mexican American community. Sánchez was indeed a man of his time, and the curricular discourse he promoted was based on the belief that integration of Mexicans into U.S. society was both desirable and necessary for the advancement of Mexican Americans. Thus his work focused on dismantling the de facto systemic segregation brought about by the bifurcated curriculum in the Southwest.

THE MANY INFLUENCES ON THE WORK
AND LIFE OF GEORGE I. SÁNCHEZ

Sánchez was a scholar influenced by the New Deal who believed academic research was a tool to transform society, and his scholarship focused on race relations and the conditions of Mexican Americans in New Mexico and Texas (Blanton, 2006). Undeniably, George Sánchez crossed multiple borders, both geographic and cultural, to help shape the history of Mexican Americans in the Southwest and Texas specifically. From his time in New Mexico, to his work with African Americans at a college in Louisiana, to his work in Venezuelan educational policy, and finally to Texas, George Sánchez's trajectory represents the breadth and depth of Mexican American curricular discourse that developed in conversation with the regional, national, and global configurations of race and politics of the times.

Undeniably, Sánchez's work with African Americans further informed his stance against segregation and his rejection of the White perspective that Mexicans were biologically and culturally inferior, which in turn shaped the politics and social policies of New Mexico and Texas. This experience shaped how he framed Mexican American curricular discourse as one engaged with segregation and the fundamentally racist practices of Southwestern schools. In one of the many jobs he took before becoming a faculty member at UT Austin, Sánchez worked for a brief time with the Julius Rosenwald Fund in Chicago, from 1935 to 1937 (Blanton, 2006, 2015). The Rosenwald Fund was a philanthropic organization that was primarily "concerned with African American rural education in the South, and in this capacity Sánchez collaborated with Fisk University's future president, the eminent sociologist Charles S. Johnson, on preparing the massive *Compendium on Southern Rural Life*" (p. 576). During his time with the Rosenwald Fund, Sánchez also traveled to Mexico to study rural schools, an endeavor that the fund hoped could inform education in the African American rural context (Blanton, 2015).

Additionally, Sánchez's work with the fund extended beyond his capacity as an educational researcher, moving him into the area of state politics. Blanton (2003) explains:

> Sánchez practiced a . . . combination of academic research and social activism. When he began his work at Grambling he had recently lost his position in the New Mexico State Department of Education due to his pointed advocacy of reform as well as his penchant for hard-hitting, publicly funded academic research on controversial topics such as the segregation of Mexican Americans in schools. He had long sparked controversy with his research on racial issues. (p. 578)

When Sánchez was tasked by the Rosenwald Fund with creating a teacher-training program at the Louisiana Negro Normal and Industrial Institute at Grambling (now known as Grambling State University), he was no stranger to state politics, but it was his first time advocating in a Southern state (Blanton, 2003). This would be Sánchez's biggest project with the Rosenwald Fund (Blanton, 2003). The goals of the program were informed by Sánchez's progressive views on education, a commitment he shared with Charles S. Johnson. Of the program created by Sánchez, Blanton (2003) notes that "Charles S. Johnson later described this Grambling teacher-training program as 'among the most progressive of the community-centered programs for the education of teachers in the country'" (p. 577), praising the program "for offering African American teachers 'opportunities for the development of creativeness and inventiveness in recognizing and solving the problems to be found in rural communities, homes, and schools'" (pp. 577–578).

Such experiences deeply influenced Sánchez's work, because he "carried over his understanding of a Southern, African American perspective to his work with Southwestern Mexican Americans in New Mexico and Texas, particularly in a 1939 study of school equalization" (Blanton, 2006, p. 580). Sánchez himself believed that his practical experiences in the South were formative for him, but he also believed that he could do such work more effectively in the Southwest: "I am intensely interested in our programs at the [Rosenwald] Fund. Such projects as the Grambling experiment, the Louisiana Survey, etc., are very close to my own particular interests. However, I'd be much more effective if I were doing this same sort of work in the Southwest" (quoted in Blanton, 2006, p. 580). Sánchez returned to New Mexico in 1938 with aspirations of bringing the type of work being done in the South and the study of race to the University of New Mexico (Blanton, 2006).

By the time he moved to Texas in 1940, Sánchez had experienced the letdown of not being able to do such work at the University of New Mexico in Albuquerque, but it was during this time that he also took up a leadership role in the League of United Latin American Citizens (LULAC), an influential Mexican American organization. Yet the influence of his work with the Rosenwald Fund on African American education, along with his lifelong work in Mexican American education in New Mexico, continued to drive his research at UT Austin. There he wanted to do work in the Mexican American community similar to the work he had done previously at Grambling. He sought funding from the Rosenwald Fund, which responded negatively: "'Unfortunately, our foundation continues to feel that it should restrict its remaining limited resources to the pressing field of Negroes and Negro-white relations'" (quoted in Blanton, p. 580). In this manner, Sánchez's life and work offer an important detail in the history of Mexican American curriculum: The political activism and the racial dynamics of the time could not be divorced from the pedagogical and curricular work schools did to influence the racialized experiences of minority groups such as African Americans (Blanton, 2006).

Sánchez's work must also be measured against the politics of his time. His community and academic work against IQ testing represented an aggressive position against White supremacy and its curriculum of segregation while affirming the larger goal of integration of Mexican American students. In many ways, his approach to Mexican American curricular discourse was ahead of his time and considered radical by many. Perhaps it was his experiences as a Mexican American informed by the specific racial politics of New Mexico that allowed him to understand the complexities and entrenched nature of systemic racial discrimination (Blanton, 2006, 2015). Meaningfully, Blanton (2006) offers us some important glimpses into Sánchez's insights:

> He [Sánchez] called for a comprehensive federal and state program to uplift down trodden Hispanic New Mexicans: "Remedial measures will not solve the problem piecemeal. Poverty, illiteracy, and ill-health are merely symptoms. If education is to get at the root of the problem schools must go beyond subject-matter instruction. . . . The curriculum of the educational agencies becomes, then, the magna carta of social and economic rehabilitation; the teacher, the advance agent of a new social order." (p. 575)

A compelling parallel comes to mind that extended beyond the insights of Sánchez. African American judge Robert Carter (2004), reflecting on the legacy of *Brown* and segregation, said:

> The theory was that segregation was the evil, and if segregation is removed, then everything is so and people are going to be okay. I wasn't really wedded to that. And, of course, it proved to be not true because once segregation was eliminated, that segregation in terms of America wasn't really the problem. Segregation was a symptom of what the disease is. White supremacy is the issue here in this country.

Both Sánchez and Carter understood that remedial measures targeting segregation would not address the larger issues of the historical and structural realities of the dominant ideology of White supremacy, though Sánchez did not himself name White supremacy. He nevertheless strongly condemned segregation, stating that "I have consistently refused to participate in any activities in connection with any segregated school. . . . The segregated school is a concentration camp—you may gold plate the fence posts and silver plate the bobbed wire and hang garlands of roses all the way around it, it is still a concentration camp" (Sánchez as quoted in Blanton, 2015, p. 165). This statement represents the commitment of Sánchez to fighting both the institutional and curricular segregation of Mexican Americans.

Sánchez believed that the federal government could enact progressive social policy such as integration that could combat the structural manifestations of racism such as poverty and lack of access to health care, a belief shared by many of his peers in the African American community of the time, a choice later put into question by Justice Carter's insights shared above. And perhaps because of his intimate knowledge of the racial caste system in New Mexico, in his later years Sánchez rejected the nationalism of Chicana/o politics, remaining committed to a coalitional politics, the African American civil rights movement, and the belief that progressive governmental reform could work (Blanton, 2006).

Indeed, under Sánchez's leadership, LULAC was involved in the civil rights cases deciding whether the segregation of Mexican Americans represented a violation of equal protection. In *Delgado v. Bastrop ISD* (1948), LULAC and the American GI Forum of Texas (both leading organizations in the fight against school segregation) joined in support of Mexican and Mexican American parents in arguing that the prohibition of Mexican American children attending schools with Whites was a violation of civil rights. The court held that the segregation of Mexican American children was unconstitutional, but that "it allowed for the loophole of curricular segregation up to three years" (Blanton, 2015, p. 170), in essence maintaining the status quo, or de facto segregation. Texas and other states skirted the issue of segregation for many years to come, finding diverse mechanisms to keep the system in place (Alemán & Luna, 2013).

Activist approaches to Mexican American curricular discourse prominent during the 1950s were thus diverse. For instance, LULAC and Sánchez came to stand at opposite ends on approaches to this fight. On the one hand, LULAC, under the leadership of Felix Tijerina, developed a radio program in Texas called Little Schools, with the goal of teaching English to young Mexican Americans so they would not enter public schools and be segregated because of their lack of English (Blanton, 2015). Sánchez perceived this as LULAC giving in to the status quo of segregation, a curricular segregation no less, which he referred to as a "genteel segregation" because it endorsed the maintenance of "special classes in public schools for our little children who may know only Spanish at the age of six" (Sánchez, as quoted in Blanton, 2015, p. 177). This, according to Blanton (2015), put him at odds with other Mexican Americans who saw such remedial programs as beneficial. For Sánchez such programs did not support the integration of Mexican Americans but rather maintained their subordinate status and the subordinate status of Spanish.

We recognize that in the context of Mexican American curricular discourse of the time (1900s–1950s), Sánchez's work and beliefs represented a formative aspect of Mexican American curricular discourse born from the first half of the 20th century that remain relevant today. Influenced by the politics and policies of the New Deal and the early civil rights movement, some Mexican Americans such as Sánchez believed that opportunity was to be found in fighting for a full measure of citizenship and equality for Mexican Americans, a position that was not shared by all within the Mexican American community. Regarding remedial approaches like the Little Schools approach, Sánchez argued that adopting these programs was in effect "acceptance of the premise that something was inherently wrong with the Mexican

American child that required abnormal energy and planning from society to fix" (Blanton, 2015, p. 178)—a maintenance of a curriculum for segregation. We believe that these differing perspectives are not surprising in light of the ambiguous nature of the off-white status of Mexicans before the turn of the century. Indeed, throughout the early to mid-20th century such a curriculum of segregation continued unabated. Turning to Sánchez's own words once more demonstrates how Sánchez viewed race as a social construct that hid far more pernicious forms of inequity: "We frequently assign to a minority group—Negro, poor-White, Mexican—characteristics that are not racial or cultural attributes but the attributes of poverty" (Sánchez, as quoted in Blanton, 2015, p. 183). In his later life, Sánchez recognized that it was indeed racism that he should have more overtly challenged, rather than his earlier belief that addressing issues of poverty and similar economic structures could remedy issues facing Mexican Americans (Blanton, 2015).

The different approaches of Mexican American and African American civil rights organizations impacted the relationship between the two. On the one hand, the National Association for the Advancement of Colored People (NAACP) presented a centralized, well-organized force in the fight for African American civil rights, while on the other hand the Mexican American groups were a conglomeration of smaller organizations that reflected the regional nature of Mexican American politics. In a letter to Roger N. Baldwin, founder of the American Civil Liberties Union (ACLU), Sánchez countered Baldwin's criticism of the failures of Mexican Americans to unite like Japanese Americans and African Americans, writing, "The Mexican-Americans *are not* and *do not regard themselves as a homogenous ethnic or cultural group*. This means that resistance to discrimination becomes fragmented, local, and personal; though the discrimination itself is generalized and does not recognize the inherent heterogeneity of the subordinate group" (quoted in Blanton, 2015, p. 200).

Ideologically, the African American civil rights movement challenged segregation as a whole while Mexican American strategies often demanded admission to White schools without also demanding an end to segregation, relying on the off-white status of Mexican Americans. This tactic ultimately failed because Whites instead turned to curricular segregation (Blanton, 2015). Subsequently, an interesting aspect of Mexican American curricular discourse informed by the experiences of Mexican Americans and segregation is exemplified by Sánchez's 1958 work comparing African American civil rights campaigns with those of Mexican Americans. He argued that while *Brown* ended the de jure segregation of Blacks, it did not end the de facto segregation of minorities in general; thus, he proposed that Black civil rights organizations look to the Mexican American civil rights movements and their experiences organizing around issues of de facto segregation (Blanton, 2015). Contrary to Sánchez, who believed that all minorities should join in one another's civil rights fights, Felix Tijerina, president of

LULAC, did not support African American civil rights, opting for an accommodationist approach to White supremacy (Blanton, 2015).

Settler colonial studies and theorizing remind us that such complexities are not unique but are rather a functional aspect of the manner in which colonial systems, such as the Spanish caste system, created regional differences and thus regional identities. Sánchez came of age in a context and place where his Hispanic or Spanish background was celebrated, occupying an ambiguous racial category that was neither White nor Black. On the other hand, we also know that many in the Mexican and Mexican American community never reaped the benefits of such inclusion and perhaps did not desire it in the same way. Nor did they believe that racial Anglo supremacy would allow for Mexicans to be equal partners with Whites. However, like Sánchez, these leaders, organizations, and communities also continued to resist.

CONCLUSION

Within the context of segregation in the Southwest, as Valencia (2005) points out, "It is . . . not surprising that the Mexican American community mounted a legal campaign to desegregate its schools" (p. 396), as evidenced by the case of *Mendez v. Westminster* (1947), in which the court held for the first time that the segregation of Mexican and Mexican American students in public schools was unconstitutional. This case and other legal battles over schooling represent the fact that the federal system was perceived to be an important mechanism through which the educational opportunities of minority communities could be improved.

Looking to the history of the Southwest, we have seen how Anglo expansion into the Southwest had to deal with "the Mexican question" and did so through a lens of racial Anglo Saxonism (Horsman, 1981) in conversation with the caste systems already in place. This legacy produced a particular type of curricular discourse in the Mexican American community in the early period of the 20th century (1900s–1950s) that centered around responses to the segregation of Mexican and Mexican American students, which ultimately recognized that in spite of legal inclusion, Whites would work to maintain a curriculum of segregation. Mexican American curricular discourse was split on how to engage such a reality. Some approaches, like the LULAC Little Schools, accommodated the curriculum of segregation. Other approaches, such as the one fought for by George I. Sánchez, perceived the challenges to be based in economics and in the poverty that permeated Mexican American communities. Such approaches did not frame Mexican Americans as needing to culturally and linguistically accommodate the Anglo segregationist curriculum.

These differing approaches perhaps owe their distinctiveness, in part, to the regional politics and racial dynamics that influenced each; the racial caste system of New Mexico allowed George I. Sánchez to see himself beyond the lens of race more starkly imposed on those in places such as Texas. More important, though, is that the legacy of both approaches are born from the complicated nature of the off-white status of Mexican Americans in the Southwest, which produces the peculiar sensation we identify at the beginning of this chapter. Racialization and colonization are ongoing processes, and we are therefore mindful to allow Du Bois's work to guide us to be aware of how race and racism might transform or reform. Today, a small percentage of the Mexican American population traces its origins to Spanish and Mexican Colonial New Mexico and Texas, and yet Mexicans (and others) migrate into the United States, carrying with them the colonial and racial legacies of their country and regional places of origin. The work we have outlined above demands that we remain vigilant to these complexities in educational work while also knowing intimately that we are living in times in which rights are being retracted, Whiteness is openly celebrated, schools are once more segregated, and curriculum is facilitating segregation.

In this context, Mexicans and Mexican Americans do not occupy an intermediate space or off-white status. States such as Arizona and Texas have adopted anti-immigrant legislation, English-only laws, and other legislation essentially targeting Mexicans. In fact, the politics of places like Arizona highlight that Mexicans and Mexican Americans are perceived as a permanent threat, like the Chinese Americans and Japanese Americans in the early and mid-20th century. One only needs to look toward the banning of the Mexican American studies curriculum in the Tucson Unified School District to see examples of how Whites fear Mexicanness (Acosta & Mir, 2012; Cabrera, Meza, & Rodriguez, 2011).

However, the pushback in Arizona has resulted in a national movement that is propelling the creation of ethnic studies and Mexican American studies programs nationwide (Pipphen, 2015), once more a curricular response to a curriculum of segregation that fundamentally maintains Whiteness. In Texas, Mexican American studies was adopted across the states in various school districts. The Texas legislature declared May 1, 2015, Mexican American Studies Day (Texas Senate, 626, 2015). And yet, despite these gains, Mexican Americans continue to be segregated in schools today.

Certainly, many of the conditions that shaped Mexican American curricular discourse in the 20th century remain unchanged, such as the need for language policy and curriculum that does not frame the linguistic capital of Mexican American students as deficient. We believe that George I. Sánchez would be a proponent of Mexican American Studies in schools. After all, he said, "The curriculum of the educational agencies becomes, then, the magna carta of social and economic rehabilitation; the teacher, the advance agent of a new social order'" (Sánchez, as quoted in Blanton, 2006, p. 575).

CHAPTER 5

African American Curriculum History

A Revisionist Racial Project

Up to this point in the book, we have shown how curricular exclusion and revision have occurred in the United States. At the core of such exclusions has been the central location of Whiteness, where White histories and experiences were at the center of the educative and curricular process. The process of exclusions has been through silence or the gross exaggeration of different non-White groups' social realities. However, despite the kind of discursive framing within official school curriculum, communities of color have consistently coalesced politically around the concerns of education and curriculum revision—or what Mills (1998) calls *revisionist ontology*. For example, in the context of Native American curricular discourse the intent of White colonial interests was to remove all signs of Native cultural and historical experiences, but students and communities consistently sought ways to disrupt the process of cultural annihilation while also seeking ways to recenter the experiences of Native Americans via the school curriculum. Asian American communities also actively engaged in discussions and actions centered on the kind of cultural losses that occurred through curriculum while seeking pathways to meet head on the contexts of curricular hegemony present throughout many of the West Coast states. For Mexican Americans as well, it was within the context of White colonial power interests that Mexican American curricular discourse took form, and efforts to redress the processes of silencing and exclusion found in school curriculum were ever present. For African Americans (the focus of this chapter), dominant discourses of Whiteness shaped the presentation of Black life in school curriculum, promoting an enduring and durable ideological discourse of anti-Blackness. However, like the other communities addressed in this volume, African Americans sought different pathways to redress the school curriculum.

This chapter first explicates the narratives about African Americans that existed during the early 20th century, with a specific attention to how the sciences and school curriculum portrayed African Americans. We then show how African Americans engaged questions of curricular critique and revision within alternative spaces. Attention is given to curriculum theorizing as found in the *Journal of Negro Education* and curriculum revisions as found in textbooks and children's literature. Similar to the other chapters in this volume, Black curriculum revision served as a mode of counterhegemony that could be found across numerous other spaces that are rarely accounted for in the existing metanarrative of U.S. curriculum history (Brown & Au, 2014).

THE CONTEXT OF AFRICAN AMERICAN CURRICULAR REVISION

The reconstruction of representations of African Americans is a vital aspect of the Black freedom movement in curricular and educational thought (Dagbovie, 2015; Grant, Brown, & Brown, 2015). As Henry Louis Gates (1988) explains, from the moment enslaved Africans arrived to Virginia, they had to begin reconstructing their own image and countering negative stereotypes from the dominant White culture. This reconstruction, however, took shape out of a long and durable history of anti-Blackness that can be traced to the 16th century. Winthrop Jordan (1968) argued that some of the earliest depictions of Black life begin as English travelers began to survey African territories, only to "discover" in the process a peculiar people of dark hue. Jordan further noted that it was through these early interactions that a conception of Blackness evolved that remains to this day circumscribed by White normative meanings of beauty, language, sociology, expression, morality, civility, and intelligence. It also helped to put in place a kind of *racial othering* whereby Blackness became ontologically excluded from the realm of democratic citizens and over time "Black people" remained durably restricted by a variety of mechanisms and racialized economies (Brown & De Lissovoy, 2011) in order to justify their conditions within society— most notably the condition of enslavement and legal segregation. In keeping with the theories of this volume, we argue that anti-Blackness is at the very core of the settler colonial project (King, 2014). In the context of African American curricular discourse, the conceptual meanings of tropes such as the brute and Sambo remained tied to an ontological project of possession of land and bodies, wherein Black bodies were constructed as functioning solely to serve White interests—including labor, leisure, amusement, entertainment, and sexual desire. Thus, the process of reconstruction and revision found within the curriculum histories produced by African Americans has remained intensely focused on the kinds of reduction and construction of Black life and Blackness found within mainstream curricular materials.

Before exploring the process African Americans undertook to reconstruct their societal image, we will first define *construction* in relation to *reconstruction*. These two terms are important because a construction is the process by which African Americans were understood in society and a reconstruction is how African Americans challenged such constructions. The Oxford dictionary provides three working definitions of a construction, but for our purposes, we take *construction* to mean two things. The first is "the manner in which a thing is artificially constructed or naturally formed; structure, formation, disposition;" and second, "a thing structured; a material structure; a formation of the mind or genius" (quoted in Gates, 1988, p. 130). We further maintain that the construction of racial representations of Blacks typically seeks to advance a set of interests to hold in place asymmetrical power relations (Hall, 1997). In this sense, the construction of racial images of African Americans helped to extend ideas that have had direct effects on African Americans' material realities. Therefore, we assert that the construction of African Americans by the dominant culture is not just about the damaged individual psyches of African Americans but that such images also helped to sustain the existing structural inequities within wider society. The politics of reconstruction for African Americans has been about revising and repudiating the existing images of Black personhood while also filling the void left by histories and stories that have not been told. Nowhere were these struggles around power and representation more visible than in the construction of school curriculum. In this chapter, we show how, within the context of anti-Black discourses, Black scholars created *counterpublic spaces* (Fraser, 1990) to challenge the existing majoritarian narratives about Black life expressed in school curriculum and society.

THE NADIR: THEOLOGY, SCIENCE, AND CURRICULUM

Historian Rayford Logan (1997 [1954]) defined "the nadir of American race relations" as a period after Reconstruction when civil rights that were gained by African Americans were taken away through legal and extra-legal measures. As historians note, the war was lost in the South, but Southern Whites looked for ways to regain what was lost (Blight, 2003; Fredrickson, 1971). Thus, the obstruction of African American integration became central to redefining the New South. The end of the Civil War and the subsequent amendments of Radical Reconstruction had ended a way of life and an over two-and-a-half-century-long division of labor that placed people of African descent at the very bottom. However, as Omi & Winant (2015) explain through their notion of racial formation theory, the abolishment of slavery did not abolish race difference; it changed the manner in which race difference would be conceptualized in the United States. Three prominent mechanisms of power helped in this remaking of anti-Black racism in the late 1800s and early 1900s. It is within this context that African American curricular discourse took form.

The first mechanism of power was racial violence and aggressive tactics intended to engender fear in African Americans. As scholars note, the practice of White violence after Reconstruction was to employ fear and intimidation to challenge Black inclusion in U.S. society as well as to prevent progressive Whites' efforts to help the recently emancipated African Americans (Fredrickson, 1971; Shapiro, 1988). White supremacists employed tactics of lynching and racial aggression to keep African American men from the voting booth and also slowed down efforts to build institutions for African Americans. The deployment of extra-legal tactics and state-sanctioned terror would continue all through the mid-1900s and would provide one of the strongest supports for the ideology of racial rule in the New South. It was during this period that many African Americans were kept from participating in the political process, relegating them to lives of peonage labor. And the process of White racial rule was not shaped by extra-legal efforts alone; it was enshrined in the legal context of the South and affirmed through the system of Jim Crow.

The coupling of extra-legal actions with the legal framework of Jim Crow would help to create a new kind of racial rule, where Whites could segregate society racially. In this context, every facet of Black life was legally blocked from any opportunity to live a flourishing life, such as voting, education, job placement, health, and housing. As such, state and federal laws systematically enclosed Black Americans in a world materially and conceptually removed from the spoils of American democracy. Although some African Americans were able to gain some level of education and prosperity, the majority of African Americans remained oppressed by the mechanisms of legal segregation as well as repressed by the hidden and overt hand of White racial violence. However, this was not enough; Whites needed a justification for their actions and it was common for scientists, social scientists, and theologians to develop grand theories about Negro capacities, temperament, and beliefs.

As scholars (Drescher, 1990; Fredrickson, 1971) note, giving scientific justification for the status of Black people helped to bolster firmly held beliefs that racial hierarchies were an outcome of a natural unfolding of human capacity. Much of this discourse emerged in the mid-1700s but remained into the early 20th century. As scholars explain, it was during the antebellum period, and particularly during the end of the slave trade, that the ideas of scientific racism flourished (Drescher, 1990; Jordan, 1968). As Drescher (1990) explains,

> They [European scientists] assumed that blacks belonged to a distinct group, whether characterized as a "race" (subspecies) or a "species." Scientific difference arose concerning the degree to which racial inheritance inhibited the progress of "civilization." The question was frequently related to the "place" of the black in nature and the role of slavery and the slave trade in future relations between Europeans and Africans. (p. 427)

The currency of racial science in Europe circulated throughout the world and in particular helped to support early philosophical beliefs about the development of an American nation. Blacks in the early American context were made into *natural slaves*, bound to their lot in life as enslaved Africans (Jordan, 1968). Furthermore, Thomas Jefferson's *Notes on Virginia* enabled racial science to gain further currency. Scholars characterized *Notes on Virginia* as a set of responses to queries by the secretary of the French legation, François Barbé-Marbois, or a kind of guidebook describing the landscape and possibilities of an American nation (Frankel, 2001; Gish & Klinghard, 2012). However, when Jefferson was asked about Black people's place in this nation, he stated that "they were a race of degenerate people who were dull and inclined to laziness. If they were not enslaved they would be unproductive, and if emancipated they starve and soon find themselves destitute" (Menchaca, 1997, p. 21). Historians note that Jefferson made such claims with some level of apprehension, calling on the empirical capacities of science to substantiate his claims about Negro inferiority (see Adelman, 2003). Jefferson's call to science ushered in a bevy of discourses throughout the 1800s that essentially argued that Blacks did not have the capacity to become full citizens due to their biological limitations and the providence of God as described through erroneous uses of biblical scripture.

After Reconstruction, these scientific theories prevailed, but within the context of Blacks' ability to function and integrate into American society as free persons—also called the "Negro Problem." The Negro Problem addressed the question of whether Blacks could be full-fledged citizens capable of living and existing within a White-dominated world. The notion that Black people were incapable of functioning as free persons in America came from some of the most influential voices of society, including politicians, scientists, theologians, and historians (See Fredrickson, 1971). This of course has been a reoccurring theme in the context of Native American, Asian American, and Mexican American curricular discourse, where questions surfaced about those groups' adaptability to U.S. White-dominated society. As historian George Fredrickson (1971) explains, it was the overarching discourse of social Darwinism, a set of ideas that rose to great popularity during the early 1900s, that provided some of the most pervasive ideas about Blacks' ability to exist within a world without bondage. The central thesis of social Darwinists was that without the patriarchy of the plantation, Black populations would degenerate and decrease over time. Fredrickson argues that noted scientist Joseph Le Conte offered one of the most well-known commentaries concerning the Negro Problem. Frederickson stated,

> In a study of "the ethnological aspects" of the "Race Problem in the South," published in 1892, Joseph Le Conte, whose contributions to geology and biology had made him the South's most distinguished natural scientist, presented probably the decade's most sophisticated application of Darwinian theory to the American race problem. Le Conte affirmed that the "laws determining the

effects of contact of species, races, varieties, etc., among animals," which "may be summed up under the formula, 'The struggle for life and the survival of the fittest,'" were "applicable to the races of men also." The destiny of the weaker varieties was either "extinction . . . or else . . . relegation to a subordinate place in the economy of nature; the weaker is either destroyed or seeks safety by avoiding competition." (Fredrickson, 1971, p. 247)

Major insurance companies and policymakers also took up the use of racial science to justify their practices.

Robert Hoffman's *Race Traits and Tendencies of the American Negro*, published in 1896, provided "a thoroughgoing and detailed exposition of exactly how and why blacks were losing out in the struggle for existence" (Fredrickson, 1971, p. 249). As Fredrickson explains, the Hoffman findings were viewed as serious science and were presented by the "prestigious imprint of the American Economic Association" (Fredrickson, 1971, p. 249). This study "became a prize source of information" (Fredrickson, 1971, p. 249) for writers who wished to support the scientific thesis that Black people were not capable of functioning in society. Through the new mathematical approach of statistical analysis, Hoffman presented an argument for Black degeneracy. He maintained that the census data of 1890 showed that the Black population was inferior due to their higher mortality rates in relation to Whites. His science rejected the idea that Black mortality rates were due to environmental conditions, positing instead that they were informed by ineradicable race traits, such as "'inferior organisms and constitutional weaknesses, which . . . is one of the most pronounced race characteristics of the American Negro'" (quoted in Fredrickson, 1971, p. 249). In the end, Hoffman argued that education and religion did little to change the life chances of African Americans due to the entrenched hereditary characteristics of Blacks. Black inferiority thus became an empirical reality as defined by Hoffman's findings. We must keep in mind that scientific studies were one of many mechanisms used to support the thesis that Blacks were inferior. As critical theorists (Hall, 1997) have argued for decades, hegemony is produced by multiple transmitters, including media, arts, and schooling. However, a case could be made for the primacy of scientific discourse over other forms of discourse made available about Blacks. Science helped to develop seemingly immutable truths about Black people that played a significant role in shaping the image of Black American culture. The negative connotations of Blackness prevailed in every aspect of society in the early 1900s. While the constructed meanings of Blackness were formed well before the early 20th century, it is important to note the unique context by which Black people were constructed discursively in the United States at that time. As historians point out, the late 19th century helped to set in place a changing racial climate in which White supremacists were compelled to hold in place centuries-old racial hierarchies (Fredrickson, 1971; Shapiro, 1988). Through this process, the school curriculum played an important role.

The characterization of African Americans as conforming to stereotypical images was a common trope, expressed in almost every facet of society. African Americans were regularly depicted as scared, simple-minded, watermelon-eating "darkies." This popular imagery of African American children found in popular culture including children's songs and counting games, in which Black children were depicted through often-violent parody, stripped Black life from its moorings in reality and portrayed Blacks as subhuman, wild-eyed, savage pickaninnies with watermelon smiles and animal-like features and limbs.

During the early part of the 20th century, much of the dominant academic discourse about African Americans focused on their biological composition. The historical depictions of Black people were mostly defined by their toil and labor in American society. Historians regularly depicted Black people as not having a history beyond the paternalism of slavery and labor. It is for certain that the history curriculum in schools also played a significant role in circulating and advancing ideas about racial inferiority that were common to this time. We define "curriculum" in a very specific sense to mean a body of knowledge that is taught in schools and supported by texts in the wider society. For this section of the chapter, we focus on the impact of children's literature and textbooks in helping to reinforce the thesis of Black inferiority. As we stated earlier, the critique and revision of curriculum was circumscribed by a socially constructed presentation of Black imagery informed by the pervasive discourses of the time. The context of Black imagery is at the very core of African Americans' project to revise and repudiate the myths and silences contained in the school curriculum.

AFRICAN AMERICAN IMAGE MAKING AND THE U.S. CURRICULUM

Curriculum played a prominent role in the process of constructing the imagery of African Americans. There were at least three purposes of curriculum in the context of racial reproduction from the late 19th to the early 20th century. The first was to make visible how African Americans were to be imagined in society. As historians (Fredrickson, 1971; Shapiro, 1988) explain, backlash against the political discourse against slavery gave rise to new images of African Americans to support the thesis that they were inherently incapable of being full-fledged citizens in the United States. Thus, school curriculum became a prominent space to reproduce ideas about Blacks as inferior, violent, uneducated, and intellectually dim-witted. The second approach to curriculum making about African Americans was to recount history in a way that diminished the manner in which racism informed the histories of African Americans. This kind of revisionist history tells the story of the past in a way that made African Americans seem agreeable and compliant to the prevailing racial hierarchies of American history. This approach was most pervasive in K–12 American history textbooks. In the section that follows, we outline how children's literature and textbooks, as forms of curricular knowledge, were used to reproduce the prevailing anti-Black ideologies of this time.

CHILDREN'S LITERATURE AND THE CURRICULUM OF RACE MAKING

The story *Ten Little Niggers* has a publishing history that spans almost 100 years, from 1875 to 1980 (Martin, 2004). The books, published and used in England, Germany, Australia, and the United States, contained songs used to promote numeracy among children. However, in the midst of learning about counting and songs, *Ten Little Niggers* helped to hold in place ideas about race that remained through most of the 20th century. The books' themes and depictions emerged from prevailing images that characterized African Americans as either violent or unintelligent.

Literature had a long history of reproducing stereotypical images of Black people. Sterling Brown (1933) powerfully made this point when he argued that antebellum literature depicted Black characters as one of seven stereotypical archetypes: "(1) The Contented Slave, (2) The Wretched Freeman, (3) The Comic Negro, (4) The Brute Negro, (5) The Tragic Mulatto, (6) The Local Colored Negro, and (7) The Exotic Primitive" (p. 180). The power of children's literature and song was twofold. The first power was its ability to reach young, impressionable minds. The context of schools, where teachers are seen as the single source of knowledge, helped to spread myths about Blackness. This was particularly effective because of the segregated racial spaces that largely created the conditions for there to be very little contact between Whites and Blacks, where anti-Black images could go unchallenged, helping to sustain the racial ideologies of that time. Thus the hegemonic capacity of children's literature was very powerful, helping to sustain a master narrative of race. The second power of children's literature and songs was their repetitive quality. To listen and sing a story over and over again has insidious capacities to instill racialized knowledge. The process of recitation within the context of schools helped to circulate in an almost harmless fashion ideas about whom and what a Black person was. The most obvious racial image was that Black people were "niggers," but even further, the content of the early children's literature helped to circulate a sociological narrative that Black pathology and inferiority were normal. As Michelle Martin (2004) explained about the content of the *Ten Little Niggers* stories:

> This song, written in the United States but popularized in England, became
> wildly popular in both countries if the proliferation of different versions is any

indication. Like "There Were Ten in the Bed" and "Ninety-Nine Bottles of Beer on the Wall," this musical story tells of elimination, but in the case of *Ten Little Niggers*, it is human beings that are successively eliminated literally. For instance, most versions of this tale begin in this way: "Ten Little Nigger Boys went out to dine; One choked his little self, and that left nine." . . . In most versions of this book prior to the 1940s, seven of the ten characters meet untimely and grizzly deaths. (p. 21)

The themes of death and violence were the two primary tropes about African American life in this story. Each page provides a graphic image of African Americans as indifferent to violence, pain, and death. In each page, one might witness Black males dealing with cut limbs, choking on food, being mauled by bears, or being burned by the sun. Across the multiple versions of *Ten Little Niggers*, different notions of Black stereotypes emerged to help support and sustain the pervasive image of Black pickaninnies, brutes, and Sambos. The pedagogical utility of song and recitation reproduced a destructive image of Black people as wild, incorrigible, dimwitted, and indifferent to violence and death. The easy rendering of death to Black characters was a hallmark approach to dehumanizing Black life through this form of curriculum. For example, the following song's lyrics offered a powerful illustration of how play and death coexisted in children's songs and picture books:

Ten little nigger boys went out to dine;
One choked his little self, and then there were nine.
Nine little nigger boys sat up very late;
One overslept himself, and then there were eight.
Eight little nigger boys traveling in Devon;
One said he'd stay there, and then there were seven.
Seven little nigger boys chopping up sticks;
One chopped himself in half, and then there were six.
Six little nigger boys playing with a hive;
A bumble-bee stung one, and then there were five.
Five little nigger boys going in for law;
One got in chancery, and then there were four.
Four little nigger boys going out to sea;
A red herring swallowed one, and then there were three.
Three little nigger boys walking in the zoo;
A big bear hugged one, and then there were two.
Two little nigger boys sitting in the sun;
One got frizzled up, and then there was one.
One little nigger boy left all alone;
He went out and hanged himself and then there were None.
(As quoted in Anderson, 2009)

Aside from the kind of graphic and stereotypical images portraying Black people as hapless, care-free, and indifferent to violence, the different editions of *Ten Little Niggers* reflected two prominent and implicit narratives. The first has to do with the nature of Black people's environs in a post-Emancipation era. Ideas about Black inferiority and pathology were often presented as an argument for African Americans to remain enslaved because of their so-called inability to self-govern. The imagery of many of these books showed Black males idly sitting in rural settings, not working or managing their daily lives. In addition, the imagery of *Ten Little Niggers* and other children's literature of the late 19th century presented a sociological context of children without mothers and fathers and thus devoid of parental guidance, again upholding the imagery that African Americans could not function in a civil society. The second important function of children's literature of this genre was to present Black people's lives as solely an outcome of their own actions without any reference to White racism. In books such as the *Coon Alphabet, Coon Town*, and *Ten Little Niggers,* the past histories of racism that have the greatest impact on Black life are nonexistent in these stories.

Textbooks promoted similar anti-Black ideologies as children's literature but with a slightly different approach. There were two primary modes of potraying Black life in American textbooks. The first was through blatant absence or silence, thus positioning people of African descent as a history-less people. The second promoted an enduring belief that Black people came from uncivilized beginnings and were not capable of reasoning or contributing to U.S. society. The context of Africa was typically constructed as a bastion of primitiveness, with no recorded history. Fredrickson (1971) argues that part of the process of promoting anti-Black discourse was to describe Africa as a place that formed the American Negro's debased character:

> The historian Joseph Tillinghast applied . . . Darwinian concepts of racial heredity to Negro history in his study *The Negro in Africa and America*, published by the American Economic Association in 1902. Describing the black man's African background in a way that was to influence a generation of scholars, he argued that the only way racial heredity could be changed was by "slow infinitesimal degrees" through the process of "selection, which tends to accumulate advantageous variation in offspring and to eliminate unfavorable ones." It was vain to think that heredity could be "manipulated by purposive human devices." The Negro character had been formed in Africa, a region which supposedly showed an uninterrupted history of stagnation, inefficiency, ignorance, cannibalism, sexual license, and superstition. (Fredrickson, 1971, p. 253)

It is important to keep in mind that the ability to record history was also premised on the ability of racial groups to contribute to society. Thus, epistemologically speaking, the recorded history was a defining characteristic of being civilized. Conversely, however, people of African descent were constructed as having no history. Prominent African American scholar Carter G. Woodson recalled the overarching ideology of Harvard's history department, which held on to the belief that Africa was a place devoid of history (Grant, Brown, & Brown, 2015). Therefore, in a similar sense, textbooks' blatant dismissal of African histories and contributions were typically consistent with the cultural logic (Goldsby, 2006) of this time.

Absence and silence also occurred in textbooks through the failure to mention the key contributions of Blacks to American history. In this context, Blacks were not present in the early American history of a developing nation in work or war. They also did not exist through the late 1800s and the end of the Civil War. Typically, textbooks also did not mention the courage of African Americans such as Harriet Tubman and the efforts of the Underground Railroad to gain freedom for Blacks. In a philosophical sense, Blacks' existence and ontological positioning as "Americans" did not exist in textbooks as a whole. The experiences of African Americans were reduced to enslavement. Therefore, in textbooks African Americans were portrayed as a collective people in bondage and enslaved. This of course presented several problems for African American activists and scholars during the early 20th century.

TEXTBOOKS AND RACE MAKING

The American textbook has been a consistent point of concern among African American scholars, educators, and thinkers (Zimmerman, 2004). Two of the more consistent concerns across the first part of the 20th century were the blatant dismissal of African Americans' historical experiences and the outwardly racist depictions. As W. E. B. Du Bois (1935a) once remarked, "One is astonished in the study of history at the recurrence of the idea that evil must be forgotten, distorted, skimmed over" (p. 722). It was clear by the 1940s that scholars recognized that textbooks were a central and vital space in which to construct problematic narratives about Black people (Du Bois, 1935a; Reddick, 1934; Woodson & Wesley, 1935). A common critique among Black thinkers and researchers was that the traditional textbook left out the histories of African Americans, while also undermining White Americans' involvement in African American oppression. Woodson and Wesley's (1935) words illustrate this sentiment:

> Practically all history teaching is propaganda; but there are significant differences between the methods as well as the contents of certain textbooks. Excessive emphasis on one type of facts and a corresponding suppression of others—the most frequent practice—conditions the child to preconceptions and false valuations which it takes much time to unlearn. The more slyly insinuated expression

of contempt for some national racial groups is apt to create antipathies which cannot always later in life be traced to their sources and so, with others, are carried along as seemingly innate. (p. 439)

During the 1930s and 1940s, African American local political organizations started to level consistent critiques against the school curriculum. For example, the National Association for the Advancement of Colored People (NAACP) met at local branches to examine how African Americans were portrayed in textbooks. The results of their findings were published in a pamphlet called *Anti-Negro Propaganda in School Textbooks* (National Association for the Advancement of Colored People, 1939). Here Walter Benjamin's commentary taken from this pamphlet summarized the NAACP's position on curriculum during this time:

Because this tremendous, overshadowing importance of the dark complexioned people in the United States goes home so directly to the most intimate problems of human existence and has so much bearing upon them, it is of the utmost importance that the young people in our schools today, laying the foundation of their future lives, should have a complete and accurate account of this most extraordinary chapter in human history. They should have it exactly as it is, true, dependable, without color or bias. But what do they get? They get a mingling of accepted fallacies, or errors that have been passed from one uninstructed writer to another, of assumptions of prejudice that have become imbedded in literature as fact, of misunderstandings and misrepresentations, often honest, always disastrous. (As quoted in *Anti-Negro Propaganda in School Textbooks*, 1939, p. 4)

Overall, issues raised by the NAACP and scholars of this time consistently made three important points about the role of textbooks in shaping the representations of African Americans in the school curriculum. The first was that much of the textbook writing during the early 20th century favored the hegemonic interests of Southern racial ideologies that sought to recast the collective memory of the South and the Civil War (Blight, 2003). The second was that, not only did textbooks provide inaccurate depictions of the past, they also advanced problematic theories about Black temperament and psyche. The third and most pervasive was that textbooks played a role in distorting the historical contributions of African Americans in the United States by either positioning White people as the progenitors of world civilization or by characterizing people of African descent as uncivilized and savage.

Historian David Blight's (2003) examination of Civil War memories explains how White organizers went to great lengths to shape the historical memory of the South. He found that it was in the context of memorializing the past that White supremacist ideologues were able to reproduce a new Southern narrative based on the bravery of Confederate soldiers and leaders.

Textbooks published during the early part of the 20th century certainly reflected Blight's assertions about the recasting of Southern racial memory. In 1934, Lawrence Reddick's comprehensive analysis of racial attitudes in textbooks found that authors discussed slavery by justifying its existence and merit. As Reddick (1934) stated,

> Most of the authors seek to justify the importation of Negroes as slaves. "In those days few persons in the world opposed slavery. Even Kings and Queens made money out of the slave traffic." "Slavery was common throughout the world at that time, and its extension to these new lands was natural." "At that time slavery was not looked upon as an evil." According to Evans, "This was the beginning of Negro slavery in our country. The Negroes were good field hands, being able to stand the summer heat better than the white man." (p. 228)

His analysis found that textbooks during this time took a pro-South approach. This finding is consistent with the post-Reconstruction discourse of the Lost Cause movement—the movement that sought to restore the image of the South through sites of memory and texts about the Civil War (Blight, 2003). Blight (2003) explained,

> As early as 1899, UDC [United Daughters of the Confederacy] chapters endorsed a pro-Southern textbook and began their decade-long crusade to fight what many perceived as a Yankee conspiracy to miseducate Southerners. When the UDC women took up the cause of history they did so as cultural guardians of their tribe, defenders of a sacred past against Yankee imposed ignorance and the forces of modernism. They built moats around their white tribe's castles to save the children from false history and impure knowledge. (p. 278)

Textbooks, however, did more than just revise the histories of slavery in the United States. They also provided a historical perspective on Reconstruction and the subsequent racial violence that ensued throughout the South. The following quotes, taken from two U.S. history textbooks, highlight a common narrative used to justify the use of White racial violence toward Blacks:

> To *overcome the negro rule* [emphasis added] a secret society was formed called the Ku Klux Klan. By making use of the negro's *instinctive fear of ghosts* [emphasis added] the Klan, dressed in white, at times with hideous masks, moved by night silently from place to place, using if necessary the harshest measures to strike terror into the negro. (Lawler, 1931, p. 390)

> The South was threatened with ruin unless something was done to break the negro control. To do this many white men joined secret societies. These societies worked to frighten the negro into staying away from the polls and to make

him realize that the white man was still to run the South. Bands of men in white robes and with fiery crosses rode the highways at night. The *superstitious negroes feared the visits of ghostly night riders* [emphasis added] who knocked at the cabin door at midnight and in a solemn voice threatened the trembling negro with terrible punishments. The work of the secret societies had the desired results. Fewer and fewer of the negroes went to the polls, and the white men gradually but surely regained control. (Marshall, 1930, p. 458)

These depictions not only provide a distorted historical record but also present myths about African American dispositions. Similar to Brown's (1933) critique of literary authors' egregious use of myth, authors of textbooks often drew on cultural anecdotes and stereotypes about African Americans.

The textbooks and children's literature of this time were informed by the racial politics and discourse of this time period. Aside from the passionate and organized attempts of African Americans to redress blatant circulation of anti-Black images, the image of the Black American remained unchanged in White supremacists' racial imagination. It is important to note that the circulation of these ideas, present in children's literature and textbooks, was not just the work of a few corrupt textbook writers and children's books authors; these ideas were part of the cultural logic (Goldsby, 2006) of that time. By cultural logic we are talking about the ways anti-Black sentiment was constructed as normal within the Black–White racial binary of the early 20th century. However, despite the preponderance of racist ideas, scholars and activists vehemently challenged the racial discourse of this time.

The socially constructed image of Blackness prevailed in every aspect of society in the early 1900s. The making of "Blackness," of course, came well before the 20th century, but it was mobilized in ways during this time that differed from the previous centuries. In the wake of the post-Reconstruction era, Blacks had entered a new racial space, constructed to sustain the interests of Whites. The making of Blackness into the proverbial "racial other" in the early 20th century required a confluence of actors, ideas, and institutions. The intentionality of the theologian, scientist, politician, children's literature author, and textbook writer all sought to "make" or construct Black people into a fixed stereotype. Anti-Blackness during this time was imbued with a cultural logic (Goldsby, 2006), meaning that anti-Blackness and all that constituted the process of marking Blacks as "less than" was viewed by White interests as a rational and necessary practice to hold in place the racial hierarchy of this time. Through this process, the school curriculum played an important and sometimes understated role in promoting these constructions of the image of Black people. Such constructions, however, did not go without ongoing and persistent critique and revision. In addition, as the disciplines of anthropology and sociology began to shift the discourse on race and culture, schools as well began to discuss the role curriculum could play in shifting racial attitudes (Burkholder, 2011).

RECONSTRUCTING THE "NEGRO":
A REVISIONIST ONTOLOGICAL PROJECT

It is safe to argue that from the very moment Africans arrived in the colonized Americas they began to reject the negative ideas that prevailed about people of African descent. The work of historians that documents the number of slave revolts and resistance to slavery indicates that Blacks persistently challenged the contexts that defined their social realities as enslaved Africans (Aptheker, 1943/1983; Genovese, 1979). This insistence on being able to resist the existing anti-Black ideologies was also reflected in the written word of African Americans in the 1800s from authors such as David Walker, Frederick Douglass, Phillis Wheatley, and Sojourner Truth, to name a few. Black history served to revise and repudiate the existing theories and histories that labeled Black people as the proverbial racial other. From the late 19th century to the early 20th century, African American scholars, novelists, and historians challenged the prevailing racial imagery of Black people as the brute or the clown. In keeping with Charles Mills's (1998) notion of revisionist ontology, the project of African American thinkers was threefold.

The first aspect of the project was to identify theories and/or ideas that presume universal truths about Black life. Theories such as racial science presumed that Black capacities were preordained by the so-called genetic make-up of Black people. Throughout the early 20th century, scholars drew from history, archeology, scientific research, and the social sciences to challenge the popular and prevailing discourse of racial science. As a whole, this work rejected the idea that people of African descent contributed nothing of value to human civilization. Thus, the work of historians was to reject these ideas through archival evidence that placed Black people within the cradle of human civilization. African American and even White scholars produced historical studies, textbooks, journal articles, and encyclopedias with the sole intent of challenging the prevailing anti-Black ideologies of science and history.

The second approach among Black scholars was to provide a space that reflected the real-life experience of Black life. The Harlem Renaissance provided one of the most comprehensive cultural movements to express Black Americans' ability to overcome and their struggle to maintain dignity and pride within a White supremacist world. This revisionist approach used novels, poetry, plays, speeches, and philosophy to allow Black people to tell their stories under their own terms. This approach was present within textbooks and other curricular spaces where the intent was to allow African Americans to tell their stories in a way that spoke truth to the contexts of Black life beyond the dominant discourses of this time.

The third approach was to develop a new method to move beyond the stereotypical images of that time. In some cases, scholars provided a new approach to documenting Black life. The work of African American social scientists such as E. Franklin Frazier and Charles Johnson each showed how the method of ethnography and qualitative research located the ecological contexts of Black life as central to the kind of cultural analysis one might conduct. Rather than theorizing in abstract ideas about Black habits and culture or through statistical methods that choose not to account for the impact of Jim Crow Southern societies on Black life, this method accounted for the voices of Black people as central to the process of documenting the social environs and historical contexts that informed Black social mobility.

Consistent across these approaches was the insistence that Black people's lives were enveloped by historical, cultural, social, and political contexts. These approaches were certainly reflected in the counterdiscourse of education as well. In the section that follows, we will show how textbooks and encyclopedias, children's literature, and African American journals served as counterhegemonic spaces where African Americans not only challenged the existing discourses but also articulated their own standpoint for curriculum making.

JOURNAL OF NEGRO EDUCATION AS COUNTERCURRICULAR SPACE

In the early 20th century, very few venues existed for African American scholars to discuss, critique, and reconceptualize the curricular discourse about African Americans. This can be explained in at least a couple of ways. First, the context of the Jim Crow South and Northern racial exclusion created the context of segregation found in every facet of society—including in academia. In a nutshell, White scholars held appointments at predominately White institutions and published articles in venues that were exclusively White, whereas Black scholars mostly attended historically Black universities and colleges and published in a small circle of journals and periodicals. Second, the reason there were few places for African Americans to engage education questions relates more to the manner in which education questions were framed historically. Interestingly, while the so-called Negro Problem was part of the existing dominant racial discourse of the time, very few curriculum discussions engaged the topic of Black education in a broad sense.

THE CRITICAL APPRAISALS OF THE *JOURNAL OF NEGRO EDUCATION*

Despite the pattern of exclusion that characterized early curricular discourse, African Americans wrote on and discussed the concerns of curriculum. Nowhere was this more visible than in the *Journal of Negro Education* (*JNE*).

The first issue and volume was published in 1932 out of Howard University. The editorial comment of this first issue here describes the purpose of *JNE*:

> The purpose of the Journal of Negro Education is three-fold: *first,* to stimulate the collection and facilitate the dissemination, of facts about the Negro; second, to present discussion involving critical appraisals of the proposals and practices relating to the education of Negroes; and, third, to stimulate and sponsor investigations of problems incident to the education of Negroes. (Editorial Comment, 1932, p. 1)

The first two decades of the journal clearly highlighted a consistent emphasis on the last two points concerning "critical appraisals" and the call for new research relating to Black education. In some cases, sections of the journal served as a straightforward report on the "state of Black education," where a whole host of ideas, theories, critiques, and philosophies emerged concerning the purpose of education for African Americans. In this same inaugural essay, the author made clear that the *Journal of Negro Education* was tending to a void in the existing curricular discourse of this time about Black education. The Editorial Comment (1932) stated,

> If one is familiar with the meetings of various organizations whose discussions are devoted, wholly or partially, to the education of the Negro, he does not need to be convinced that very little critical appraisal has been present in their "deliberations." Most of the discussions have consisted of inspirational talks rather [than] critical appraisals of the assumptions underlying certain basic procedures and proposals. (p. 2)

The author further stated,

> A combination of circumstances, too well known to recount here, makes this field unique. Unfortunately, we have separately organized school systems in more than forty per cent of the states, and a majority of the Negro school population comes from a minority, underprivileged in practically every manner in which this term can be constructed. As a result there are involved, not only all of the problems common to every school system, but as well those peculiar and indigenous to the social environment in which Negroes find themselves in this country. (p. 2)

The overarching emphasis of *JNE* was to address the intellectual and practical needs of Black education, which, the author notes, were "not adequately met by any other agency at the present time" (Editorial Comment, 1932, p. 2). In this sense, *JNE* exemplified what we are calling an alternative curricular space, where ideas, discourse, philosophy, and policies were discussed concerning American curriculum—albeit Negro America.

Looking across the journal over the first 10 years, three kinds of "critical appraisals" of curriculum and pedagogy emerged. The first was the critical appraisal of prevailing ideas about the capacities of Black folk. The second kind of critical appraisal was to discuss the state of Black education and provide redirection. The third critical appraisal was to rethink the way in which ideas and concepts such as race and culture were employed within educational discourse. In the section that follows, we outline the manner in which these critical appraisals were present within the curricular discourse of *JNE*.

Critical Appraisal 1

During the early part of the 20th century, racial science was pervasive within the educational discourse of the progressive era (Baker, 2001; Fallace, 2015). Curriculum historian Thomas Fallace (2015) argues that "child-centered education emerged directly from the theory of recapitulation, the idea that the development of the White child retraced the history of the human race" (p. 73). Even within the development of Black educational institutions, Watkins (2001) notes that racial theories prevailed with the intent of producing an educational system specifically tailored for the so-called capacities of the Negro.

Leading the pack in terms of proffering racist ideologies about Black education was the field of race psychology. Therefore, it made sense that in 1934 the *Journal of Negro Education* would publish a special issue titled "The Physical and Mental Capacities of the American Negro." In this issue scholars provided conceptual, historical, and meta-analyses about the merits of racial psychology and its implications for Black education. Thomas R. Garth (1934) argued,

> The whole problem turns on this question of mobility of races. The problem of race psychology, then, is to prove true or false the belief that races are immutable. We may call this the racial difference hypothesis, meaning by racial differences, racial differences in mental traits. (p. 320)

In this issue scholars first critiqued whether the problem was adequately defined, pointing to the fact that the data instruments were not used properly and that interpretations of the racial data collected during the early 20th century were grossly misinterpreted. A common argument raised throughout the special issue was that scientists seemed to overlook the rules of science when drawing conclusions about the immutability of race. Scholars noted that when educational psychologists discussed the so-called capacities of Black Americans, they tended to draw conclusions about African American achievement based on findings that were not empirically valid. However, at the core of this issue was a critical appraisal of the racial thesis that Blacks' capacities were defined by their immutable biological composition.

Doxey Wilkerson (1934) forcefully made the point here when he stated that "No test or battery of tests has yet been devised which is capable of segregating racial groups on the basis of either mental ability or scholastic achievement" (p. 454). In his exhaustive analysis, Montague Cobb (1934) also cogently found interpretations about the physical constitution of the Negro and the methods used to derive them to be flawed and significantly inaccurate. Cobb (1934) found that "neither eugenic nor dysgenic effects from the Negro-white crossings have been demonstrated" (p. 532). Implicit across each of the essays was the argument that race is a social construct and our attention as researchers should be focused on ecological and sociological effects on the development and achievement of Blacks. Robert Daniel (1934) made this point quite clearly when he stated,

> There is very little point in studies of racial comparison in order to ascertain the possession or nonpossession of traits without realizing the background of habits and differences in racial circumstance socially imposed which may make personality traits complex in characterization, varied in manifestation according to the situation, and different from that of another racial group.
>
> There is a tremendous difference between the term "racial difference" and the term "differences between races." Tests may reveal a difference in responses of Negroes and whites, but the finding of this statistical difference cannot immediately be considered as an innate difference due to race. It may just as well be due to difference imposed by social forces as a consequence of racial identity. (p. 423)

Through critical review of the major research in racial psychology and racial difference studies, the scholars of this issue challenged every dimension of the racial difference thesis of this period. The racial logic of this time had gone through a shift, and *JNE* played an important role in challenging the discourse of race that prevailed during this time.

Critical Appraisal 2

JNE also provided a venue to discuss the needs of Black education. The journal focused on curriculum, pedagogy, teacher education, and policy. An important and enduring ideological tension common to many of the discussions about the redirection of Black education focused on whether education for Black children should be segregated or integrated into White society. However, given the context of the Jim Crow South and racial exclusion in the North, the topic of inclusion was the central issue of Black education in the 1930s. Implicit in much of the discussions about education was a profound belief that racial integration was key to the future of African Americans. Also consistent across each issue during this period were reports and overviews about the state of Black education, including issues of cost and redevelopment for many of the Black teacher colleges and universities.

As it pertains to curriculum, Walter G. Daniel in 1932 provided some of the most innovative analyses about curriculum for the Negro child. Daniel early on in the essay pointed out that the need to have a discussion about Negro curriculum resulted from the the lack of attention to Negro pupils' curricular needs in the mainstream discussions. He stated,

> The Department of Superintendence of the National Education Association, the National Society for the Study of Education, and others have set forth the American point of view as to the objectives and content of the curriculum of the school. Ideally we would expect that these statements would be applied in making curricula for all of the children who attend the public school; but actually this ideal situation does not exist. (Daniel, 1932, p. 277)

Thus this venue of *JNE* in 1932 was the ideal counterpublic space to engage in discussions about school curriculum for the American Negro. Daniel goes on to note that much has been said about what is lacking for the curriculum provisions for African Americans, but few discussions tended to the issues of what succession of experiences the Negro child should have in order to meet some set of desired goals. Daniel's sense of critical pragmatism argued simply that if the desired outcome of curriculum is to produce educated individuals who help to make the desired adjustments to meet their current social circumstance, then the school curriculum must reflect these goals. This was "culturally responsive" before the educational discourse started to use those terms. Daniel (1932) stated:

> In accordance with needs dictated by the locality, and in harmony with the psychological needs of the individual, the adaption of the selection, approach to, and organization of the experiences is essential. That is to say for the lifelikeness of the Negro child, the home, race agriculture and industrial activities, and indications of the need for supplementation and enrichment of curricular experiences. The basis of adaption hence is in individual and local needs, rather than undetermined, and non-existent, racial needs. (p. 295)

For Daniel, curriculum for the Black child was contextual and local, thus critiquing the notion that there was a single curriculum. His anthropological approach certainly was consistent with that of the counterhegemonic discourse of theorizing Black education as a whole. Through the 1930s, other Black educators and scholars such as Charles Johnson and Ambrose Caliver called for changes to Black education, focusing specifically on curriculum development and knowledge acquisition. For example, in 1936, Johnson addressed the need for "realism" in Black education, arguing that the current education process had failed at reflecting African Americans' social life. Johnson recommended a *realist* approach that would provide African American students with (1) a curriculum reflective of the reality of their lives; (2) basic tools and techniques for the modern technological age; (3) a sound interpretation of their own history and traditions; and (4) a sound character education.

Johnson (1936) asserted that the education process should be tied to the realities of social life. He believed that formal education was only a part of the education process and that school and teaching should be in mutual coordination with the home, the church, the press, and the public generally. For example, Johnson (1936) stated, "Insofar as this process is a conscious and artificial one it can be selective, and it becomes important in the education of a maladjusted group that its procedures should be adjusted to its cultural needs. Only in such a manner can any material social development be expected" (p. 376). In addition, drawing from John Dewey, Johnson (1936) pointed to the error of only considering education as "preparation for life." In short, Johnson (1936) called for a redirection of Black education that considered the experiences of the student, which could also provide intellectual guidance "related to the larger world of knowledge" (p. 378).

Johnson (1936) argued that one of the problems facing African Americans was mastering the techniques imposed by technological changes. He recommended that African Americans become equipped with practical and psychological tools in order to adjust to a "new age" premised on competition and rapid technological advances. He cautioned against providing a training that was outdated merely because it served as a simple skill for the Black child to acquire. In addition, he rejected programs that sought to impart a technical skill for the intensely specialized and rapid advances of modern industry. Johnson (1936) suggested an alternative knowledge acquisition for the adjustment to rapidly changing technical knowledge:

> What seems to be required now is the development in Negro youth of a technique of manipulation, with the thoroughness attempted by the liberal arts colleges in developing an undifferentiated *cultural competence*. And, as is the presumption of the liberal arts colleges, this technique may be transferred and applied to the specific task demanding it. (p. 379, emphasis added)

For Johnson (1936), this type of "undifferentiated" knowledge acquisition would enable African Americans to adjust to advanced technological changes.

The reinterpretation of Black history was the third aspect to Johnson's (1936) redirection of Black education. He insisted that this reinterpretation impart knowledge about Black history and contributions in order to imbue and stimulate social development, self-confidence, and self-respect to the African American student. In addition, that history should neither impart distorted knowledge about a glorious past nor focus on aspects of history that promote "self-disparagement." He pointed out that past historical texts had only focused narrowly on the image of the docile African slave without giving recognition to African Americans' progress and contributions. Johnson claimed that attention given to this history would encourage and stimulate the Black child to develop self-consciousness that compensated for their inferior social status.

The fourth and final aspect of redirecting Black education was to impart *character education* to the African American child. Johnson (1936) defined *character education* as "habits of self-discipline" that would stimulate the Black child to develop beyond the limited historical and social aspects of Black life. He suggested that the African American child develop a sense of self that would encourage progress beyond the relative definitions of "success." According to Johnson, this mold of character education would incite the Black child to understand that different educational outcomes were not a result of "innate" biological racial differences but were an outcome of hard work and effort to exceed mediocrity or limited conceptions of aptitude. This kind of comprehensive discourse was a hallmark of *JNE* essays. Education scholar Ambrose Caliver's published speech in 1933 also reflected a deep philosophical concern for pedagogy and curriculum.

Caliver placed great value on the importance of the African American teacher to infuse the curriculum with culturally and historically relevant education practices. During an address delivered at the convention of the National Association of Teachers in Colored Schools, Caliver (1933) suggested the need for a philosophy of Black education and Black teachers. In his address to African American teachers, he first discussed the historical context of the developing modern society and how this related to the future of African American education. For example, although he found the achievements of modern science and technology necessary to a developing nation, he felt that such "dominant motives" had undermined the pursuits of moral and social purpose. Caliver (1933) stated,

> In spite of the marvelous progress which has been made in science and technology; in the general growth of the intellectual powers; and in the increase in material wealth, our civilization, when measured in balance of moral values, is found wanting. . . .
>
> Theoretically, our moral and social life has improved greatly, yet social maladjustments abound and we are morally corrupt. Our intellectual and religious advancement have increased beyond the most sanguine hopes, still we are unable to think straightly and clearly, and, we are without spiritual moorings. (p. 434)

Caliver (1933) suggested that Black teachers redirect their education practices to combat this social and moral dilemma. He felt that Black teachers must rethink the question: *What and how shall we teach?* First, he suggested that teachers reconsider the use of science to solve education problems. He asserted that, although science could provide solutions to education problems, its use must be put in proper context. For Caliver, science could only serve as an objective practice if the teacher understood the cultural and social forces that inform the practice. Second, Caliver argued that learning and life must be coordinated. He felt that teachers must understand the social issues of the day in order to "coordinate learning to life." Caliver further pointed out that the Black teacher must take the responsibility to understand the culture and social context of the child. He stated, "Reduced to its simplest terms this means that subjects of instruction should not be taught in isolation from life and without reference to the ultimate goals of the pupils, but they should be taught with definite reference to their social relation and use" (Caliver, 1933, p. 441). Third, Caliver (1933) argued that the education process must be infused with a moral and social purpose.

For Caliver (1933), the teacher should represent the highest moral, social, and intellectual ground, serving as a skillful guide to moral integrity. He argued that in order to accomplish such a goal, African American teachers must teach the Black child about the accomplished past of the African American race. He stated that "teaching the Negroes something about the history and accomplishments of their race in order to engender the spirit of personal and race pride becomes a matter of great importance" (Caliver, 1933, p. 444). In closing, he cautioned Black teachers to not fall victim to selfish individualism and materialism. He called for Black teachers to instead see the mission of teaching as tied to the greater "fortunes of the Negro race." Caliver (1933) made this point:

> One individual here a small group somewhere else. Their intercommunication finally results in a community of ideas and beliefs, which, likewise, eventually unites with another similar group, until the spreading of ideas, attitudes, beliefs, and patterns become the dominating culture pattern of the race. (p. 446)

Through the 1930s, other Black educators and scholars addressed the need for developing a philosophy for Black education and teaching. In 1935 in a special edition of *JNE* titled "The Courts and the Negro Separate School," Du Bois (1935b) posed the following question: "Does the Negro need separate schools?" He asserted that in situations in the North where African Americans were placed in mostly White schools, the African American child was often ridiculed, neglected, and undereducated. Du Bois (1935b) illustrated this context:

I have repeatedly seen wise and loving colored parents take infinite pains to force their little children into schools where the white children, white teachers, and white parents despised and resented the dark child, made mock of it, neglected or bullied it, and literally rendered its life a living hell. Such parents want their child to "fight" this thing out—but, dear God, at what cost! Sometimes to be sure, the child triumphs and teaches the school community a lesson; but even in such cases, the cost may be high, and the child's whole life turned into an effort to win cheap applause at the expense of healthy individuality. In other cases, the result of the experiment may be complete ruin of character, gift, and ability and ingrained hatred of school and men. (p. 331)

For this reason, Du Bois (1935b) argued that African American children would require a separate school where they would be happy and inspired. He argued that, in the United States, where the African American was still subject to White racism and social inequality, a separate school would guard against such treatment. Du Bois (1935b) further qualified that the need for separate schools was not to suggest that the African Americans must receive an education "suited" for their intellectual and mental capacity, but must serve to develop young minds in school settings that welcome their race, history, and experiences. Such a classroom setting should (a) foster a sympathetic touch between teacher and pupil based on perfect social equality and (b) infuse in the curriculum the knowledge, history, and background of class and group. While Du Bois saw the Black teacher as best suited to foster such a learning environment, he saw this effort as the part of the collective responsibility of the African American community.

Critical Appraisal 3: Racial Understanding

In 1944, *JNE* published a special issue relating specifically to the topic of racial understanding. The goal of the special publication was to outline the core issues relating to racial understanding—which can be broken down into at least three categories of analysis. The first was to examine the barriers to racial understanding in the United States and the role education can play in addressing the challenges of race relations. The second approach was to seek solutions to the issue of racism through a variety of educational and school spaces, such as K–12 schooling, federal intervention programs, and community nonprofit efforts. Unlike the special issues discussed earlier where the authors were seeking to trouble the existing intellectual paradigm of race research, here they explored the topic of race as a problem of society, thus requiring a comprehensive discussion of how the problem is defined and what can be done to redress the pervasive issues of racism in society. Similar to the authors' diverse perspectives on the redirection of Black education in *JNE*, a wide variety of topics, theories, and concerns were raised.

In the section that follows, we discuss some of the approaches authors addressed in this issue.

A few scholars noted that issues of race understanding had to be addressed outside of the schooling context. One scholar in particular, Lawrence Reddick (1944), made clear that race understanding not only occurs in the context of schools but is also defined and sustained over time within popular culture. Similar to the work of cultural studies scholarship (Hall, 1997), Reddick showed that anti-Negro discourse occurs in the context of media and culture. Reddick stated,

> If the main task of the educative process is the transmission of the culture of the society, then the great educational agencies of the United States are not its schools and colleges; rather, its movie houses, newspapers and magazines, its radio broadcasting stations and public libraries. Beside them, the formal institutions of learning pale into comparative insignificance. While there are but 30,000,000 persons enrolled in all schools and colleges in the United States, 90,000,000 children and adults attend the movies each week; 30,000,000 homes share with other places the 57,000,000 radio receiving sets, 44,000,000 copies of newspapers are read daily and more than 425,000,000 books are circulated each year to 96,000,000 readers by the public libraries. In a word, what the citizens of this nation think about any broad question is determined, largely, by what these citizens read about it in their newspapers and libraries, hear about it over the radio, or see and hear about it at the movie. (p. 367)

So for Reddick, the attention to race must focus on the popular discourses that helped to shape the public imagination of Black people. Roy Wilkins's (1944) essay supported Reddick's claims, arguing that mediums such as radio and film serve a significant function in reproducing stereotypes about African Americans. Again similar to Reddick, Wilkins maintained that the process of learning about race must occur within multiple spaces. He stated, "While the program for the use of the schools will be effective, to a degree, with children and young people, thus teaching future parents, it is important that every method be employed to change the attitudes of parents, and to build a community pattern which will make for racial understanding" (Wilkins, 1944, p. 438). In a sense, Wilkins called for a pedagogical approach to race understanding that focused on newspapers, magazines, and film as playing a primary role in race understanding in society. This approach to the topic of racial understanding was akin to the critical theorists from the Frankfurt school and the cultural studies scholars of the 1990s that focused on the production of hegemony in the context of media.

However, in this special issue numerous scholars also called for an approach to the school curriculum that focused on the function of curriculum to foster cross-cultural understanding and to support the identities of African American children. Echoing a common critique of this period, several authors (Johnson, 1944; Wilkins, 1944) in this issue addressed the insidious power of textbooks and school knowledge to produce negative stereotypes of Black people. Scholars argued that the acquisition of racial understanding came through the pervasiveness of racist school knowledge. However, authors in this issue saw the schools as key spaces to shift Black and White people's understandings of race. Then there were essays from scholars such as Hortense Powdermaker (1944) and Alain Locke (1944) that highlighted the problematic theoretical assignment of race, forcefully arguing that race is a social construct. Locke's words here powerfully summarized the intent and purpose of this issue:

> Beyond that the authorities, like the doctors, disagree considerably both in diagnosis and prognosis of solution; with an increasing number of intellectuals, however, on the side of the optimists and mentally prepared, at least, to meet the issue head-on and not so much for the sake of the Negro as for the sake of democracy itself. And among them, with horizons widened beyond selfish or narrow racialism, are many intelligent, sober but militant and morally aroused Negroes, who see no sanity or safety in half-way solutions. (p. 406)

It was clear that the intent and purpose of this issue of *JNE* was to reconceptualize the discourse on race, while also taking into consideration new pedagogies to redress the problematic ways African Americans were understood in society. The analysis of the race problem in this issue was reconceptualized on two planes of analysis. The first plane related to understanding how the dissemination of ideas in schools and society helped to reproduce race narratives that circulated a problematic imagery. The second plane was at the level of the individual and the child in particular. In this context, scholars noted the powerful ways that school curriculum can negate and undermine the personhood of Black children. However, the school curriculum in this context was also a place to reexamine the histories of African Americans and challenge old stereotypes about Black life. The third plane of examination was at the level of race relations between Whites and African Americans.

JNE in Summary

There certainly is much more that we could address in the contents of *JNE*, but it is clear that *JNE* was central to the early African American curricular discourse. It is in this journal that you find some of the earliest conversations about cultural difference and critiques against culturally or racially deficit educational theories. It is within this curricular space that critical appraisal of the pervasive theories about Black people and Black education occurred. *JNE* also presented critical appraisal of the state of Black education by highlighting the quality and purpose of education in helping to transform the dire inequities of Black life in schools and society. Overall, we define *JNE* as a transformative curricular space to establish what Watkins (1993) called *black curriculum orientations*.

AGAINST ANTI-BLACK CURRICULUM:
TEXTBOOKS, ENCYCLOPEDIAS, AND CHILDREN'S LITERATURE

As discussed earlier in this chapter, K–12 curriculum in the United States circulated some of the most racially offensive ideologies about Black people and Black life—what we are calling anti-Black curricular discourse. There were two prominent ways in which curriculum helped to promulgate the White supremacist, anti-Black racial imagery. The first was through the absence of stories, histories, and contexts that engaged the full spectrum of African Americans' historical experiences. The second was by adding inaccurate histories, myths, and theories that helped to perpetuate some of the most graphic stereotypical images about Black people. However, similar to *JNE,* several authors wrote textbooks, encyclopedias, and children's literature that challenged the existing anti-Black curricular discourse. In the section that follows, we lay out how varied scholars used textbooks, encyclopedias, and children's literature to provide a counterhegemonic curricular discourse.

Textbooks and Encyclopedias

Historian John Ernest (2004) refers to the historical materials produced by African Americans produced in the 19th century as *liberation historiography*. During this time, African Americans produced texts that addressed the contributions of African Americans in military service as well as the great accomplishments of Black people from all walks of life. Some of the earliest textbooks and compendiums were written at a time when the existing theories of race were based on fixed notions about the biological and sociological limitations of African Americans (Brown, 2010). These textbooks and encyclopedias consistently selected biographies and histories that challenged the presumptions of racial capacity and U.S. loyalty. Nowhere was this more present than in the textbooks produced by the prolific historian Carter G. Woodson (Grant, Brown, & Brown, 2015). Woodson understood that there was a preponderance of ideas and histories that were ideological and propagandistic.

Overall, there were two goals of textbooks and compendiums produced from the late 19th century through the early 1930s. The first was to provide histories and biographies that challenged the existing theories of race and culture during this time period. For example, texts such as *Negro Builders and Heroes* by Benjamin Brawley (1937), *The American Negro: His History and Literature* by George W. Williams (1968/1883), and *Black Phalanx: African American Soldiers in the War of Independence, the War of 1812 and the Civil War* by Joseph Wilson (1994/1887) all provide biographies of accomplished African Americans in the context of a racialized world. The following section of text illustrates this point:

> In the early years of the nineteenth century the Negro most frequently referred to as proof of the intellectual capacity of his people was Benjamin Banneker, of Maryland. To understand the career of this man it is necessary to go back two hundred years, to a time when Baltimore was still a village of thirty houses and white servitude system of labor in the colonies. The Negro had yet to prove his ability in mental pursuits. (Brawley, 1937, p. 25)

The second goal of textbooks and compendium texts was to locate African Americans' histories and experiences within the historical trajectory of the American nation. The point was that America could not have become a great or exceptional nation without the labor, service, and contributions of African Americans. This was most reflected in the text and curricular materials that highlighted the military service of African Americans. Here are two examples of this approach to curricular texts.

> SOLDIERS: As a mark of esteem and respect for your patriotic devotion to the cause of human freedom, I desire to dedicate to you this record of the services of the negro soldiers, whom you led so often and successfully in the struggle for liberty and union during the great war of 1861-'65.

> Your coming from the highest ranks of social life, undeterred by the prevailing spirit of caste prejudice, to take commands in the largest negro army ever enrolled beneath the flag of any civilized country, was in itself a brave act. The organization and disciplining of over two hundred thousand men, of a race that for more than two centuries had patiently borne the burdens of an unrequited bondage, for the maintenance of laws which had guaranteed to them neither rights nor protection, was indeed a magnificent undertaking. (Wilson, 1994/1887, dedication page)

> When the war-clouds gathered in 1812, there was no time wasted in discussing whether it would be prudent to arm the Negro, nor was there a doubt expressed as to his valor. His brilliant achievements in the war of Revolution, his power of endurance, and martial enthusiasm, were the golden threads of glory that bound his memory to the victorious cause of the American Republic. (Williams, p. 23, 1968 [1883])

The quotes above are illustrative of the some of the early efforts to address the kinds of silences found in school curriculum and history as a whole. This approach is sometimes referred to as *vindicationist*, in that it sought to vindicate African Americans from the kinds of negative images that were pervasive during this time.

Children's Literature: The Case of *The Brownies' Book*

These similar tenets of revision are also reflected in the children's literature produced by African Americans. While there were several instances in which African Americans produced children's literature that challenged the dominant ideologies (see Harris, 1990), our focus in this chapter will be given to *The Brownies' Book*, a magazine for children that was created by Jessie Fauset and W. E. B. Du Bois.

Children's literature scholar Violet Harris (1990) has powerfully argued that

> the inclusion or exclusion of an author or a group of authors from children's literature canons results from a variety of factors and symbolizes one aspect of the "politics" of children's books. These factors include tradition, the literary knowledge of those who contribute to the canonizing process, the availability of literary works, awareness of works, and socio-cultural forces such as elitism and bias. (p. 108)

In essence, similar to curriculum theorists who have analyzed the ideological aspects of school curriculum, Harris is suggesting that children's literature has a curriculum of its own that has also been concerned with issues of power and hegemony. However, scholars have argued that, despite the kinds of symbolic violence that occurred in children's literature, Black scholars developed children's literature that presented positive and accurate imagery of Black life. Again, similar to the concerns regarding school curriculum, scholars and activists during the early 20th century understood that affecting change in the context of children's interaction with literature was essential to rectifying the image and perception of Black people. Jessie Fauset and W. E. B. Du Bois's children's magazine *The Brownies' Book* provides one of the strongest illustrations of creating a space for African Americans to challenge the anti-Black ideologies.

In the October 1919 issue of *The Crisis*, W. E. B. Du Bois's essay "The True Brownies" announced the creation of *The Brownies' Book*. In setting the context for producing a curricular space to challenge the pervasive ideologies of racial hatred, Du Bois proposed a seven-step plan:

1. To make colored children realize that being "colored" is a normal, beautiful thing.
2. To make them familiar with the history and achievements of the Negro race.

3. To make them know that other colored children have grown into beautiful, useful and famous persons.

4. To teach them a delicate code of honor and action in their relations with white people.

5. To turn their little hurts and resentments into emulation, ambition and love of their homes and companions.

6. To point out the best amusements and joys and worthwhile things of life.

7. To inspire them to prepare for definite occupations and duties with a broad spirit of sacrifice. (Cited in Harris, 1989, p. 192)

As indicated by this seven-point plan, Du Bois understood the context of children's literature as an intervening counterhegemonic, curricular discourse. Harris (1989) maintained that *The Brownies' Book* was imbued with what she called a "New Negro" philosophy—a renewed ideology to reject anti-Blackness. The more specific task of the stories found in *The Brownies' Book* was to provide stories that were not in the stereotypical vein. From this "New Negro" philosophy Harris maintains that the following eight themes emerged from these texts: "race pride, duty and allegiance to the race, intelligent Blacks, beautiful Blacks, moderation, political and social activism, knowledge of and respect for African culture, and the inculcation of specific values such as kindness, truthfulness, egalitarianism, and love" (p. 193).

This theme would remain part of the discourse of Black children's literature all through the 20th century. However, for Du Bois and children's literature writers of this time, this was not simply about exposing Black children to positive images; it was about challenging the racist discourse on Black children of this time. If the children's literature and folk songs of Black debasement were the dominant hegemonic texts of this time, *The Brownies' Book* stood in direct contrast to the preponderance of these stories.

Black Curriculum Revision in Summary

The history of African American curriculum is intricately tied to the process of revising the wider image-making context surrounding depictions of African Americans occurring outside of schools. It was clear that scholars understood the powerful connection between official texts and the way young people made sense of their histories and identities. As Brown and Brown (2015) argue, children's literature and school curriculum possess the capacity to support and sustain existing racial narratives about the debasement of Black life. However, they further argued that what made the context of K–12 curriculum dangerous was the continuity of the racial narrative over time. Scholars understood that from kindergarten through high school the repetitiveness of anti-Black racial narratives normalized the cultural and racial meanings ascribed to Black people, which would have a destructive impact on the public image of African Americans as well as on how African

Americans see themselves. Therefore, the racial politics of the school curriculum was viewed as a central space to combat the bevy of images that depicted Black people as a brutish, simple-minded, historyless people. What is clear is that K–12 curriculum and children's literature were vital spaces to reimagine Black people's history and experiences. While novels, plays, and editorials were key spaces to challenge the existing racial norms, the school curriculum was a vital space to advance the transformative racial project of the early 20th century.

CONCLUDING THOUGHTS ON
AFRICAN AMERICAN CURRICULAR HISTORY

The absence of African Americans within the narrative of the founding of the U.S. curriculum is startling. Given the persistent and ongoing critique and revision of school curriculum throughout most of the 20th century, it is hard to imagine how curriculum scholars missed this rich history. The publication of encyclopedias and compendium texts about the experiences of Black people in the United States continued from the late 19th century all the way through the late 20th century. From the publication of George Washington Williams's *The American Negro* in 1883 to the publication of Anthony Appiah and Henry Louis Gates's *Encarta Africana* in 1999, the concerns of African American history in schools and in the popular imagination have remained an enduring concern of Black freedom and Black curricular discourse. The early history highlights the urgency around the importance of understanding the effects of school curriculum in extending a lasting racial narrative (Brown, 2010).

This chapter, however, only scratches the surface of the extent to which African American scholars and activists presented the most forceful critiques within the American curriculum. Much of the literature on U.S. curriculum focuses on the differing White ideologies and interests, and the voices of Black scholars have been summarily left out of these histories. The history of African American curriculum at times is informed by the same discourses of progressive era educational thought, but in large part the scholarship of this time period provided detailed critiques about the problematic anti-Black constructions and silences in school curriculum. The Black curricular discourse of this time was not just about images in the curriculum but about presenting questions and treatises about the meaning and purpose of schooling for Black people and society as a whole.

What the curriculum history of African Americans powerfully provides is a detailed analysis of the problems with the "American" curriculum. While early-20th-century academics such as Charles Eliot, John Dewey, G. Stanley Hall, and William Torrey Harris quibbled over the meaning and purpose of schooling, African American scholars (along with the Native,

Asian American, and Mexican American scholars and community members described in this book) were able to shed light on a problem endemic to the American curriculum—the dilemma of race. In the context of "objective" social science, the so-called elephant in the room of American curriculum at that time was the inability to acknowledge the kinds of subjective reasoning and racial fallacies of the American curriculum. Similar to the insightful critiques of school curriculum formulated within Native American, Asian American, and Mexican American communities, the Black curriculum scholarship of W. E. B. Du Bois, Lawrence Reddick, and Carter G. Woodson offers a rich analysis of what the American curriculum was really about—sustaining the White racial ideologies of that time.

So much more can be explored on this topic. The foundational histories of this chapter are only intended to extend our conceptions of curriculum history by locating the spaces in which curriculum was conceptualized. For African American curriculum history, this has meant the deliberation of ideas and content present in the schools. The process of critical deliberation often took place outside of the traditional spaces where U.S. curriculum history is documented, such as meetings of the NAACP and the Association of Negro Life and History, and cultural movements such as the Harlem Renaissance and Chicago Realism. These spaces helped to engage a new discourse about what it meant to be Black in America. These counterpublic spaces (Fraser, 1990) also created the condition for new knowledge to be produced and canonized over time. For example, the Black bookstore for decades served as a space to imagine new ways of thinking about the histories of African Americans and the entire African Diaspora. From these cultivated spaces emerged purveyors of new knowledge via books, speeches, pamphlets, and meetings that helped to call into question the surrounding discourses about the nature of Black life.

CHAPTER 6

Conclusion

The work for this book really began in 2010, when we (Anthony and Wayne), who had been classmates at the University of Wisconsin–Madison, sat down to catch up on life and talk about educational politics. At the time we both realized that we had been teaching curriculum studies classes and that the major curriculum studies textbooks available to us were dominated by academic Whiteness. It was through that conversation that we began to openly wonder, "Might it be that the foundational story of curriculum studies in the United States is told this way in all of the field's major textbooks?" And we wondered this because we both know our communities' histories fairly well, so we knew that communities of color had long been engaged in discussions about curriculum for their children *at exactly the same period of time* that the typically identified "founders" of curriculum studies were holding their committee meetings, doing their research, and producing their reports. Eventually after a review of dozens of curriculum studies texts, we mostly had our wondering confirmed: A historical canon had developed in curriculum studies, and this canon really did consist mainly of White men in the academy, with the occasional woman (e.g., Jane Adams) and the even-more-occasional mention of an African American figure (e.g., Carter G. Woodson) thrown in for good measure (Brown & Au, 2014). Asian Americans didn't exist at all in this narrative, and save for a single, more recent chapter, the story of Native American curricular discourse was invisible as well. Hence our peculiar sensations (Du Bois, 1904/1994) as scholars of color within the field of curriculum studies were affirmed.

Upon finishing the article for *Curriculum Inquiry*, we knew that a book needed to be written because, frankly speaking, our paper (Brown & Au, 2014) fell short by necessity: There was so much curriculum history and discourse taking place in communities of color during the field's founding that we simply did not have the space but to barely scratch the surface. That is why we started writing *Reclaiming the Multicultural Roots of the U.S. Curriculum*. As we alluded to in the introduction, this project took a tremendous amount of research and historical digging, and after over a year of working on the text, we realized that we needed help—with the sheer amount of research and writing at hand, but also with the content expertise needed to develop histories of Native American and Mexican American curricular discourses. At that point we approached Dolores because of her expertise in curriculum studies and her work on both Indigenous and Latino epistemologies. Even with the addition of Dolores, it took us as a group of coauthors well over a year to pull the full text together.

Even though this book is historical in focus, its very existence is a testament to the fact that the issues of racism, White supremacy, and exclusion still operate within and through our contemporary institutions. Indeed, our own struggles to piece together a curricular history that is our own and that pushes back against historic racism in our field serves as a metacommentary in and of itself. These multicultural roots of the U.S. curriculum shouldn't have to be "reclaimed," and despite the work we have done here, we are aware that there is so much more "reclaiming" of curricular discourse that we were unable to fit into this single volume. There is so much more to be told, more regions and communities to include. For instance, we know Hawaii, with its own curriculum history specific to both Native Hawaiians and Asian immigrant communities, is missing here. We also know that there is more to be told about Asian American curricular discourse and history generally. The story of Mexican Americans outside of Texas and New Mexico is missing here. The colonial curriculum projects of what became U.S. territories in the Pacific (e.g., the Philippines) and the Caribbean (e.g., Puerto Rico) at the end of Spanish-American War are missing here and could be the focus of their own volumes.

That said, we feel the stories that we have included in *Reclaiming the Multicultural Roots of the U.S. Curriculum* are important and help offer a corrective to how we understand the historical foundations of not just the field of curriculum studies but education more generally. Our four central chapters attempt to do just what our book title suggests. We want to "reclaim" a curriculum history that was not only forgotten or neglected but systematically denied existence because of the lens of Whiteness pervading our field. In doing so we took up the historical curricular discourses of Native Americans, Chinese and Japanese Americans on the West Coast of the United States, African Americans, and Mexican Americans in the Southwestern United States. In the case of Native American curricular discourse (Chapter 2), we found a story of curriculum as a White supremacist manifestation of settler colonialism, which positioned anything Native/Indigenous as savage, barbaric, and uncivilized (and, of course, those things White and Christian as the civilized ideal). This created a context for Native American curricular discourse where the struggle was over curriculum sovereignty for Natives in the face of a curriculum of genocide being enacted by colonizing Whites and U.S. federal education policy. Thus, Native communities engaged in long, often contested conversations about what kind of education was best for their peoples—particularly given the ravages of settler colonialism on their land and culture. In ways big and small, Native communities also resisted the inculcations of the curriculum genocide being imposed upon them by

White Christians, finding ways to escape, build community, and generally continue cultural maintenance in the spaces they could carve out.

The Chinese American and Japanese American curricular discourse in and around the turn of the 20th century in the United States was characterized by similar tensions to those experienced by their Native counterparts, albeit under different conditions and in different contexts. Both Chinese Americans and Japanese Americans had to negotiate a context of White supremacy, xenophobia, and nationalism that was operationalized within a framework of anti-"Orientalism" and "yellow peril." Similar to Native communities during this time period, these Asian American communities engaged in deep and substantive conversations about what would be the best curricular path for their children in such an anti-Asian context, especially given their tenuous and sometimes changing legal status as immigrants. In response, both Chinese American and Japanese American communities each in their turn fought to gain access to the existing public school structures (as a legal right) while also building their own educational institutions for linguistic and cultural maintenance. There were, of course, some critical contextual differences between these Asian American communities and Native communities at this time, including (but not limited to) the fact that the entirety of Asian American curricular discourse took place on what was once sovereign, Native land colonized by Whites. Additionally, unlike with Native communities, the politics of international relations between the United States and Japan and China influenced the positioning of Chinese Americans and Japanese Americans within the U.S. power structure.

Mexican Americans in the Southwestern United States faced a similar curricular dilemma, and in many ways this community's struggles and experiences over curriculum represent a synthesis of many of the issues facing both Asian Americans and Native Americans. In this context, Mexican Americans are a part of the history of both Spanish and U.S. settler colonialism, *and* their community experiences also carry aspects of the immigrant experience. As such, the curricular discourse among Mexican Americans in the Southwest during the founding of curriculum studies was a result of contending with this mix of community complexity as they too engaged in deeply involved conversations about what kind of curriculum and education was best for Mexican American children. Similar to Asian Americans, the Mexican American community in the Southwest also contended with the tensions between curricular Americanization (with its manifest Whiteness) and the desire for linguistic (Spanish) and cultural maintenance (Mexican and Indigenous). Also similar to Asian Americans, Southwestern Mexican Americans had to negotiate their curricular discourse within the context of White supremacy, racism, and xenophobia, and there were ongoing political relations between the United States and Mexico that undoubtedly shaped official governmental responses on all sides. Similar to Native Americans, the Southwestern Mexican Americans also had to think about their educational positioning within a context of Anglos constantly seeking to expand their landholdings by legal and extralegal means. Thus in the history of Mexican Americans in New Mexico and Texas, we see a curricular discourse that speaks to not only the issues of curricular sovereignty highlighted in Native American communities but also the tensions manifested in transnational curricular discourse exhibited within Asian American communities. One key difference, however, was the issue of segregation. Where Asian Americans were often legally segregated (even if this segregation was not put into consistent practice in all areas), Mexican Americans in Texas and New Mexico faced no official or de facto segregation and instead were contending with unofficial or de jure segregation.

In some important ways we might say that African American and Native American discourse had significant parallels, the most important of which would be the extent to which both communities were pushing back against the White construction of Blackness and Nativeness—a construction that took place through official school texts in ways that were specifically different for Asian Americans and Mexican Americans. The White gaze on African Americans, as with other communities, was often expressed through popular media and children's books, but the contextual legacy of the enslavement of Africans, the institution of slavery itself, and the context of Black reconstruction gave African American curricular discourse a distinctive trajectory of pushing back directly, explicitly, and publicly against the imposition of Whiteness in a manner that was different from other communities. That said, we also have to point out that both the African American and Mexican American curricular discourse explicitly took on the scientific racism of the time through the work of prominent scholars in both communities (e.g., George Sánchez and W. E. B. Du Bois), and the Black, Japanese American, and Mexican American communities all had developed their own community institutions as foundations to advocate for their own voices in curricular discourse. However, we also have to note that the African American community had a more developed body of scholars and intelligentsia, in part due to the long history of specifically African American institutions of higher education. As such, of all the communities we have discussed in this book, the African American community had the strongest collection of university-educated scholars to launch curriculum critiques and undertake the project of Black curriculum revision through their own, non-White institutions (e.g., journals and schools).

One of the overwhelming themes across all of the chapters here in *Reclaiming the Multicultural Roots of the U.S. Curriculum* is that all of the communities we highlight had to contend with White supremacy, racism, xenophobia, and nationalism in various forms—and all within a context of settler colonialism as well. Consequently, the curricular discourse of these communities was necessarily born of oppression and the heartfelt struggle to resist that oppression. Such resistance carried a particularly heavy weight too, since these communities were engaged in not just a fight over what curriculum should be taught but a fight over *how they wanted their children to be in the world*. In this regard we would argue that the histories, stories, and voices we have shared here should be seen and understood as early expressions of not just community activism but, more specifically, a legacy of educational activism by communities of color in the United States. From lawsuits, to petitions, to academic scholarship, to testimonies, to fleeing White institutions of education, to maintaining language and culture by any means necessary, these parents and community members, individually and collectively, fought for the educational rights—indeed, the cultural souls—of their children.

Afterword: What We Must Know

At a 2014 town hall for his new My Brother's Keeper initiative, President Obama took a question from a Native high school student from Montana. "My question for you, Mr. President," the boy asked, "is how is the United States government helping American Indian people revitalize their language and culture? Because so many of our young men and boys don't know who they are because they've lost their culture and language, and the United States government has tried so hard for the past 200 years to destroy that" (The White House, 2014).

The president responded by first lamenting the "heartbreaking" stories he had heard from Indigenous young people he had met on a recent trip to a reservation in South Dakota. He then reminded the Native questioner that "we live in the 21st century" and instructed him that "you can't just live in the past." "Young Native Americans are also going to have to learn math, science, computer sciences, engineering," he insisted. Even as young Native people are looking "back to [their] roots," he said, they will also have to adapt to "what is increasingly a world culture."

For the Native student, the primary concern is securing the futurity of Native peoples and resisting the U.S. nation-state's efforts to systematically erase the Indigenous knowledges that are so important in providing foundation and direction for that futurity. President Obama, representing that nation-state, argued that the knowledge that Indigenous youth need in the new "world culture" would have to emphasize studies in science, technology, engineering, and mathematics, either eschewing or transcending Indigenous knowledges. Thus, for the state, a legitimate curriculum must prioritize the advancement of capitalist accumulation and consumption over and against any other aims.

What we must know as peoples of color—what we must know to survive, to understand who (and where) we are, to imagine freer and more joyful futurities—demands curricula that honor the knowledge production of our ancestors; engage the yearnings of our children, families, and communities; and interrogate the enduring tradition of White supremacist subjugation and misrepresentation. What we must know is positioned against the interests of the nation-state, against the imperatives of capital. Understanding this, we must proceed with the understanding that "the multicultural roots of U.S. curriculum" are planted in the fertile soil of our peoples' freedom dreams (Kelley, 2002)—soil that is also soaked with the blood of so many who have gone before and who continue to dream and to die, fighting.

Although we must know *and continue to know* that we have dreamed and fought together—that, as peoples of color in the United States, our roots share some common soil—we must also attend to the specificity of our dreamings, the specificity of the roots of curriculum. As detailed by the authors of this book, it becomes deeply important to make sense of how our different peoples have produced and disseminated knowledges in strikingly different material and cultural-ideological contexts and with decidedly and differently imposed relationships to land, to the nation-state, to White people, to our own bodies. There is a specificity to what we must know about our own people, and about each other, in order to advance multicultural curricula that move in solidarity, that yearn together, while also producing and growing the knowledges that sustain the humanity embodied in the specificities of Indigenous life; of Black life; of Japanese, Chinese, and Mexican American lives; and of the lives of so many others for whom curriculum is a site of ongoing dreaming and struggle.

In President Obama's admonishment of the Native high school student, Indigenous curriculum is constructed as an artifact of earlier centuries, best left "in the past," a past in which we cannot live. Roots, as imagined here, are always already dead. This, then, is an official, national imagination that must be refused. The roots of multicultural curriculum must be understood as yearnings that refuse such strangling, morbid linearity. We must know that those roots are still ever alive, straining against drought, breaking through rock, stretching toward deeper, darker ground.

—Michael J. Dumas, University of California, Berkeley

REFERENCES

Kelley, R. D. G. (2002). *Freedom dreams: The black radical imagination*. Boston, MA: Beacon.

The White House. (2014). *Remarks by the President at "My Brother's Keeper" town hall*. The White House. Retrieved from www.whitehouse.gov

Notes

Chapter 1

1. Pinar's (2012) *What Is Curriculum Theory?* does provide one of the more comprehensive discussions of African Americans and curriculum. Unlike most curriculum volumes, he writes an entire chapter about African Americans' struggle for curriculum revision in the 1930s and 1940s—although the chapter draws almost entirely from Zimmerman's (2002) *Whose America?* But this again highlights a pattern found in many new volumes of curriculum history, where new voices are more present but still not positioned as foundational to the field.

Chapter 4

1. Certainly, a follow-up piece is needed to explore how Spanish and Mexican colonialism and Indigenous resistance and life in New Mexico in its complex diversity interacted to shape educational ideas and practices.

2. Pueblo Indians represented a paradox for Anglo settler colonists and the U.S. government because the diverse Pueblos appeared to be "civilized" and had legally been granted Mexican citizenship. However, this granting of citizenship in the Mexican settler context was most likely given—as was common in Mexican colonialism— "to strip them [Pueblos] of protections on their land grants [from Spain] and, thus, facilitate dispossession of Indian lands into Mexican hands" (Gomez, 2005, p. 31).

3. In 1910 Congress specified that Pueblo lands were included in *Indian country,* the federal designation of Indigenous lands (Gomez, 2007). Certainly, before and after this date, Pueblo Indians, like Mexicans, occupied a strange status (Cotera & Saldaña-Portillo, 2014), but in the end the logics of settler colonialism resulted in laws that favored dispossession of Pueblo lands (even when they intended to protect them). For example, legal arguments were made in a series of cases that Pueblos were not Indians in the U.S. context as they entered the United States with Mexican citizenship (*United States v. Lucero*), exemplified by the caste category of civilized Indians within the Spanish and Mexican caste system, and therefore were not accorded the same status as tribes in the United States (Gomez, 2007; Lucero, 2007). Ultimately this issue was about land. Because Pueblos were not treated as Indians during this time, Pueblo lands could thus be sold, as they were deemed to be held privately (Cotera & Saldaña-Portillo, 2014; Gomez, 2007). This enabled the expropriation of Pueblo lands by White and Mexican encroachers (Gomez, 2007; Lucero, 2007).

4. Ironically, the history of Los Padillas is tied intimately to the history of one of the authors, which is not a surprise as families from Rio Abajo in New Mexico and the eastern Pueblos interacted both peacefully and violently. Diego de Padilla,

the original grantee of Los Padillas, was the son of José de Padilla. Their stories were intimately tied to the Pueblo Revolts, the ensuing exodus, the establishment of Senecú del Sur Pueblo (Piro Indians) in what is today El Paso, Texas, near Ysleta del Sur Pueblo (Tiwa Indians). Dolores Calderón's family is Tiwa/Piro and Mexican from this region (see Sisneros, n.d.).

References

Acosta, C., & Mir, A. (2012). Empowering young people to be critical thinkers: The Mexican American Studies Program in Tucson. *Voices in Urban Education, 34*(Summer), 15–26.

Acuña, R. (1988). *Occupied America* (3rd ed.). New York, NY: HarperCollins.

Adams, D. W. (1988). Fundamental considerations: The deep meaning of Native American schooling, 1880–1900. *Harvard Educational Review, 58*(1), 1–28.

Adams, D. W. (1995). *Education for extinction: American Indians and the boarding school experience 1875–1928.* Lawrence: University of Kansas Press.

Adelman, L. (Executive Producer) (2003). *Race: The power of an illusion* [DVD]. Available from California Newsreel: http://newsreel.org/video/race-the-power-of-an-illusion

Alaniz, Y., & Cornish, M. (1983). The Chicano struggle: A racial or a national movement? *Freedom Socialist: Voice of Revolutionary Feminism, 8*(4). Retrieved from www.socialism.com/drupal-6.8/bulletins/chicano-struggle-liberation-provides-lessons-all

Alaniz, Y., & Cornish, M. (2008). *Viva la raza: A history of Chicano identity and resistance.* Seattle, WA: Red Letter Press.

Alemán, E., & Luna, R. (producers) & Luna, R. (director). (2013). *Stolen education* [motion picture] United States: AlemanLuna Productions.

Alvarado v. El Paso Independent School District, 593 F. .2d 577 (5th Cir. 1979)

Anderson, T. (2009) "Ten Little Niggers": The making of a Black man's consciousness. Retrieved from folkloreforum.net/2009/05/01/%E2%80%9Cten-little-niggers%E2%80%9D-the-making-of-a-black-man%E2%80%99s-consciousness/

Aptheker, H. (1983). *American Negro slave revolts.* New York, NY: International Publishers.

Apple, M. W. (1971). The hidden curriculum and the nature of conflict. *Interchange, 2*(4), 27–40.

Apple, M. W. (1999). The absent presence of race in educational reform. *Race Ethnicity and Education, 2*(1), 9–16.

Apple, M. W. (2000). *Official knowledge: Democratic education in a conservative age* (2nd ed.). New York, NY: Routledge.

Apple, M. W. (2004). *Ideology and curriculum* (3rd ed.). New York, NY: RoutledgeFalmer.

Apple, M. W. (2010). Fly and the fly bottle: On Dwayne Huebner, the uses of language, and the nature of the curriculum field. *Curriculum Inquiry, 40*(1), 95–103.

Apple, M. W. (2012). *Education and power* (2nd ed.). New York, NY: Routledge.

Aptheker, H. (1983/1943). *American Negro slave revolts.* New York, NY: International Publishers.

Arriola, C. (1995). Knocking on the schoolhouse door: *Mendez v. Westminster* equal protection, public education and Mexican Americans in the 1940s. *La Raza Law Journal, 8,* 166.

Asato, N. (2005). Americanization vs. Japanese cultural maintenance: Analyzing Seattle's Nihongo Tokuhon, 1920. In L. Fiset & G. Nomura (Eds.), *Nikkei in the Pacific Northwest* (pp. 95–119). Seattle: University of Washington Press.

Asato, N. (2006). *Teaching Mikadoism: The attack on Japanese language schools in Hawaii, California, and Washington, 1919–1927.* Honolulu: University of Hawaii Press.

Assmann, J., & Czaplicka, J. (1995). Collective memory and cultural identity. *New German Critique, 65,* 125–133.

Au, W. (2007). High-stakes testing and curricular control: A qualitative metasynthesis. *Educational Researcher, 36*(5), 258–267.

Au, W. (2009). Model minority myth. In W. Ng, P. Chua, & E. Chen (Eds.), *The Greenwood encyclopedia of contemporary Asian American issues* (pp. 221–228). Westport, CT: Greenwood Publishing.

Au, W. (2011). *Critical curriculum studies: Education, consciousness, and the politics of knowing.* New York, NY: Routledge.

Au, W. (2012). The long march towards revitalization: Developing standpoint in curriculum studies. *Teachers College Record, 114*(5), 1–30.

Azuma, E. (2005). *Between two empires: Race, history, and transnationalism in Japanese America.* New York, NY: Oxford University Press.

Baker, B. (1996). The history of curriculum or curriculum history? What is the field and who gets to play on it? *Curriculum Studies, 4*(1), 105–117.

Baker, B. (2001). *In perpetual motion: Theories of power, educational history, and the child.* New York, NY: Peter Lang.

Baker, B. (2002). The hunt for disability: The new eugenics and the normalization of school children. *Teachers College Record, 104*(4), 663–703.

Baker, B. (Ed.). (2009). *New curriculum history.* Rotterdam, The Netherlands: Sense.

Barnhardt, C. (2001). A history of schooling for Alaska Native people. *Journal of American Indian Education, 40*(1), 1–48.

Barrera, A. (2006). The "Little Schools" in Texas, 1897–1965. *American Educational History Journal, 33*(2), 35–45.

Bell, D. A. (1980). Brown v. Board of Education and the interest-convergence dilemma. *Harvard Law Review, 93*(3), 518–533.

Blanton, C. K. (2003). From intellectual deficiency to cultural deficiency: Mexican Americans, testing, and public school policy in the American Southwest, 1920–1940. *Pacific Historical Review, 72*(1), 39–62.

Blanton, C. K. (2006). George I. Sánchez, ideology, and whiteness in the making of the Mexican American civil rights movement, 1930–1960. *The Journal of Southern History, 72*(3), 569–604.

Blanton, C. K. (2012). A legacy of neglect: George I. Sanchez, Mexican American education, and the ideal of integration, 1940–1970. *Teachers College Record, 114*(6), 1–34.

Blanton, C. K. (2015). *George I. Sánchez: The long fight for Mexican American integration.* New Haven, CT: Yale University Press.

Blight, D. W. (2003). *Race and reunion: The Civil War in American memory*. Cambridge, MA: Belknap Press of Harvard University Press.

Bowman, K. L. (2001). The new face of school desegregation. *Duke Law Journal, 50,* 1751–1808.

Brawley, B. (1937). *Negro builders and heroes*. Chapel Hill: University of North Carolina Press.

Brown, A. L. (2010). Counter-memory and race: An examination of African American scholars' challenges to early 20th century K–12 historical discourses. *Journal of Negro Education, 79*(1), 54–65.

Brown, A. L., & Au, W. (2014). Race, memory, and master narratives: A critical essay on U.S. curriculum history. *Curriculum Inquiry, 44*(3), 358–389.

Brown, A. L., & Brown, K. D. (2015). The more things change, the more they stay the same: Excavating race and the enduring racisms in U.S. curriculum. *National Society for the Study of Education, 114*(2), 103–130.

Brown, A. L., & De Lissovoy, N. (2011). Economies of racism: Grounding education policy research in the complex dialectic of race, class, and capital. *Journal of Educational Policy, 26*(5), 595–619.

Brown, S. A. (1933). Negro character as seen by white authors. *Journal of Negro Education, 2*(2), 179–203.

Burkholder, Z. (2011). *Color in the classroom: How American schools taught race, 1900–1954*. New York, NY: Oxford University Press.

Byrd, J. A. (2011). *The transit of empire: Indigenous critiques of colonialism*. Minneapolis: University of Minnesota Press.

Cabrera, N. L., Meza, E. L., & Rodriguez, R. C. (2011). The fight for Mexican American studies in Tucson. *NACLA Report on the Americas, 44*(6), 20.

Calderón, D. (2008). Indigenous metaphysics: Challenging western knowledge organization in social studies curriculum (Doctoral dissertation). Available from ProQuest (304654538)

Calderón, D. (2011). Locating the foundations of epistemologies of ignorance in normative multicultural education. In N. Jaramillo and E. Malewski (Eds.), *Epistemologies of ignorance and studies of limits in education*. Charlotte, NC: Information Age.

Calderón, D. (2014a). Speaking back to manifest destinies: A land education-based approach to critical curriculum inquiry. *Environmental Education Research, 20*(1), 24–36.

Calderón, D. (2014b). Uncovering settler grammars in curriculum. *Educational Studies, 50*(4), 313–338.

Caliver, A. (1933). Negro college students and the need of personnel work. *Journal of Negro Education, 2*(3), 359–378.

Carlson, D. (2009). Tales of future past: The living legacy of eugenics in American education. *Journal of the American Association for the Advancement of Curriculum Studies, 5,* 1–10.

Carrigan, W. D. (2004). *The making of a lynching culture: Violence and vigilantism in Central Texas, 1836–1916*. Urbana: University of Illinois Press.

Carter, R. (2004). *Brown v. Board of Education: Fifty years later* (video transcript). Smithsonian National Museum of American History. Retrieved from americanhistory.si.edu/brown/history/6-legacy/brown-video-transcript.html

Castenell, L., & Pinar, W. F. (Eds.) (1993). *Understanding curriculum as a racial text*. Albany: State University of New York Press.

Chan, S. (1993). *Asian Americans: An interpretive history*. New York, NY: Twayne Publishers.

Chan, S. (1998). Race, ethnic culture, and gender in the construction of identities among second-generation Chinese Americans, 1880s to 1930s. In K. S. Wong (Ed.), *Claiming America* (pp. 127–164). Philadelphia, PA: Temple University Press.

Chang, B., & Au, W. (2007). You're Asian, how could you fail math? Unmasking the myth of the model minority. *Rethinking Schools, 22*(2), 14–19.

Chen, S. (2002). *Being Chinese, becoming Chinese American*. Chicago: University of Illinois Press.

Cheung, C. (1924, August 21). *Life history as a social document of Mr. Chin Cheung*. Retrieved from collections.stanford.edu/pdf/10100000000027_0042.pdf.

Child, B. J. (1998). *Boarding school seasons: American Indian families, 1900–1940*. Lincoln: University of Nebraska Press.

Churchill, W. (2004). *Kill the Indian, save the man: The genocidal impact of American Indian residential schools*. San Francisco, CA: City Lights Books.

Cobb, A. (2000). *Listening to our grandmothers' stories: The Bloomfield Academy for Chickasaw females, 1852–1949*. Lincoln: University of Nebraska Press.

Cobb, W. M. (1934). The physical constitution of the American negro. *Journal of Negro Education, 3*(3), 340–388.

Coleman, M. C. (1993). *American Indian children at school, 1850–1930*. Jackson: University Press of Mississippi.

Connelly, F. M, He, M. F., & Phillion, J. (Eds.). (2008). *The Sage handbook of curriculum and instruction*. Thousand Oaks, CA: Sage.

Cotera, M. E., & Saldaña-Portillo, M. J. (2014). Indigenous but not Indian? Chicana/os and the politics of Indigeneity. In R. Warrior (Ed.), *The World of Indigenous North America* (pp. 549–568). New York, NY: Routledge.

Counts, G. S. (1932). *Dare the schools build a new social order?* New York, NY: John Day.

Cushman, E. (2011). *The Cherokee syllabary: Writing the people's perseverance*. Norman: University of Oklahoma Press.

Dagbovie, P. G. (2015). *What is African American history?* Malden, MA, Cambridge: Polity Press.

Daniel, R. P. (1934). Negro-white differences in non-intellectual traits, and in special abilities. *Journal of Negro Education, 3*(3), 411–423.

Daniel, W. G. (1932). The curriculum. *Journal of Negro Education, 1*(2), 277–303.

Daniels, R. (1988). *Asian America: Chinese and Japanese in the United States since 1850*. Seattle: University of Washington Press.

Delgado v. Bastrop Independent School District, Civil No. 388 (W.D. Tex. 1948)

Delgado, R., & Stefancic, J. (2012). *Critical race theory: An introduction* (2nd ed.). New York: New York University Press.

Desai, C. (2012). Do we want something new or just repetition of 1492? Engaging with the "next" moment in curriculum studies. *Journal of Curriculum and Pedagogy, 8*(1), 153–167.

Deyhle, D., & Swisher, K. (1997). Research in American Indian and Alaska Native education: From assimilation to self-determination. *Review of Research in Education, 22*, 113–194.

Deyhle, D., Swisher, K., Stevens, T., & Galvan, R. T. (2008). Indigenous resistance and renewal: From colonizing practices to self-determination. In F. M. Connelly, M. F. He, & J. Phillion (Eds.), *The Sage handbook of curriculum and instruction* (pp. 329–348). Thousand Oaks, CA: Sage.

Donato, R. (1997). *The other struggle for equal schools: Mexican Americans during the civil rights era*. Albany: State University of New York Press.

Donato, R. (2003). Sugar beets, segregation, and schools: Mexican Americans in a Northern Colorado community, 1920–1960. *Journal of Latinos in Education, 2*(2), 69–88.

Donato, R., & Hanson, J. (2012). Legally white, socially "Mexican": The politics of de jure and de facto school segregation in the American Southwest. *Harvard Educational Review, 82*(2), 202–225.

Drescher, S. (1990). The ending of the slave trade and the evolution of European scientific racism. *Social Science History, 14*(3), 415–450.

Du Bois, W. E. B. (1920). *Darkwater: Voices from within the veil*. New York, NY: Dover.

Du Bois, W. E. B. (1935a). *Black reconstruction in America 1860–1880*. New York, NY: Simon and Schuster.

Du Bois, W. E. B. (1935b). Does the Negro need separate schools? *Journal of Negro Education, 4*(3), 328–335.

Du Bois, W. E. B. (1994). *The souls of Black folk*. New York, NY: Gramercy Books. (Original work published 1904)

Du Bois, W. E. B. (1998). Black reconstruction in America: 1860–1880. New York, NY: Free Press. (Original work published 1935)

Dunbar-Ortiz, R. (2007). *Roots of resistance: A history of land tenure in New Mexico*. Norman: University of Oklahoma Press.

Duncan-Andrade, J. M. (2005). An examination of the sociopolitical history of Chicanos and its relationship to school performance. *Urban Education, 40*(6), 576–605.

Duran, L. (2013, April). *The life and legacy of New Mexico's own Dr. George I. Sánchez, a belated tribute*. Public addressed delivered at the 40th Annual Conference of the New Mexico Association for Bilingual Education, Albuquerque, New Mexico.

Editorial: Why a journal of Negro education. (1932). *Journal of Negro Education, 1*(1), 1–4.

Ephraim, C. W. (2003). *The pathology of Eurocentrism: The burden and responsibilities of being black*. Trenton, NJ: Africa World Press.

Ernest, J. (2004). *Liberation historiography: African American writers and the challenge of history, 1794–1861*. Chapel Hill: University of North Carolina Press.

Estrada, L. F., Garcia, F. C., Macias, R. F., & Maldonado, L. (1981). Chicanos in the United States: A history of exploitation and resistance. *Daedalus, 110*(2), 103–131.

Fallace, T. (2012). Recapitualition theory and the new education: Race, culture, imperialism and pedagogy, 1894–1916. *Curriculum Inquiry, 42*, 510–533.

Fallace, T. (2015). The savage origins of child-centered pedagogy, 1871–1913. *American Educational Research Journal, 52*(1), 73–103.

Flinders, D. J., & Thornton, S. J. (Eds.). (2012). *The curriculum studies reader* (4th ed.). New York, NY: RoutledgeFalmer

Foley, N. (1997). *The white scourge: Mexicans, blacks, and poor whites in Texas cotton culture*. Berkeley: University of California Press.

Frankel, M. C. (2001). "Nature's nation" revisited: Citizenship and the sublime in Thomas Jefferson's notes on the state of Virginia. *American Literature, 73*(4), 695–726.

Fraser, N. (1990). Rethinking the public sphere: A contribution to the critique of actually existing democracy. *Social Text, 25/26*, 56–80.

Fredrickson, G. (1971). *The Black image in the White mind: The debate on Afro-American character and destiny, 1817–1914*. New York, NY: Harper & Row.

Garcia, M. T. (1984). Mexican Americans and the politics of citizenship: The case of El Paso, 1936. *New Mexico Historical Review, 59*(2), 187–204.

Garth, T. R. (1934). The problem of race psychology: A general statement. *The Journal of Negro Education, 3*(3), 319–327.

Gates, H. L. (1988). The trope of the new Negro and the reconstruction of the image of the Black. *Representations, 24*, 129–155.

Genovese, E. D. (1979). *From rebellion to revolution: Afro-American slave revolts in the making of the modern world*. Baton Rouge: Louisiana State University Press.

Gillborn, D. (2008). *Racism and Education: Coincidence or Conspiracy?* New York, NY: Routledge.

Gish, D. A., & Klinghard, D. P. (2012). Republican constitutionalism in Thomas Jefferson's notes on the state of Virginia. *Journal of Politics, 74*(1), 35.

Godfrey, P. C. (2008). The "Other White": Mexican Americans and the impotency of whiteness in the segregation and desegregation of Texan public schools. *Equity and Excellence in Education, 41*(2), 247–261.

Goldsby, J. D. (2006). *A spectacular secret: Lynching in American life and literature*. Chicago, IL: University of Chicago Press.

Gomez, L. E. (2005). Off-White in an age of White supremacy: Mexican elites and the rights of Indians and Blacks in nineteenth-century New Mexico. *Chicano-Latino Law Review, 25*, 9.

Gomez, L. E. (2007). *Manifest destinies: The making of the Mexican American race*. New York: New York University Press.

Gonzalez, G. G. (1974). *The system of public education and its function within the Chicano communities, 1920–1930*. Los Angeles: University of California.

Gonzalez, G. G. (1978). Educational reform in Los Angeles and its effects upon the Mexican community, 1900–1930. *Explorations in Ethnic Studies, 1*, 5–26.

Gonzalez, G. G. (1979). The historical development of the concept of intelligence. *Review of Radical Political Economics, 11*(2), 44–54.

Gonzalez, G. G. (1982). *Progressive education: A Marxist interpretation*. Minneapolis, MN: Marxist Educational Press.

Gonzalez, G. G. (1985). Segregation of Mexican children in a southern California city: The legacy of expansionism and the American southwest. *Western Historical Quarterly, 16*(1), 55–76.

Gonzalez, G. G. (1990). *Chicano education in the era of segregation*. Philadelphia, PA: Balch Institute Press.

Gonzalez, G. G. (2013). *Chicano education in the era of segregation*. Denton, TX: University of North Texas Press.

Goodwin, A. L. (2010). Curriculum as colonizer: (Asian) American education in the current U.S. context. *Teachers College Record, 112*(12), 3102–3138.

Gordon, B. (1993). Toward emancipation in citizenship education: The case of African-American cultural knowledge. In L. Castenell & W. F. Pinar (Eds.), *Representations of identity and difference in education* (pp. 263–284). Albany: State University of New York Press.

Gould, S. J. (1996). *The mismeasure of man* (Revised and expanded). New York, NY: Norton.

Grande, S. (2015). *Red pedagogy: Native American social and political thought* (10th anniversary ed.). New York, NY: Rowman & Littlefield.

Grant, C. A., Brown, K. D., & Brown, A. L. (2015). *Black intellectual thought in education: The missing traditions of Anna Julia Cooper, Carter G. Woodson and Alain Locke*. New York, NY: Routledge.

Gross, A. J. (2003). Texas Mexicans and the politics of whiteness. *Law and History Review, 21*(1), 195–205.

Hall, S. (Ed.). (1997). *Representation: Cultural representations and signifying practices*. London, England: Sage.

Hamme, L. V. (1995). American Indian cultures and the classroom. *Journal of American Indian Education, 35*(2).

Lopez, I. F. H. (1994). The social construction of race: Some observations on illusion, fabrication, and choice. *Harvard Civil Rights-Civil Liberties Law Review, 29,* 1–62.

Harris, V. J. (1989). Race consciousness, refinement, and radicalism: Socialization in *The Brownies' Book*. *Children's Literature Association Quarterly, 14*(4), 192–196.

Harris, V. J. (1990). From Little Black Sambo to Popo and Fifina: Arna Bontemps and the creation of African-American children's literature. *The Lion and the Unicorn, 14*(1), 108–127.

Harris, W. J. (1914). *Chinese and Japanese in the United States 1910* (Bulletin 127). Washington, DC: Department of Commerce, Bureau of the Census.

Hendrick, I. (1977). *The education of non-Whites in California, 1849–1970*. San Francisco, CA: R & E Associates.

Hendry, P. (2011). *Engendering curriculum history*. New York, NY: Routledge.

Horsman, R. (1981). *Race and manifest destiny: The prigins of American Anglo-Saxonism*. Boston, MA: Harvard University Press.

Huebner, D. E. (1970, March 2). Curriculum as the accessibility of knowledge. Paper presented at the Curriculum Theory Study Group, Minneapolis, MN.

Huebner, D. E. (1999). Knowledge and the curriculum. In V. Hillis (Ed.), *The lure of the transcendent: Collected essays by Dwayne E. Huebner* (pp. 44–65). Mahwah, NJ: Lawrence Erlbaum.

Ichioka, Y. (1988). *The Issei: The world of the first generation Japanese immigrants, 1885–1924*. New York, NY: Free Press.

In re Rodriguez, 81 F. 337 (W.D. Tex. 1897)

Indian Nations at Risk Task Force. (1991). *Indian nations at risk: An educational strategy for action*. Washington, DC: U.S. Department of Education.

Interview with a Chinese student. (1925, October 13). Retrieved from collections .stanford.edu/pdf/10100000000028_0033.pdf.

Johnson, C. S. (1936). On the need of realism in Negro education. *Journal of Negro Education, 5*(3), 375–382.

Johnson, C. S. (1944). The next decade in race relations. *Journal of Negro Education, 13*(3), 441–446.

Jordan, W. D. (1968). *White over black: American attitudes toward the Negro, 1550–1812*. Raleigh, NC: UNC Press.

Kawai, Y. (2005). Stereotyping Asian Americans: The dialectic of the model minority and the yellow peril. *Howard Journal of Communications, 16*(2), 109–130.

Kidwell, C. S. (1985). Native knowledge in the Americas. *Osiris, 1,* 209–228.

Kincheloe, J. L., Steinberg, S. R., Rodriguez, N. M., & Chennault, R. E. (Eds.). (2000). *White reign: Deploying whiteness in America*. New York, NY: Palgrave Macmillan.

King, J. E. (1991). Dysconscious racism: Ideology, identity, and the miseducation of teachers. *The Journal of Negro Education, 60*(2), 133–146.

King, T. (2014, June 10) Labor's aphasia: Toward antiblackness as constitutive to settler colonialism. *Decolonization, Indigeneity, and Society.* Retrieved from decolonization.wordpress.com/2014/06/10/labors-aphasia -toward-antiblackness-as-constitutive-to-settler-colonialism/

Kliebard, H. M. (2004). *The struggle for the American curriculum, 1893–1958* (3rd ed.). New York, NY: RoutledgeFalmer.

Klos, G. (1994). "Our people could not distinguish one tribe from another": The 1859 expulsion of the Reserve Indians from Texas. *Southwestern Historical Quarterly, 97*(4), 598–619.

Kuo, J. (1998). Excluded, segregated and forgotten: A historical view of the discrimination of Chinese Americans in public schools. *Asian American Law Journal, 5*(7), 181–212.

Lai, H. M. (2004). *Becoming Chinese American: A history of communities and institutions*. Walnut Creek, CA: Alta Mira Press.

Lai, H. M. (2005). Teaching Chinese Americans to be Chinese: Curriculum, teachers, and textbooks in Chinese school in America during the exclusion era. In S. Chan (Ed.), *Chinese American transnationalism: The flow of people, resources, and ideas between China and America during the exclusion era* (pp. 194–210). Philadelphia, PA: Temple University Press.

Lawler, T. B. (1931). *Essentials of American history*. New York, NY: Ginn and Co.

Le Goff, J. (1992). *History and memory*. New York, NY: Columbia University Press.

Ledesma, M. C. (2013). Revisiting Grutter and Gratz in the wake of Fisher: Looking back to move forward. *Equity & Excellence in Education, 46*(2), 220–235.

Lee, E. (2015). *The making of Asian America: A history*. New York, NY: Simon and Schuster.

Lee, E., & Shibusawa, N. (2005). What is transnational Asian American history? Recent trends and challenges. *Journal of Asian American Studies, 8*(3), vii–xvii.

Leung, L. (1924, August 12). Interview with Lillie Leung. Retrieved from collections .stanford.edu/pdf/10100000000025_0026.pdf.

Lim de Sanchez, S. (2003). Crafting a Delta Chinese community: Education and acculturation in twentieth-century southern Baptist mission schools. *History of Education Quarterly, 43*(1), 74–90.

Locke, A. (1944). Whither race relations? A critical commentary. *Journal of Negro Education, 13*(3), 398–406.

Logan, R. W. (1997 [1954]). *The betrayal of the Negro, from Rutherford B. Hayes to Woodrow Wilson* (1st Da Capo Press ed.). New York, NY: Da Capo Press.

Lomawaima, K. T. (1999). The unnatural history of American Indian education. In K. Swisher & J. Tippeconnic III (Eds.), *Next steps: Research and practice to advance Indian education* (pp. 1–32). Charleston, WV: ERIC Clearinghouse on Rural Education and Small Schools.

Lomawaima, K. T., & McCarty, T. L. (2006). *To remain an Indian: Lessons in democracy from a century of Native American education.* New York, NY: Teachers College Press.

Lopez, H. (1996). *White by law: The legal construction of race.* New York: New York University Press.

Lucero, R. L. (2007). *State v. Romero*: The legacy of Pueblo land grants and the contours of jurisdiction in Indian country. *New Mexico Law Review, 37,* 671–700.

Malewski, E. (Ed.). (2010). *Curriculum studies handbook: The next movement.* New York, NY: Routledge.

Maramba, D. C., & Bonus, R. (Eds.). (2013). *The "other" students: Filipino Americans, education and power.* Charlotte, NC: Information Age.

Marshall, J. D., Schubert, W. H., & Sears, J. T. (2000). *Turning points in curriculum: A contemporary curriculum memoir.* Columbus, OH: Prentice Hall.

Marshall, T. M. (1930). *American history.* New York, NY: Macmillan.

Martin, M. (2004). *Brown gold: Milestones of African American children's books, 1845–2002.* New York, NY: Routledge.

McCarthy, C. (1988). Rethinking liberal and radical perspectives on racial inequality in schooling: Making the case for nonsynchrony. *Harvard Educational Review, 58*(3), 265–279.

McCarthy, C. (1990a). Multicultural education, minority identities, textbooks, and the challenge of curriculum reform. *Journal of Education, 172*(2), 118–129.

McCarthy, C. (1990b). Race and education in the United States: The multicultural solution. *Interchange, 21*(3), 45–55.

Menchaca, M. (1993). Chicano Indianism: A historical account of racial repression in the United States. *American Ethnologist, 20*(3), 583–603.

Menchaca, M. (1997) Early racist discourses: Roots of deficit thinking. In R. R. Valencia. (Ed.), *The evolution of deficit thinking: Educational thought and practice* (pp. 13–40)

Menchaca, M. (2001). *Recovering history, constructing race: The Indian, black and white roots of Mexican Americans.* Austin: University of Texas Press.

Menchaca, M., & Valencia, R. R. (1990). Anglo-Saxon ideologies in the 1920s–1930s: Their impact on the segregation of Mexican students in California. *Anthropology and Education Quarterly, 21*(3), 222–249.

Mendez v. Westminister [*sic*] School Dist. of Orange County, 64 F.Supp. 544 (S.D. Cal. 1946), aff'd, 161 F.2d 774 (9th Cir. 1947)

Mihesuah, D. A. (1997). *Cultivating the rosebuds: The education of women at the Cherokee Female Seminary, 1851–1909.* Champaign: University of Illinois Press.

Miller, J. L. (2005). The American curriculum field and its worldly encounters. *Journal of Curriculum Theorizing, 21*(2), 9–24.

Mills, C. (1998). *Blackness visible.* Ithaca, NY: Cornell University Press.

Montejano, D. (1987). *Anglos and Mexicans in the making of Texas, 1836–1986.* Austin: University of Texas Press.

Moran, A. (2002). As Australia decolonizes: Indigenizing settler nationalism and the challenges of settler/indigenous relations. *Ethnic and Racial Studies, 25*(6), 1013–1042.

Morimoto, T. (1997). *Japanese Americans and cultural continuity: Maintaining language and heritage*. New York, NY: Garland.

National Association for the Advancement of Colored People. (1939). *Anti-Negro propaganda in school textbooks* [pamphlet]. New York, NY: NAACP.

Ngugi, W. T. (1986). *Decolonising the mind: The politics of language in African literature*. Portsmouth, NH: Heinemann.

Nieto, S. (2007). School reform and student learning: A multicultural perspective. In J. A. Banks & C. A. McGee Banks (Eds.), *Multicultural education: Issues and perspectives* (pp. 425–44) Boston, MA: Allyn and Bacon.

Nieto-Phillips, J. M. (2008). *The language of blood: The making of Spanish-American identity in New Mexico, 1880s–1930s*. Albuquerque: University of New Mexico Press.

Omi, M., & Winant, H. (2015). *Racial formations in the United States* (3rd ed.). New York, NY: Routledge.

Padilla, F. (1980). Early Chicano legal recognition in 1846–1897. *Journal of Popular Culture, 13*(3), 564–574.

Paraskeva, J. (2011). *Conflicts in curriculum theory: Challenging hegemonic epistemologies*. New York, NY: Palgrave Macmillan.

Perdue, T. (1994). The Sequoyah syllabary and cultural revitalization. In P. Kwachka (Ed.), *Perspectives on the Southeast: Linguistics, archaeology, and ethnohistory* (pp. 116–125). Athens: University of Georgia Press.

Perea, J. F. (2001). Fulfilling manifest destiny: Conquest, race, and the insular cases. In C. D. Burnett and B. Marshall (Eds.), *Foreign in a domestic sense: Puerto Rico, American expansion, and the constitution* (pp. 140–166). Durham, NC: Duke University Press.

Perea, J. F. (2003). Law and the border: A brief history of race and the U.S.-Mexican border: Tracing the trajectories of conquest. *UCLA Law Review, 51*, 283–312.

Pinar, W. F. (Ed.). (1975). *Curriculum theorizing: The reconceptualists*. Berkeley, CA: McCutchan.

Pinar, W. F. (1978). The reconceptualization of curriculum studies. *Curriculum Studies, 10*(3), 205–214.

Pinar, W. F. (2006). *The synoptic text today and other essays: Curriculum development after the reconceptualization*. New York, NY: Peter Lang.

Pinar, W. F. (2012). *What is curriculum theory?* (2nd ed.). New York, NY: Routledge.

Pinar, W. F., Reynolds, W. M., Slattery, P., & Taubman, P. M. (1995). *Understanding curriculum: An introduction to the study of historical and contemporary curriculum discourses*. New York, NY: Peter Lang.

Pipphen, J. W. (2015, July 19). How one law banning ethnic studies led to its rise. *The Atlantic*. Retrieved from www.theatlantic.com/education/archive/2015/07/how-one-law-banning-ethnic-studies-led-to-rise/398885/

Plessy v. Ferguson,163 U.S. 537 (1896)

Powdermaker, H. (1944). The anthropological approach to the problem of modifying race attitudes. *Journal of Negro Education, 13*(3), 295–302.

Powers, J. M. (2008). Forgotten history: Mexican American school segregation in Arizona from 1900–1951. *Equity and Excellence in Education, 41*(4), 467–481.

Reddick, L. D. (1934). Racial attitudes in American history textbooks of the South. *Journal of Negro History, 19*(3), 225–265.

Reddick, L. D. (1944). Educational programs for the improvement of race relations: Motion pictures radio, the press, and libraries. *Journal of Negro Education, 13*(3), 367–389.

Reyhner, J., & Eder, J. (2004). *American Indian education: A history*. Norman: University of Oklahoma Press.

Reynolds, W. M. (1990). Perspectives and imperatives: Comprehensiveness and multidimensionality in synoptic curriculum texts. *Journal of Curriculum and Supervision, 5*(2), 189–193.

Roediger, D. R. (1994). *Towards the abolition of whiteness: Essays on race, politics, and working class history*. New York, NY: Verso Press.

Romo, R. (1983). George I. Sánchez and the civil rights movement: 1940–1960. *La Raza Law Journal, 1*, 342.

Rosenbaum, J. E. (1976). *Making inequality: The hidden curriculum of high school tracking* (1st ed.). New York, NY: John Wiley & Sons.

Rosenfelt, D. M. (1973). Indian schools and community control. *Stanford Law Review, 25*(4), 489–550.

Rosiek, J., & Kinslow, K. (2016). *Resegregation as curriculum: The meaning of the new racial segregation in U.S. public schools*. New York, NY: Routledge.

Rugg, H. (1929). *An introduction to American civilization: A study of economic life in the United States*. Chicago, IL: Ginn and Company.

Rugg, H. (1931). *A history of American government and culture: America's march towards democracy*. Chicago, IL: Ginn and Company.

Ruiz, V. L. (2001). South by southwest: Mexican Americans and segregated schooling, 1900–1950. *OAH Magazine of History, 15*(2), 23–27.

San Miguel, G., Jr. (1983). The struggle against separate and unequal schools: Middle class Mexican Americans and the desegregation campaign in Texas, 1929–1957, *History of Education Quarterly, 23*(1), 343–359.

San Miguel, G., Jr. (1986). Status of the historiography of Chicano education: A preliminary analysis. *History of Education Quarterly 26*, 523–536.

San Miguel, G., Jr. (1987). *"Let them all take heed": Mexican Americans and the campaign for educational equity in Texas, 1910–1981*. College Station: Texas A&M University Press.

San Miguel, G., Jr., & Valencia, R. (1998). From the Treaty of Guadalupe Hidalgo to Hopwood: The educational plight and struggle of Mexican Americans in the Southwest. *Harvard Educational Review, 68*(3), 353–413.

Sánchez, R., & Pita, B. (2014). Rethinking settler colonialism. *American Quarterly, 66*(4), 1039–1055.

Schubert, W. H. (1986). *Curriculum: Perspective, paradigm, and possibility*. New York, NY: Macmillan.

Schubert, W. H. (2010). Journeys of expansion and synopsis: Tensions in books that shaped curriculum inquiry, 1968–present. *Curriculum Inquiry, 40*(1), 17–94.

Schubert, W. H., Schubert, A. L. L., Thomas, T. P., & Carroll, W. M. (2002). *Curriculum books: The first hundred years* (2nd ed.). New York, NY: Peter Lang.

Scudder, H. E. (1884). *A history of the United States of America: Preceded by a narrative of the discovery and settlement of North America*. Boston, MA: J. H. Butler.

Senese, G. (1991). *Self-determination and the social education of Native Americans.* New York, NY: Praeger.

Shapiro, H. (1988). *White violence and Black response: From Reconstruction to Montgomery.* Amherst: University of Massachusetts Press.

Shim, D. (1998). From yellow peril through model minority to renewed yellow peril. *Journal of Communication Inquiry, 22*(4), 385–409.

Simmons, M. (1977). *New Mexico: An interpretive history.* Albuquerque: University of New Mexico Press.

Sisneros, S. (n.d.). The life and times of Esteban Padilla: How the acquisition of land changed his social status and place in the Padilla family hierarchy. Retrieved from newmexicohistory.org/people/esteban-padilla.

Spack, R. (2002). *America's second tongue: American Indian education and the ownership of English, 1860–1900.* Lincoln: University of Nebraska Press.

Spring, J. (2010). *Deculturalization and the struggle for equality: A brief history of the education of dominated cultures in the United States* (6th ed.). San Francisco, CA: McGraw-Hill.

Standing Bear, L. (1978). *Land of the spotted eagle.* Lincoln: University of Nebraska Press. (Original work published 1933)

Szasz, M. C. (2006). Through a wide-angle lens: Acquiring and maintaining power, position, and knowledge through boarding schools. In C. E. Trafzer, J. A. Keller, & L. Sisquoc (Eds.), *Boarding school blues: Revisiting American Indian educational experiences* (pp. 187–201). Lincoln: University of Nebraska Press.

Takaki, R. (1998). *Strangers from a different shore: A history of Asian Americans* (Updated and revised). New York, NY: Little, Brown and Company.

Taliaferro-Baszile, D. (2010). In Ellisonian eyes, what is curriculum theory? In E. Malewski (Ed.), *Curriculum studies handbook: The next movement* (pp. 483–495). New York, NY: Routledge.

Tanner, D., & Tanner, L. (1995). *Curriculum development: Theory into practice.* Eaglewood Cliffs, NJ: Prentice-Hall.

Texas Senate. (2015). Texas Senate Resolution 626.

Tom, K. F. (1941). The function of the Chinese language school. *Sociology and Social Research, 25*(6), 557–561.

Tom, K. F. (1944). *The participation of the Chinese in the community life of Los Angeles* (Master's thesis). University of Southern California, Los Angeles.

Trafzer, C. E., Keller, J. A., & Sisquoc, L. (Eds.). (2006a). *Boarding school blues: Revisiting American Indian educational experiences.* Lincoln: University of Nebraska Press.

Trafzer, C. E., Keller, J. A., & Sisquoc, L. (2006b). Introduction: Origin and development of the American Indian boarding school system. In C. E. Trafzer, J. A. Keller, & L. Sisquoc (Eds.), *Boarding school blues: Revisiting American Indian educational experiences* (pp. 1–33). Lincoln: University of Nebraska Press.

Trouillot, M. (1995). *Silencing the past: Power and the production of history.* Boston, MA: Beacon Press.

Trujillo, O. V., & Alston, D. A. (2005). Report on the status of American Indians and Alaska Natives in education: Historical legacy to cultural empowerment. Washington, DC: National Education Association of the United States.

Tuck, E. (2011). Rematriating curriculum studies. *Journal of Curriculum and Pedagogy, 8*(1), 34–37.

Tuck, E., & Gaztambide-Fernandez, R. A. (2013). Curriculum, replacement, and settler futurity. *Journal of Curriculum Theorizing, 29*(1), 72–89.

Tuck, E., & Yang, K. W. (2012). Decolonization is not a metaphor. *Decolonization: Indigeneity, Education and Society, 1*(1), 1–40.

United States v. Lucero, 1 N.M. 422 (N.M. Terr. 1869)

U.S. Department of Commerce. (1921). *14th Census of the United States.* Washington, DC: U.S. Deparment of Commerce, Bureau of the Census. Retrieved from www2.census.gov/prod2/statcomp/documents/1921-02.pdf

Valencia, R. (2005). The Mexican American struggle for equal educational opportunity in *Mendez v. Westminster*: Helping to pave the way for *Brown v. Board of Education. Teachers College Record, 107*(3), 389–423.

Valencia, R. R. (2008). *Chicano students and the courts: The Mexican American legal struggle for educational equality.* New York: New York University Press.

Vizenor, G. R. (1994). *Manifest manners: Postindian warriors of survivance.* Hanover, MA: Wesleyan University Press.

Vizenor, G. R. (Ed.). (2008). *Survivance: Narratives of native presence.* Lincoln: University of Nebraska Press.

Ward, C. J. (2005). *Native Americans in the school system: Family, community, and academic achievement.* New York, NY: Altamira Press.

Watkins, W. H. (1993). Black curriculum orientations: A preliminary inquiry. *Harvard Educational Review, 63,* 321–338.

Watkins, W. H. (2001). *The white architects of black education: Ideology and power in America, 1856–1954.* New York, NY: Teachers College Press.

Weinberg, M. (1997). *Asian-American education: Historical background and current realities.* Mahwah, NJ: Lawrence Erlbaum.

Wilkerson, D. A. (1934). Racial differences in scholastic achievement. *Journal of Negro Education, 3*(3), 453–477.

Wilkins, D. E. (2002). *American Indian politics and the American political system.* Lanham, MD: Rowman and Littlefield.

Wilkins, D. E. (2010). *American Indian sovereignty and the US Supreme Court: The masking of justice.* Austin: University of Texas Press.

Wilkins, D. E., & Stark, H. K. (2010). *American Indian politics and the American political system.* Lanham, MD: Rowman and Littlefield.

Wilkins, R. (1944). Next steps in education for racial understanding. *Journal of Negro Education, 13*(3), 432–440.

Williams, G. W. (1968). *The American Negro: His history and literature.* New York, NY: Arno and New York Times Press. (Original work published 1883)

Williams R. A. (1990). *The American Indian in Western legal thought: The discourses of conquest.* Cambridge, England: Oxford University Press.

Willis, P. (1977). *Learning to labor: How working class kids get working class jobs.* New York, NY: Columbia University Press.

Wilson, J. T. (1994). *The Black Phalanx: African American soldiers in the war of independence, the War of 1812, and the Civil War* (1st Da Capo Press ed.). New York, NY: Da Capo Press. (Original work published 1887)

Winfield, A. G. (2007). *Eugenics and education in America: Institutionalized racism and the implications of history, ideology, and memory.* New York, NY: Peter Lang.

Wolfe, P. (2006). Settler colonialism and the elimination of the Native. *Journal of Genocide Research, 8*(4), 387–409.

Wollenberg, C. (1976). *All deliberate speed: Segregation and exclusion in California schools, 1855–1975*. Berkeley: University of California Press.

Woodson, C. G., & Wesley, C. (1935). *The story of the Negro retold*. Washington, DC: Associated Publishers.

Wraga, W. G. (1998). Interesting, if true: Historical perspectives on the "reconceptualization" of curriculum studies. *Journal of Curriculum and Supervision, 14*(1), 5–28.

Wraga, W. G. (1999). "Extracting sun-beams out of cucumbers": The retreat from practice in reconceptualized curriculum studies. *Educational Researcher, 28*(1), 4–13.

Young, D. (1924, August 29). Life history and social document of David Young. Retrieved from collections.stanford.edu/pdf/10100000000029_0022.pdf

Zimmerman, J. (2002). *Whose America? Culture wars in the public schools*. Cambridge, MA: Harvard University Press.

Zimmerman, J. (2004). Brown-ing the American textbook: History, psychology, and the origins of modern multiculturalism. *History of Education Quarterly, 44*(1), 46–69.

Zinn, H. (1995). *A people's history of the United States: 1492–present* (Revised and updated). New York, NY: Harper Perennial.

Index

Absence from curricular discourse, 2–3, 4–8, 18. *See also* African Americans: absence from curriculum

Access to public schools. *See* Public school access

ACLU (American Civil Liberties Union), 111

Acosta, C., 113

Activism of people of color, 2–3. *See also* Resistance by group

Acuña, R., 84, 85, 86, 87

Adams, D. W., 18, 25, 28, 29, 30, 31, 32, 33, 34, 35, 36, 37, 38, 39, 40, 41, 42

Adelman, L., 118

African American civil rights organizations, 111, 125, 145

African Americans. *See also Journal of Negro Education*
  absence from curriculum, 80n1 (Ch. 1), 120, 123–124, 140–142, 144, 147
  Black scholarship, 128–129, 140–144, 145
  construction and *reconstruction* concepts, 115–116
  historical stereotypes, 93–94, 114–115, 120–127
  and the New South, 116–118
  and other minorities, 114, 149
  and racial science, 117–120, 131–132, 145
  resistance, 128–129, 140–144, 145, 149–150
  as topic of book, 16–17

Alaniz, Y., 85, 87, 90

Alaska, 21

Alcorn, W. A., 60

Alemán, E., 100, 110

Alien Land Law, 69

Allotment Act, 21, 22

Alston, D. A., 21

Alvarado v. El Paso Independent School District, 97

Alvarez, L., xi

American Civil Liberties Union (ACLU), 111

American GI Forum of Texas, 110

American Indian. *See* "Indian education"; Indigenous peoples

Americanization goal
  and Chinese Americans, 50–51
  and Indigenous peoples, 21
  and Japanese Americans, 50–51, 72–76, 78
  and Mexican Americans, 81, 93, 94, 97, 98, 148

American Legion, 65, 69

American Negro, The (Williams), 140–141, 144

Anderson, T., 122

Anglo as term, 83

Anglo expansion, 80, 88–89, 90, 112

Anglo Saxonism, 91–93. *See also* Racism; Settler colonialism; White supremacy

Anti-Black racism, 115, 116, 127

Anti-Chinese Congress, 52

Anti-Chinese policies, 52–53, 62, 77–78

Anti-immigrant legislation, 62, 113. *See also* U.S. immigration law

Anti-Japanese policies, 65, 66, 69

Anti-Japanese sentiment, 65, 68–70, 76–77

Anti-Mexican exclusions, 80, 83

Anti-Negro Propaganda in School Textbooks (National Association for the Advancement of Colored People), 125

Aoki v. Deane, 66–67

Apple, M. W., 3, 7, 13, 14, 25, 36

Aptheker, H., 128

Arizona and anti-immigrant policy, 113

Arriola, C., 96

Asato, N., 65, 66, 67, 69–70, 71, 72, 73, 74, 77, 78
Asian Americans. *See also* By group
  and choices made in writing this book, 16, 46–50
  and cultural maintenance, 48, 51
  historical context, 47–48
Asian Pacific Islander, 49
"Asian problem," 47
Assimilation goal, 20, 21, 42, 50–51, 82, 98, 101
Assmann, J., 13
Association of Japanese Language Schools, 74, 76
Au, W., 2, 3, 4, 5, 6, 8, 10, 11, 13, 18, 25, 28, 35, 48, 50, 71, 81, 115, 146
Azuma, E., 47, 67

Baker, B., 3, 4, 131
Baldwin, R. N., 111
Banks, J. A., ix, xi
Barbé-Marbois, F., 118
Barnhardt, C., 21
Barrera, A., 95, 99
Beikoku Kashu Kyoiku-kyoku Kentei, Nihongo Tokuhon (Japanese Reader), 75
Bell, D. A., 47, 77, 78
Biographies of African Americans, 140–141
Biological determinism. *See* Eugenics; Racism: and science
Black Phalanx (Wilson), 140–141
Blacks. *See* African Americans; *Journal of Negro Education*
Blanton, C. K., 82, 83, 85, 102, 103, 104–105, 106, 107, 108, 109–111, 113
Blight, D. W., 116, 125, 126
Boarding schools. *See* Federal boarding schools
Bonus, R., 49
Bowman, K. L., 92
Brawley, B., 140–141
Brown, A. L., 2, 3, 4, 5, 6, 8, 10, 11, 18, 50, 81, 115, 124, 140, 143, 144, 146
Brown, K. D., 3, 5, 115, 124, 140, 143
Brown, S. A., 121, 127
Brownies' Book, The (Fauset & Du Bois), 141–142
Buddhist Church of Honpa Honganji Bukkyodan, 70
Buddhist Church of Sacramento, 70
Bukholder, Z., 127–128

Burlingame Treaty, 54
Byrd, J. A., 13, 14, 84, 87

Cabrera, N. L., 113
Calderón, D., 3, 8, 13, 14, 25, 33, 84, 89, 105n4
California and the Oriental (California State Board of Control), 69
California law, 67. *See also* By name
California Oriental Exclusion League, 69
California School Law, 54, 55–56, 65
California State Board of Education, 75
California State Federation of Labor, 69
California Supreme Court, 55–56
Caliver, A., 135–136
Camarota, S. A., x
Capitelli, S., xi
Carlisle boarding school, 31
Carlson, D., 3
Carrigan, W. D., 97
Carroll, W. M., 4
Carter, R., 109
Castenell, L., 4
Caste system. *See* Citizenship: caste system; Racial caste system
Catholic schools, 93
Cattle industry, 91
Central California Japanese Language School Association, 76
Central Japanese Association of Southern California, 72
Chan, S., 10, 47–48, 50, 52, 53, 59, 78
Chang, B., 48
Chapters overview, 15–17
Character education, 135
Chen, S., 52, 53, 61, 62, 78
Chennault, R. E., 6
Cherokee Nation, 27–29
Cherokee Nation v. The State of Georgia, 34
Cheung, C., 46, 53
Chicanos. *See* Mexican Americans
Chickasaw Nation, 28–29, 39–40
Chico, CA, 52
Chief Sequoyah, 27
Child, B. J., 29, 38, 39, 41, 44
Children's literature and portrayal of African Americans, 121–123, 142–143
Chinese Americans. *See also* Asian Americans
  assimilation goal of, 50–51
  Chinese-language schools, 46, 55–59, 61–64

Christianizing goal, 55
    cultural maintenance goal, 46, 61, 63
    historical context, 49–53, 59
    integrated schools, 53–54
    in Mississippi, 59–60
    nationalism, 64
    public school path, 46, 53–55, 60–61
    transnational curricular discourse,
        77–78
Chinese Central High School, 62
Chinese Consolidated Benevolent
    Association (CCBA), 62
Chinese Exclusion Act, 52, 62
Christianizing goal, 20–21, 25–26, 55
Christian missionary schools, 28, 55
Christian names, 36
Churchill, W., 18, 29, 30, 34, 38
Church-run schools, 28, 55, 94, 95
Citizenship
    anti-Japanese movement, 69
    caste system, 81, 85–86, 87–88, 92
    education, 32–33
    hierarchy of types, 85–86
    and League of United Latin American
        Citizens (LULAC), 99
Civics testing requirement, 73
"Civilized" status, 23, 86, 88n2, 88n3
Civilizing goal, 20–21, 25–28, 31, 32, 43
Civil War, 116
Class status, 85, 88, 95, 97, 110. *See also*
    Citizenship: caste system; Racial caste
    system
Cloud, H. R., 40–41
Cobb, A., 26, 28, 29, 39
Cobb, W. M., 132
Coleman, M. C., 29
Collier, J., 41
Colonialism. *See* Settler colonialism
Colonial legacy, 113
Committee of One Hundred, 40
Committee on Indian Affairs, 26
Commodore Stockton School, 57
Compendium on Southern Rural Life
    (Rosenwald Fund), 107
Compendium texts, 140–141
Conference of the Japanese Association on
    the Pacific Coast, 74
Connelly, F. M., 4
Construction term, 115–116
Cornish, M., 85, 87, 90
Cotera, M. E., 84, 85, 86, 87, 88, 88n3
Cotton, 90, 91
Counts, G. S., 42
Courtland district, 67, 68

*Courts and the Negro Separate School,
    The* (Du Bois), 135–136
Creek Nation, 29
Criollos, 85
Crisis, The (journal), 142
Critical appraisals. *See under Journal of
    Negro Education*
Critical race theory (CRT), 13–14
Critical theory, 13
Culturally responsive curriculum, 133
Cultural maintenance goal
    and Asian Americans, 48, 51
    and Chinese Americans, 46, 61, 63
    and Indigenous peoples, 46
    and Japanese Americans, 71, 72, 74, 76,
        77, 78
    and Mexican Americans, 81, 95, 99,
        148
Cultural memory and historical narrative,
    13–14
Curricular colonization concept, 25
Curricular genocide, 24–25, 43–44,
    147–148
Curricular genocide term, 24–25
Curricular self-determination term, 24–25
Curriculum (Schubert), 6
Curriculum Development (Tanner &
    Tanner), 6
Curriculum studies field
    absences/omissions, 4–5, 9–11
    context of, 3–4, 10
    critical turn, 7–8
    irony in, 7–9
    master narrative, 4–9
    and "peculiar sensation," 1–3
    and racism, 9–11
Curriculum Studies Reader (Flinders &
    Thornton), 5
Cushman, E., 27, 28, 32
Czaplicka, J., 13

Dagbovie, P. G., 115
Daniel, R. P., 132
Daniel, W. G., 133
Daniels, R., 50, 66
Daqing Qiaomin Xuetang (Great Overseas
    Chinese School), 62, 63
Daqing Shuyan, 62, 63
Dawes Act, 21
Day schools, 21, 41
Debt peonage system, 90
Decolonization as term, 24
De facto segregation, 97, 99–101, 103,
    110, 111, 115, 149

Deficit curriculum, 94, 97
Dehumanization of Black people, 121–122
De jure segregation, 101, 111, 149
Delgado, R., 13–14
Delgado v. Bastrop ISD, 110
De Lissovoy, N., 115
Desai, C., 3
Dewey, J., 41, 42, 134
Deyhle, D., 6, 18, 20, 25, 38
"Digging in the crates" metaphor, 11–13
Dispossession of land. *See also* Territorial
    acquisition
    and Indigenous peoples, 18, 23, 33
    and Japanese Americans, 69
    and Mexican Americans, 81, 85, 88–91,
        88n2, 88n3, 100
Donato, R., 81, 92, 96–97, 99, 100, 101,
    102
Double consciousness, 1
Drescher, S., 117
Du Bois, W. E. B., 1–2, 3, 12, 44, 94, 124,
    136–137, 145
Dunbar-Ortiz, R., 85, 91
Duncan-Andrade, J. M., 84
Duran, L., 105
Dysconscious racism, 5

Early childhood education, 75
Eck, D. L., xi
Eder, J., 29, 40, 41
Editorial, 130
Eliot, J., 25–26
El Paso, TX, 97
Encarta Africana (Appiah & Gates), 144
English colonizers, 26
English language, 94
English-only law, 94, 113
Enrollment of girls, 62
Enslavement. *See* Slavery
Environmental design of boarding schools,
    35, 43
Ephraim, C. W., 1
Equalization Act, 106
Equal Protection clause. *See* Fourteenth
    Amendment
Ernest, J., 140
Escuelitas, 95
Estrada, L. F., 80, 88, 89, 90–91
Eugenics, 34, 102, 103. *See also* Racism:
    and science
Exclusion. *See* Anti-Chinese policies; Anti-
    Japanese policies; Jim Crow system

Fallace, T., 3, 10, 131
Fear tactics, 116–117
Federal boarding schools, 29–30, 35–37,
    41, 43
Federal citizenship, 85–86
Federal Indian policy. *See* "Indian
    Education"
Federal land policy, 88–89
Female enrollment, 62
First Continental Congress, 26
First Nations peoples. *See* "Indian
    education"; Indigenous peoples
Flinders, D. J., 2, 5
Florin district, 67–68, 73
Foley, N., 96–97
Food/food rites at boarding schools, 35, 41
Forced removal, 78. *See also* Dispossession
    of land; Territorial acquisition
Foreign Language School Control Law, 75
Fourteenth Amendment, 55, 56, 60
Frankel, M. C., 118
Fraser, N., 116
Frazier, E. F., 129
Fredrickson, G., 116–117, 118–120, 123
Fresno, CA, 76

Galvan, R. T., 6, 18, 25, 38
Garcia, F. C., 80, 88, 89, 90–91
Garcia, M. T., 98
Garth, T., 102
Garth, T. R., 131
Gates, H. L., 115
Gaztambide-Fernandez, R. A., 8, 9, 10, 11,
    14–15, 25, 33
Geary Act, 52
Gendered roles, 19
Genovese, E. D., 128
Gilborn, D., 4
Gish, D. A., 118
Godfrey, P. C., 81, 90, 99, 100, 101, 102
Golden Gate Institute, 72
Goldsby, J. D., 124, 127
Gomez, L. E., 80, 81, 83, 84, 85, 86, 87–
    88, 88n3, 89, 90, 92, 96, 104–105
Gong Lum v. Rice, 59
Gonzalez, G. G., 82, 91, 93, 95, 96–97,
    100, 102, 103
Goodwin, A. L., 48, 49, 79
Gordon, B., 3, 8
Gould, S. J., 103
Grande, S., 20
Grant, C. A., 3, 5, 115, 124, 140

Great Qing Overseas Chinese School, 62
Grizzly Bear, 69–70
Gross, A. J., 92

Haciendas, 85
Hair cutting, 35–36
Hall, G. S., 40, 42
Hall, S., 116, 119, 138
Hamme, L. V., 21
Hanson, J., 81, 92, 97, 99, 100, 101, 102
Harlem Renaissance, 128
Harris, V. J., 142–143
Harris, W. J., 65
He, M. F., 4
Hendrick, I., 103
Hendry, P., 3
Hernandez v. Texas, 84
Higher-learning institutions and racism,
    10–11
High schools, 22, 62
Hip-hop metaphor for methodology,
    11–13
Hip Wo Chinese school, 62
History of the United States of America, A
    (Scudder), 33
Hokubei Hyoron, 75
Horsman, R., 83, 92, 112
House Concurrent Resolution 108, 22
Huebner, D. E., 35

Ichioka, Y., 72
Identity, 1, 47, 48, 63, 64, 95–96
Immigrant demographics, x, 95
Immutability-of-race notion, 131
Imperial Japanese government, 78
Imperial Japanese Monbushō, 71
Indian American community, 50
Indian Civilization Fund Act, 28
Indian country, 88n3
"Indian education"
    about, 18, 43–44, 46
    academic subjects, 31–33
    boarding schools, 21, 29–30, 35–37,
        41, 43
    colonial context, 20–21, 25–26, 147
    curricular genocide, 31–37
    day schools, 21, 41
    federal policy periods, 20–23
    power and White supremacy, 43–45, 46
    Progressive Era reform, 40–43
    public schools, 41
    reappropriating curriculum, 38–40

resistance, 36–38
self-determination, 22–23, 26–29
state role, 21, 22
and students, 37–38, 41, 67, 72–73
Indian Nations at Risk Task Force, 23
Indian Removal Act of 1830, 28
Indian Reorganization Act, 22, 41
Indigenous Hawaiians, 48, 147
Indigenous peoples. *See also* By group;
    "Indian education"
    and analytical lenses, 14
    and assimilation goal, 20, 21, 42–43
    Christianizing goal, 20–21, 25–26
    culture of, 19, 32, 44, 46
    and curricular discourse, 6, 23–25, 147,
        149
    dispossession of lands, 18, 21, 23, 28, 33
    historical portrayal, 19
    and identity, 36, 43, 44
    southeastern tribes, 26–27
    as topic of book, 15
    traditional educational systems, 19, 28
    tribal schools, 22–23, 27–29
    worldview, 32
    written language, 27–28
Indios bárbaros, 86
Indios civilizados, 86
Individualism, 34
Industrialization, 95
Institute for Government Research, 40
Institutes (Japanese American schools),
    73, 75
Integrated versus segregated schooling,
    132, 136–137
Intellectual capacities, 34, 40, 97, 117,
    128, 131–132
Intellectual inferiority, 97, 102
Interdenominational Mission Congress, 66
International relations, 47, 67, 77, 78, 148
Interview with a Chinese student, 58
Invisible narrative concept, 4–5
IQ testing, 102–103, 105
Isleton district, 67, 68
Isolation of Mexican community, 98
Issei, 65, 71. *See also* Japanese Americans
Issei teachers, 74

Japan, government of, 67, 68
Japanese Americans. *See also* Asian
    Americans
    anti-Japanese movement, 65, 68–70,
        76–77

Japanese Americans *(continued)*
  assimilation goal, 50–51
  cultural maintenance goal, 71, 72, 74, 76, 77, 78
  dispossession of land, 69, 78
  historical context (pre-WWII), 65–68
  names and terms, 65
  nationalism, 74, 75
  resistance, 66
  rise of Japanese-language schools, 70–71
  school curriculum, 71–74
  school textbooks, 74–78
  transnational curricular discourse, 77–78
Japanese Association of America, 66, 71, 72
Japanese Association of Oregon, 72
Japanese Consul, 66
Japanese Exclusion League, 65, 69
Japanese Language Institutes of Northern California, 73, 75
Japanese Language School Association, 74, 76
Japanese Language Schools of Northern California, 73
Japanese nationalism, 74, 75
Japanese Reader, 76
Japanese Teachers Association of America, 72, 73, 75
Japanese Teachers Association of Northern California, 75
Japanese Teachers Association of Southern California, 75
Japanese Teachers of America, 74
Jefferson, T., 118
Jim Crow system, 97, 117
Johnson, C. S., 107, 129, 133–135, 138–139
Johnson-O'Malley Act (OM). *See* Indian Reorganization Act
Jordan, W. D., 115, 117–118
Journal of Negro Education
  inclusion curriculum, 132–137
  and racial science, 131–132
  racial understanding, 137–139
  role in curriculum discourse, 129, 139–140
Judeo-Christian names, 36

Kando Ikeda, 75
Kawai, Y., 50, 77
Kawamura, Y., 74
Keller, J. A., 10, 19, 25, 26, 27, 28, 29, 31, 36, 37, 38, 39

Kelley, R. D. G., 152
Kidwell, C. S., 19
Kincheloe, J. L., 6
King, J. E., 6
King, T., 106, 115
Kinslow, K., 94, 96
Kliebard, H. M., 2, 5, 42
Klinghard, D. P., 118
Klos, G., 91
Korean American community, 50
Kuo, J., 47, 54, 55, 56, 57, 59, 60, 62, 66, 67, 77
Kyoiku Chokugo (Japanese Imperial Rescript on Education), 72
Kyoiku Chosa-kai (Education Survey Committee), 72

Lai, H. M., 49, 61, 62, 63
Land grant system, 85, 91
Land of the Spotted Eagle (Standing Bear), 18
Land tenure system. *See* Land grant system
Language deficit position, 97, 100–101, 113
Latinos. *See* Mexican Americans
Lawler, T. B., 126
Leadership education/skills, 19
League of United Latin American Citizens (LULAC), 82, 98–99, 108, 110, 111, 112
Le Conte, J., 118–119
Ledesma, M. C., 84
Lee, E., 10, 49, 50, 51, 52, 78
Legal segregation. *See* De facto segregation
Le Goff, J., 13
Leung, L., 58–59
Liberation historiography, 139–140
Lim de Sanchez, S., 59, 60
Linguistic deficit position, 97, 100–101, 113
Little Schools radio program, 110, 112
Locke, A., 4–5, 139
Logan, R., 116
Lomawaima, K. T., xi, 19, 20, 22, 25, 26, 29, 30, 31, 34, 35, 39, 43, 44
Lopez, H., 47, 60, 100
Lopez, I. F. H., 100
Los Padillas, NM, 105, 105n4
Louisiana Negro Normal and Industrial Institute at Grambling (Grambling State University), 107–108
Lucero, R. L., 88n3
Lum, M., 59–60
Luna, R., 100, 110

Macias, R. F., 80, 88, 89, 90–91
Maguire, J., 56
Maldonado, L., 80, 88, 89, 90–91
Malewski, E., 3, 4
Maramba, D. C., 49
Marshall, J. D., 8
Marshall, T. M., 126–127
Martin, M., 121–122
Math instruction, 32
Mayo, C., xi
McCarthy, C., 8
McCarty, T. L., xi, 19, 20, 22, 29, 30, 34,
    35, 39, 44
McClatchy, V. S., 69
McKinley (W.) Administration, 34
Media role in racial understanding, 138
Meiji Shogakko, 70
Menchaca, M., 81, 83, 84, 85, 86, 87, 88,
    90, 93, 96–97, 100, 102, 103, 118
Mendez v. Westminster, 112
Mental capacities. See Intellectual
    capacities
Meriam, L., 40
Meriam Report, 22, 40, 41
Mestizos, 86
Mexican Americans
    and assimilation goal, 82, 98, 101
    cultural maintenance goal, 81, 95, 99,
        148
    dispossession of land, 81, 85, 88–92,
        88n2, 88n3, 100
    historical context, 80–82, 84–85
    history of activism, 104–111, 112–113
    identity, 11
    as laborers, 93, 97, 100
    and language-deficit view, 97, 100–101,
        113
    New Mexico context, 80, 85–89, 92–96
    and racial ambiguity, 92–96
    recent discourse, 113
    resistance, 94–95, 97–98, 103–104
    school segregation and colonialism,
        96–101, 112
    school segregation and racism, 102–103,
        112–113
    Texas context, 80, 84, 89–92
Mexican American Studies Day, 113
Mexican American studies programs, 113
Mexican–American War, 85
Mexican citizenship, 88n2
Mexico, government of, 90
Meza, E. L., 113
Mihesuah, D. A., 28
Military-style schooling, 31, 35

Miller, J. L., 8
Mills, C., 10, 14, 114, 128
Mir, A., 113
Mississippi Circuit Court, 60
Mississippi constitution, 60
Mississippi delta region, 59–60
Mississippi Supreme Court, 59
Mokuyobi Kai (Thursday Club), 71–72
Monbusho textbooks, 75, 76
Montejano, D., 96–97
Moral dilemma, 135–136
Moral education, 72
Moran, A., 34
Morimoto, T., 54, 56, 57, 66, 68, 70, 71,
    72, 73, 74, 75, 76, 78
Morning Bell School, 62, 63
Mortality rates in United States, 119
Moulder, A., 56
Murillo, N., ix
Mutualistas, 98, 99

(NAACP) National Association for the
    Advancement of Colored People.
    See National Association for the
    Advancement of Colored People
    (NAACP)
Name changes, 36
Names and terms used in this book, 24,
    65, 83, 115–116
Nam Hoy Fook Yum Tong, 62
Nam Kue School, 63
National Association for the Advancement
    of Colored People (NAACP), 111,
    125
National Association of Teachers in
    Colored Schools, 135–136
National Center for Education Statistics, x
Native Americans. See "Indian education";
    Indigenous peoples
Native Daughters of the Golden West, 65,
    69
Native Hawaiians, 48, 147
Native Sons of the Golden West, 65, 69
Negro Builders and Heroes (Brawley),
    140–141
"Negro inferiority," 117–118
"Negro Problem," 118
New Deal, 22, 110
New Mexico, 87, 149. See also Mexican
    Americans: New Mexico context
New Mexico Education Association, 106
"New Negro" philosophy, 143
New South. See Reconstruction
Ngugi, W. T., 24

Nieto, S., 97
Nieto-Phillips, J. M., 104–105
Nihongo Tokuhon, 76
Nihon Shogakko (Japanese Elementary
   Schools), 70
Nikkei, 65, 72–73, 76–77. See also
   Japanese Americans
Nisei, 65, 71–73. See also Japanese
   Americans
Nixon Administration, 22
Nonresident fees, 21
Norm of Whiteness, 1, 27, 115
Northern Circuit Court of California, 57
Northman, The, 69
Northwest American Japanese Association,
   72
Notes on Virginia (Jefferson), 118

O'Brien, P., xi
Off-reservation schools. See Federal
   boarding schools
Off-white concept, 80, 86–87, 92, 95, 101,
   104, 111, 113
Omi, M., 13, 47, 116
Omission from curriculum discourse. See
   Absence from curricular discourse
Omissions from this book, 147
Oral educational tradition, 19
Organic Act, 21
"Oriental School," 57–59, 62, 65, 66
Ozawa v. United States, 60

Pacific Coast Japanese Association
   Deliberative Council (PCJADC), 72,
   74
Pacific Islanders, 49
Padilla, D., de, 105n4
Padilla, F., 84
Paraskeva, J., 3
"Peculiar sensation," 1–2, 3
Perdue, T., 27
Perea, J. F., 86, 90
Phillion, J., 4
Pinar, W. F., 2, 4, 5, 6, 6n1 (Ch. 1), 7, 8
Pipphen, J. W., 113
Pita, B., 80, 86, 87, 88, 89–90, 91, 105
Plessy v. Ferguson, 60
Political alliances, 87–88
Population demographics
   Chinese American, 50, 52–53, 65
   immigrant, x
   Japanese American, 65
   of Texas and New Mexico, 87
Possessive individualism, 34, 36

Powdermaker, H., 139
Power (relations) and analysis of field,
   13–14
Powers, J. M., 92, 95, 96–97
Pratt, Captain R. H., 31
Private School Control Law, 73–74
Progressive education, 40–43, 107–108
Progressive Education (journal), 41
Project to correct anti-Black ideologies,
   143–144
Pro-South approach in textbooks,
   125–126
Public school access, 16, 53–57, 60–61,
   65–68, 77, 78, 148
Pueblos, 86, 88, 88n2, 88n3, 105n4
Purpose of book/authors' objectives, 15
Putnam, R. D., x

Race
   and Anglo Saxonism, 91–93
   and curriculum studies, 5, 8
   and Native peoples, 46
   as social construct, 127, 132, 139
   as societal problem, 137–138
Race psychology, 131–132
Race Traits and Tendencies of the
   American Negro (Hoffman), 119
Racial ambiguity
   and Asian Americans, 47, 60, 79
   Mexican Americans, 80, 82, 84, 88,
      92–96, 99, 101
Racial caste system, 86, 87, 88, 88n3, 92,
   95, 104, 112
Racial othering concept, 115
Racism
   and African Americans, 115, 116–120,
      125–126
   and Asian Americans, 50, 51
   and Chinese Americans, 52, 53–54,
      58–62
   of colonialism, 8, 9–10
   and curriculum studies, 6, 147–150
   and Indigenous people, 42, 44, 91
   and Japanese Americans, 60, 67, 68–70,
      72–73, 76–77
   and Mexican Americans, 80, 95,
      102–103, 108–109, 111, 113
   and science, 34, 102, 103, 117–120,
      131–132, 145
   in textbooks, 125–126
Radical Reconstruction. See
   Reconstruction
Railroad construction, 88
"Realism" in Black education, 133–134

Reconstruction, 125–127
Reconstruction term, 115–116
Recreational activities and segregation, 59
Reddick, L. D., 3, 124, 126, 138–139, 145
Redirection of Black education, 133–135
Reel, E., 34
Reservations. *See* Dispossession of land:
    and Indigenous peoples; Territorial
    acquisition
Resettlement. *See* Dispossession of land;
    Territorial acquisition
Resistance to absences in curriculum
    studies, 2–3. *See also* Resistance by
    group
Revisionist history, 14–15, 120–121,
    125–127
Revisionist ontology project, 13, 14,
    43–44, 114, 128–129
Reyhner, J., 29, 40, 41
Reynolds, W. M., 2, 5, 7
Rhodes, C., 41
Right to public education. *See* Public
    school access
Roche, A., ix–x
Rodriguez, N. M., 6
Rodriguez, R. C., 113
Roediger, D. R., 6
Roman Catholic missionaries, 25–26
Romo, R., 101, 105
Roosevelt, T., 66–67
Roosevelt (Franklin D.) Administration, 41
Rosedale, MS, 59–60
Rosenbaum, J. E., 7
Rosenfelt, D. M., 21, 22, 37
Rosenwald Fund, 107, 108
Rosiek, J., 94, 96
Rugg, H., 42
Ruiz, V. L., 94, 95–96, 98
Ryan, W. C., Jr., 40–41

Sakura Gakuen, 70
Saldaña-Portillo, M. J., 84, 85, 86, 87, 88,
    88n3
Sánchez, G. I.
    background, 82, 83
    influences on, 106–112
    life and work, 104–106
    role in Mexican American curricular
        discourse, 82, 83, 108–112,
        112–113
Sánchez, R., 80, 86, 87, 88, 89–90, 91, 105
San Francisco public schools, 65–66
San Francisco School Board, 53–54, 55,
    56–58, 65, 66, 67

San Francisco Superior Court, 56
San Miguel Jr., G., 81, 93, 94, 95, 96–97,
    98, 99, 100, 102
Schubert, A. L. L., 4
Schubert, W. H., 4, 6, 7, 8
Scientific racism. *See* Racism: and science
Scott Act, 52
Scudder, H. E., 33
Sears, J. T., 8
Seattle, WA, 52, 72, 76–77
Secularization of schools, 94
Segregated schooling. *See also* "Indian
    education": boarding schools; "Indian
    education": day schools
    and African Americans, 132, 136–137
    and Chinese Americans, 54, 55–56, 57,
        59–60, 67–68
    and Japanese Americans, 65–68
    and Mexicans/Mexican Americans, 80,
        81, 93, 102, 111, 112
    and Mississippi, 59–60
    and the Southwest, 96–97
    and White supremacy, 109
Segregation. *See* De facto segregation
Senese, G., 23
Settler colonialism, 9–10, 13, 14–15,
    25–26, 80, 147, 148
Settler nationalism, 33
Seven-step plan for challenging racial
    hatred, 142–143
Shapiro, H., 117, 120
Sheep industry, 91
Sheldon, W., 102
Shibusawa, N., 51
Shim, D., 50
Shin Sekai (New World), 71
Silence concept, 5–6
Silence in curricular discourse. *See* Absence
    from curricular discourse
Simmons, M., 89
Sisneros, S., 105
Sisquoc, L., 10, 19, 25, 26, 27, 28, 29, 31,
    36, 37, 38, 39
Slattery, P., 2, 5, 7
Slavery, 90, 91, 115, 116, 125–127
Social Darwinism, 118–119
Social dilemma, 135–136
"Sojourner" orientation, 62
Southern California Japanese Language
    Association, 76
Spack, R., 32
Spanish colonizers, 25–26
Spanish land grant system, 85, 90
Spanish language, 94

Spanish missions, 25–26
Spanish settlers, 85
Spring, J., 38
Standing Bear, L., 39
Stark, H. K., 81
State citizenship, 85–86
Stefancic, J., 13–14
Steinberg, S. R., 6
Stephens, W. D., 69
Stevens, T., 6, 18, 25, 38
Stiglitz, J. E., x
St. Mary's Chinese school, 62
Structural inclusion, x–xi
Struggle for the American Curriculum
    (Kliebard), 5
Survival capacity, 27–28
Survival education/skills, 19
Swisher, K., 6, 18, 20, 25, 38
Szasm, M. C., 29, 39

Takaki, R., 49, 50
Taliaferro-Baszile, D., 3
Tanner, D., 6
Tanner, L., 6
Tape, M., 56
Tape v. Hurley, 56
Taubman, P. M., 2, 5, 7
Taxation and land dispossession, 88–90
Teachers at "Oriental School," 58
Teacher testing requirement, 73–74
Teaching Mikadoism (Asato), 77
Ten Little Niggers, 121–123
Terman, L., 102
Termination and relocation period, 22
Territorial acquisition, 87, 88–89
Testing of IQ, 102
Texas, 87, 149. See also Mexican
    Americans: Texas context
Texas Rangers, 90
Texas Revolution, 90
Texas Senate, 113
Textbooks
    for Chinese-language schools, 63–64
    curriculum studies, 5–6
    for Japanese-language schools, 74–77
    and portrayal of Blacks, 124–128, 139,
        140–142
Theoretical lenses (this work), 13–15
"The Physical and Mental Capacities of
    the American Negro" (JNL), 131
"The Problem of Indian Administration."
    See Meriam Report
"The True Brownies" (Du Bois), 142–143
Thomas, T. P., 4

Thornton, S. J., 2, 5
Tijerina, F., 110, 111
Tom, K. F., 54, 62–63, 64
Trafzer, C. E., 10, 19, 25, 26, 27, 28, 29,
    31, 36, 37, 38, 39, 43
Transnational curricular discourse.
    See under Chinese Americans:
    transnational curricular discourse;
    Japanese Americans: transnational
    curricular discourse
Transnational identity, 64, 67
Treaty of Guadalupe Hidalgo, 82, 84,
    85–86, 92
Tribal schools, 22–23, 27–29
Tribal self-determination period, 22
Trouillot, M., 7
Trujillo, O. V., 21
Tuck, E., 3, 8, 9, 10, 11, 13, 14–15, 24,
    25, 33, 84
Tucson Unified School District, 113

Understanding Curriculum (Pinar et al.),
    5–6
Undifferentiated knowledge acquisition,
    134
United States v. Lucero, 88n3
United v. Thind, 60
U.S. Census Bureau, xi
U.S. Congress, 88n3
U.S. Department of Commerce, 65
U.S. history testing requirement, 73
U.S. House of Representatives Committee
    on Immigration and Naturalization,
    69
U.S. immigration law, 48–49, 62, 65, 67
U.S. military, 88
U.S. social studies instruction, 32
U.S. Supreme Court, 22, 34, 60, 75

Valdés, G., xi
Valencia, R., 83, 93, 94, 96, 102, 103, 112
Valencia, R. R., 93, 96–97
Vindicationist approach, 142–143
Visibility narrative concept, 4–5
Vizenor, G. R., 44
Vocational education, 22, 28, 34–35, 134
Voter obstruction, 117

Walnut Grove district, 67, 68
Ward, C. J., 20
Ward v. Flood, 55–56
Washington, B. T., 5
Washington Grammar School, 57–58
Washington state, 76–77

Washington Territory, 52
Watkins, W. H., 3, 8, 131, 140
Weinberg, M., 50, 53, 54, 56, 57, 58, 59,
    66, 67, 68
Welcher, W., 56
Wesley, C., 124–125
What Is Curriculum Theory? (Pinar), 80n1
    (Ch. 4)
Wheeler-Howard Act. *See* Indian
    Reorganization Act
White as term, 83
White House, 151
White male dominance in curriculum
    studies, 4–6
Whiteness norm, 1, 6, 10, 27
White supremacy, 47, 86, 87, 91, 97, 99.
    See also Anglo Saxonism; Racism;
    Settler colonialism
Whose America? (Zimmerman), 80n1
    (Ch. 4)
Wilkerson, D. A., 132
Wilkins, D. E., 20, 22, 23, 81, 86
Wilkins, R., 138–139
Williams, G. W., 140–141
Williams, R. A., 86
Willis, P., 36
Wilson, J. T., 140–141
Winant, H., 13, 47, 116

Winfield, A. G., 3
Wolfe, P., 87
Wollenberg, C., 54, 56, 57, 65, 66, 67, 68,
    70, 96–97, 102, 103
Wood, W. C., 73
Woodson, C. G., 124–125, 140–141, 145
Work, H., 40
Workforce competition, 34–35
World War I, 65
World War II, 78
Wraga, W. G., 8
Writing instruction, 31–32
Wyoming Territory, 52

Yamato Minzoku (Japanese race), 74–75
Yang, K. W., 13, 14, 24, 33, 84
"Yellow peril" perception, 50, 52, 77, 78,
    148
Yeong Wo School, 62
Young, D., 57–58
Yrisarri, NM, 105
Yu, A. F., 58

Zaibei Nihonjim Kyoiku Kai, 72
Zhunghua Qiaomin Gongli Xuexiao
    (Chinese Public School), 62
Zimmerman, J., 88n3, 124
Zinn, H., 27, 47

About the Authors

Wayne Au is an associate professor in the School of Educational Studies at the University of Washington Bothell. A former public high school teacher and long-time editor for the social justice teaching magazine *Rethinking Schools*, his work focuses broadly on critical education policy, theory, and practice—with emphases on critiquing corporate education reform, examining the racial politics of high-stakes testing and curriculum, and supporting local and national educational justice movements. Most recently he edited *Rethinking Multicultural Education: Teaching for Racial and Cultural Justice* and co-edited *Mapping Corporate Education Reform: Power and Policy Networks in the Neoliberal State*, and he has been published in *Teachers College Record* and *Educational Researcher*, among other journals.

Anthony L. Brown is an associate professor of curriculum and instruction in social studies education at the University of Texas at Austin. He is also an affiliated faculty in the areas of cultural studies in education, the John Warfield Center of African and African American Studies, and the Department of African and African Diaspora Studies. His research agenda falls into two interconnected strands of research, related broadly to the education of African Americans. His first strand of research examines how educational stakeholders make sense of and respond to the educational needs of African American male students. The second strand examines how school curricula portray the historical experiences of African Americans in official school knowledge (such as standards and textbooks) and within popular discourse. He has been published in *Teachers College Record, Harvard Educational Review*, and the *Journal of Educational Policy*.

Dolores Calderón is an associate professor of youth, society, and justice at Fairhaven College of Interdisciplinary Studies at Western Washington University. As a researcher who embodies the complicated subjectivities of the U.S./Mexico border—Mexican (settler/arrivant), Indigenous (Pueblo), and U.S. citizen—she is interested in researching and participating in work that untangles and unpacks the complicated way multiple colonialisms impact decolonial thinking and practices, specifically in educational curriculum. As a former social studies teacher and educational outreach worker, she is interested in exposing problematics often overlooked in larger educational research. Areas of study include critical Indigenous studies in education, curriculum, multicultural education, and epistemology and education. She has published in *Qualitative Inquiry, Harvard Educational Review*, and *Anthropology and Education Quarterly*.